Mother Earth Spirituality

Native American Paths to Healing Ourselves and Our World

Ed McGaa, Eagle Man

Illustrated by Marie N. Buchfink

HarperSanFrancisco

A Division of HarperCollins*Publishers*

Library of Congress Cataloging-in-Publication Data
McGaa, Ed.
    Mother Earth spirituality / Ed McGaa ; illustrated by Marie N. Buchfink,
      p.   cm.
    ISBN 0–06–250596–3 (pbk.)
    1. Oglala Indians—Religion and mythology. 2. Oglala Indians—
Philosophy. 3. New Age movement. I. Title.
E99.03M34   1990   89–46149
                                                 CIP

91 92 93 94 RRD(H) 10 9 8 7 6 5

Contents

Foreword

A question that will be asked is why I am willing to teach non-Indians about Native American spirituality and about my own spiritual experiences. I believe, like Fools Crow, Eagle Feather, Sun Bear, Midnight Song, Rolling Thunder, and a host of other traditional peoples, that it is time that spirituality is shared.

Frank Fools Crow, Oglala holyman and ceremonial chief of the Teton Sioux, said in reference to the pipe and the sweat lodge, "These ceremonies do not belong to Indians alone. They can be done by all who have the right attitude . . . and who are honest and sincere about their beliefs in Wakan Tanka (Great Spirit) and follow the rules."

We do not have any choice. It is one world that we live in. If the Native Americans keep all their spirituality within their own community, the old wisdom that has performed so well will not be allowed to work its environmental medicine on the world where it is desperately needed.

Global warming, acid rain, overpopulation, and deforestation are real. It is a mess, and all of us two-leggeds will have to work together to get ourselves out of it. A spiritual fire that promotes a communal commitment to a worldwide environmental undertaking is needed. Native or primal ways will fuel that fire and give it a great power. I call on all experienced Native American traditionalists to consider coming forward and sharing their knowledge. Come forth and teach how Mother Earth can be revered, respected, and protected.

Acknowledgments

To the many friends, supporters, and critics who have contributed to my path: My thanks to each of you. May the six powers of our universe send rewarding rains of refreshment upon your earth walk journeys.

Special appreciation to Mary Ray and my inspiring children.

To Mark Salzwedel, my editor at Harper & Row, *Pilamaya aloh* (thank you very much) for your perception, advice, and direction. Also special appreciation to Arla Ertz, production editor, and Joanne Sandstrom, copyeditor.

To Raymond Oneglia, Hilda Neihardt, Judith Favia, Evie Ketcham, Fred Wolf, Kathleen O'Sullivan, Jack Weatherford, Cynthia Bend, Jim Brown, Thunder Owl of the Mdewakantons, Herb Dorr (Assiniboine), Buddy Red Bow, and my mentors, Grey Eagle and Molly Poets, your support and input are equally appreciated.

To my adopted sisters, Freida Tapio, Jamie Sams, and Tayja Wiger, and adopted brother, Tim Ryan, a special Pilamaya. To my creative sister LaVerne for her writing of our children stories, to Mildred for her welcome lodge at the Sun Dance, to the spirit of generous brother Russ and to oldest brother Mick for his memories. To Dad and Mom for talking Indian.

Of course, a full circle of appreciation to Bill Eagle Feather, Frank Fools Crow, and Ben Black Elk, who took me as a warrior and began my adventurous journey into the ceremonial world; to all sun dancers and especially those pledgers back when there were but a few of us; and to all the strong dominant grandmothers of all tribes who would never let the Mother Earth Spirit die and kept whispering it into our ears when we were little ones.

The Great Chief in Washington sends word that he wishes to buy our land. The Great Chief also sends us words of friendship and good will. This is kind of him, since we know he has little need of our friendship in return. But we will consider your offer. For we know that if we do not sell, the white man may come with guns and take our land.

How can you buy or sell the sky, the warmth of the land? The idea is strange to us. If we do not own the freshness of the air and the sparkle of the water, how can you buy them?

Every part of this earth is sacred to my people. Every shining pine needle, every sandy shore, every mist in the dark woods, every clearing, and every humming insect is holy in the memory and experience of my people. The sap which courses through the trees carries the memories of the red man. So, when the Great Chief in Washington sends word that he wishes to buy our land, he asks much of us. . . .

Whatever befalls the earth befalls the sons of the earth. Man did not weave the web of life; he is merely a strand in it. Whatever he does to the web, he does to himself. But we will consider your offer to go to the reservation you have for my people. We will live apart, and in peace.

It matters little where we spend the rest of our days. Our children have seen their fathers humbled in defeat. Our warriors have felt shame, and after defeat they turn their days in idleness and contaminate their bodies with sweet foods and strong drinks. It matters little where we spend the rest of our days. They are not many. A few more hours, a few more winters, and none of the great tribes that once lived on this earth or that roam now in small bands in the woods will be left to mourn the graves of a people once as powerful and hopeful as yours. But why should I mourn the passing of my people? Tribes are made of men, nothing more. Men come and go, like the waves of the sea. Even the white man, whose God walks and talks with him as friend to friend, cannot be exempt from the common destiny.

One thing we know, which the white man may one day discover—our God is the same God. You may think now that you own Him as you wish to own our land: but you cannot. He is the God of man; and his compassion is equal for the red man and the white. This earth is precious to Him and to harm the earth is to heap contempt on its Creator. The whites too shall pass; perhaps sooner than all other tribes. *Continue to contaminate your bed, and you will one night suffocate in your own waste.**

But in your perishing you will shine brightly, fired by the strength of the God who brought you to this land and for some special purpose gave you dominion over this land and over the red man. That destiny is a mystery to us, for we do not understand when the buffalo are all slaughtered, the wild horses are tamed, and the view of the ripe hills blotted by talking wires. Where is the thicket? Gone. Where is the eagle? Gone. And what is it to say goodbye to the swift pony and the hunt? The end of living and the beginning of survival. So we will consider your offer to buy the land.

If we agree, it will be to secure the reservation you have promised. There, perhaps, we may live out our brief days as we wish. When the last red man has vanished from this earth, and his memory is only the shadow of a cloud moving across the prairie, these shores and forests will still hold the spirits of my people. For they love this earth as a newborne loves its mother's heartbeat. So, if we sell our land, love it as we've loved it. Care for it as we've cared for it. Hold in your mind the memory of the land as it is when you take it. And with all your strength, with all your mind, with all your heart, preserve it for your children, and love it . . . as God loves us all. One thing we know. Our God is the same God. This earth is precious to Him. Even the white man cannot be exempt from the common destiny. We may be brothers after all. We shall see. . . .

*Emphasis added.

Introduction

The ceremonies within these pages have arisen from a mystical tapestry of cultured tradition that has woven earthly spirituality into every aspect of life. The perspective of Native Americans in regard to Mother Earth spirituality holds great potential for the environmental movement as it emerges as a world political and social issue. The cause of the environment is a song of love, and the Indians have drummed its rhythm. Just as the Indians have given us a Mother Earth spirituality, so too they have given us the concept of a worthy warrior who has the qualities to fight for what she or he holds sacred.

In the past, warriors were honored when they defended their family and tribe. Today, the new tribal members are planetary citizens, and the threat to the quality of life—indeed, to its very survival—goes far beyond the constricted view shaped by military consideration. As the threat changes, so too the qualities we honor in a warrior must change. Guns and swords are ineffective against the complex and varied assaults of an environment thrown out of natural balance. A true earth warrior must be imbued with the determination to let nature restore her inherent harmony. Although we can expect great progress from the greening of technology and the inventiveness of the human spirit, we should not allow ourselves to be beguiled that information and technological advance will be sufficient. The Indians talk of "mystic warriors." They would understand what Einstein meant when he said:

> The more knowledge we acquire, the more mystery we find. . . . A human being is part of the whole, called by us the Universe, a part limited in time and space. He experiences himself, his thoughts and feelings as something separate from the rest—a kind of optical illusion

of his consciousness. This delusion is a kind of prison for us, restricting us to our personal desires and to affection for a few persons nearest to us. Our task must be to free ourselves from this prison by widening our circle of compassion to embrace all living creatures and the whole of nature in its beauty. Nobody is able to achieve this completely, but the striving for such achievement is in itself a part of the liberation and a foundation for inner security.[1]

The warrior who feels the great mystery of existence is marked by a profound humility. Such new warriors will not see themselves as titans standing astride the universe demanding dominion over the earth. Instead, they will be like the vision-questing Indian who stares at the stars in the black sky and feels humility before nature's power and awesome beauty.

Native American Indians learned how to live with the earth on a deeply spiritual plane. Their intuitive sense of intimate connection with all of existence from Brother Bear to Sister Stone to Father Sky to Mother Earth provides the deep ecological wisdom that the present-day environmental prophets have rediscovered and begun to teach to an alienated world. At some point, these environmentalists will ask why their passion is so strong, their commitment so intense, their pain from earth's suffering so terrible, their ecstasy with earth's healing so exquisite. They will look inside. When they are ready and their quest is sincere, they will experience what the Indians know as the Great Spirit.

I recently bought my son a chart of human history. It measured eight feet by three feet and the industrial age was only two inches in the bottom of the graph. Yet if Chief Seattle returned today to see what we have done in a short time to his sacred land, his heart would surely fill with tears.

He might ask, as I do, what it takes to inject a sense of urgency into this country. Do we have to tear a hole in the sky before we wake up? Well, we've done it. Do we have to see the life-giving rain be turned so acidic that it kills fish and trees and endangers human health? Well, we've done it. Do we have to watch the great seas rise, inundate our coastlines, and disrupt agricultural patterns through global warming? Well, we're doing it. Do we have to see the great Rhine River run with a current of death caused by a disastrous pesticide spill? Well, we've seen it. Does cancer have to rise up among us like a modern plague because of radon and toxics? Well, we've seen it. Do the clouds of Chernobyl have to spew radioactivity around the globe for us to declare enough is enough? What does it take to inject a sense of urgency? What does it take to wake up world governments to the global environmental threat? Can we not see that the miner's canary is dying—that we must save the earth if we are to save ourselves?

I do not want to be an old man who tells his offspring in the glow of nostalgic reflection about the good old days when we used to have primeval forests and great whales and clean, fresh water. I want neither nostalgia nor bitterness, but I am tired of waiting while the earth is dying. I want to see the earth flourish, and I want to see the ways of regeneration.

If killing Mother Earth is a sin, as the Indians believe, then avoiding sin becomes a step on the path of illumination. The theologian Rheinhold Niebuhr declared that sin is a separation from the truth. If the truth, as seen in the Native American's holy visions, is the profound interconnectedness of all existence, then sin becomes inevitable when one becomes alienated from nature. Yet has there ever been a time when humanity has been so torn from nature's embrace? Thoreau wrote that "the mass of men lead lives of quiet desperation." People living in the modern age have become alienated, feeling alone, isolated, and separated. Modern myths have created the perception of an atomistic society, where all connections have been cut. Yet nothing is further from the truth. Interdependence is at the center of all things. The separation between us and nature is a mirage. The perception of separation is the result of ignorance. It springs from the arrogant belief that a human being is unlike animal beings and plant beings and rock beings. It is reinforced by the false teaching that technology has lifted us above the web of life. The sin of hubris made modern people believe that human beings are superior to and independent of nature. The Indians knew the meaning of humility when they stood beneath the Great Spirit in ceremony and prayed. "Oh, *Wakan Tanka* [Great Spirit, Great Mystery] make me worthy." We must realize, it is an unbroken flow that runs from humankind to the glory of creation. We do not seek a "back to nature" movement; instead we emphasize the realization that we can never leave nature.

As we leave behind the worldview of a dead, mechanistic earth, it is only natural to begin to envision the great transformation that lies ahead. The worn-out age built on fossil fuels is drawing quickly to its end, and the glimpses of a postmodern civilization are beginning to excite a new generation of futurists. Poised as we are on the verge of a new dawn, we need to draw upon the sacred traditions and values of the Indian people. Black Elk, the Oglala Sioux, told us that he would always rise early to greet the daybreak star, for it is the star of understanding. He told of a four-rayed herb of understanding that would be dropped upon the earth and would flower and bloom. Could it be that we are now upon the threshhold of the Oglala holy man's age of understanding?

As the Indians have known for centuries, and as the environmentalists are now discovering, often with experiential instruction from the Indians' sacred traditions, we are not living on a dead earth. Mother Earth is alive, our most intimate relation. As unfortunate as it might be, we can, if we must, live without fathers, mothers, brothers, sisters, ancestors, spouses, friends, and acquaintances. However, a person depends every moment of every day upon Mother Earth. We breathe her air into our lungs, we drink her waters, we eat her nutrients. Our cells are dying and are constantly being replaced. The flow between nature and ourself is always in process. We degenerate and regenerate with nature's help. I used to think the Indians were talking metaphorically about sister mountains and brother buffalo, but I have now known the quest and seen the vision. I am beginning to understand! If there were no rocks, my body would have no minerals and I would die. If there were no sun, the plants would not grow and I would die. If there were no water, my cells would dry up and I would die. If there were no Great Spirit moving in all aspects of the vast creation, I would not have awakened with a consciousness of this cosmic dance of life. Rising from the dreams of their holy ones, the Indians long ago awakened to the Great Mystery that lies at the core of the profound Oneness. They were not only taught but through their ceremonies truly comprehended the phrase "dust to dust," and more than perhaps any other people, have looked upon the earth as sacred. They have known that if we profane the earth, we will corrupt ourselves. What we do to Mother Earth, we do to ourselves.

Within the pages of Eagle Man's *Mother Earth Spirituality,* we have the opportunity to learn, as the Indians have learned in their ceremonies. In the Sweat Lodge Ceremony, we relax in the cosmic flow; we are charmed by it, revel in it, celebrate it, are awed by it, and are wonderfully satisfied that we are truly a part of all that is. We are part of the great cosmic flow that never ceases. Such a new consciousness, that we have awakened after more than fifteen billion years of evolution, should give us a sense of excitement about the mysterious journey of which we are now becoming a part.

The Vision Quest can produce a flash of profound insight. The immensity of space, the sighing of the breeze through the trees, the movement of the winged, or an immense mountain gale that demonstrates the power of nature can all be a teacher as we sit upon a mountain.

Many understand, many more will. Fyodor Dostoevski understood: "Love every leaf, every ray of light. Love all the animals, love each separate thing. If you love everything, you will perceive the mystery of God in all, and when you perceive this you will grow every day in fuller understanding of it, until you come at last to love the whole world with a love that will be all-embracing and universal."[2] Yet its attainment involves a quest that will require the characteristics of true protectors of the earth. The new mystic warriors will impart the values of life, not death; of relationship, not violence; of peace, not war. *"Mitakuye oyasin,"* the Sioux say in ceremony: "We are related to all things." The new mystic warriors will be strong in their love and powerful in their compassion. They will be imbued with the willpower to save the voiceless ones, the plants and animals, because they understand our earthly relationship.

As the modern age ends and the new age is being born, *Homo sapiens*—the two-legged—must learn to evolve so as to survive. The law of evolution—adapt or die—will move to a new stage. People must adapt spiritually, not physically. The great challenge to save the planet cannot be met without the soul power of the spirit.

Native Americans tell the environmentalists that they are right to listen to the wisdom of Mother Earth. "To the four quarters [nature's power and wisdom] you shall run for help, and nothing shall be strong before you." Black Elk was reassured. The philosophy of today's ecology is built in accordance with Indian spiritual tradition. If the trillions of cells in our bodies can run amazingly complex functions without our conscious effort, then we can only imagine the wisdom of Mother Earth that we have not yet learned. The Mother Earth ceremonies place our bodies, our minds, our spirits within the wisdom of Mother Earth. Are these trillions of cells not responding euphorically when they are bathed within the warm womb of our Mother Earth when we undergo the Sweat Lodge? Do our thoughts, our perceptions not expand vastly like the great galaxies above us when we vision quest upon the sacred mountains? Surely the new age should enact policies that will direct very substantial resources into the study of the earth, the study of true natural relationships, creating a rich renaissance for the universities and think tanks around the world.

So let us, in walking gently on the earth, leave behind a simple legacy—that we loved the earth and were new warriors, mystic warriors who had the courage to try to save it. We are motivated by the words of Albert Schweitzer: "The noblest instinct of them all is the reverence for life." And we are reassured by Black Elk's vision. After the herb of understanding was imparted to the earth, a voice went all over the universe and filled it. It was such a beautiful voice that nothing could keep from dancing. All life danced. Leaves, grasses, waters, four-leggeds, two-leggeds, and winged all danced together. Black Elk looked down and saw that everything was beautiful and green with fruits growing and all things kind and happy. The voice said: "Behold this day, for it is yours to make."

Jan Hartke
Environmental Liaison
Earth Day 1990

MOTHER EARTH SPIRITUALITY

PART ONE

WATER

The Spiritual Character of the Native American

Ceremonial beseechment led the Sioux safely westward. The Buffalo Calf Woman appeared to them on the plains, and one of their own, Black Elk, had a foretelling vision. The tribe's values and virtues are representative of most North American tribes. Their stewardship of Earth was so exemplary that now, with the impending environmental disaster besieging our planet, we must consider their spiritual values as well.

Buffalo Calf Woman: The Coming of the Sacred Pipe

The Sioux were taught and understood that all things are of the Great Spirit. Trees, rivers, mountains, grass, four-legged animals, two-legged animals, and winged creatures all came from the Great Spirit, called *Wakan Tanka*, who is the Supreme Being. In modern times, traditional Sioux still practice their Way. Holy men and holy women can be found on the reservations, and the ceremonies are still conducted. Some of these ceremonies are now taking place in the non-Indian world.

Before the appearance of the Buffalo Calf Woman, the Indian honored the Great Spirit. But among the Sioux, the coming of Buffalo Calf Woman brought a most important instrument, the pipe, which is now used in all ceremonies.

The sacred pipe came into being many, many years ago. Two men of a small band of the Sioux tribe, the Sans Arc, were hunting and saw something approaching in the distance. As the figure drew close, they observed a beautiful maiden, dressed in white buckskin, carrying a bundle wrapped in buffalo hide.

> Behold me.
> Behold me,
> For in a sacred manner
> I am walking.

She sang this out and repeated the song as she walked slowly toward them.

One of the men had evil thoughts about this maiden and moved toward her. The other hunter tried forcibly to restrain him, but the evil man pushed the good warrior away. A cloud descended on the evil one, and when it lifted, his body was a skeleton being devoured by worms. This symbolized that one who lives in ignorance and has evil in his heart may be destroyed by his own actions.

The good hunter knelt in fear, trembling as the buckskin-clad woman approached. She spoke to him, telling him not to be afraid, but to return to his people and prepare them for her coming. This was done, and the beautiful maiden appeared in their midst, walking among them in a sunwise, or clockwise, direction. She held forth her bundle and said:

> This is a sacred gift
> And must always be treated in a holy way.
> In this bundle is a sacred pipe
> Which no impure man or woman should ever see.
>
> With this sacred pipe
> You will send your voices to *Wakan Tanka*.
> The Great Spirit, Creator of All.
> Your Father and Grandfather.
>
> With this sacred pipe
> You will walk upon the Earth
> Which is your Grandmother and Mother.
> All your steps should be holy.
>
> The bowl of the pipe is red stone
> Which represents the earth.
> A buffalo calf is carved in the stone facing the center
> And symbolizes the four-legged creatures
> Who live as brothers among you.
>
> The stem is wood and represents all growing things.
> Twelve feathers hang from where the stem fits the bowl
> And are from the Spotted Eagle.
> These represent all the winged brothers
> Who live among you.
>
> All these things are joined to you
> Who will smoke the pipe and send voices to *Wakan Tanka*.
> When you use this pipe to pray,
> You will pray for and with every thing.
> The sacred pipe binds you to all your relatives;
> Your Grandfather and Father,
> Your Grandmother and Mother.

The red stone represents the Mother Earth
On which you will live.
The Earth is red
And the two-legged creatures who live upon it are also red.
Wakan Tanka has given you a red road—
A good and straight road—to travel,
And you must remember that all people
Who stand on this earth are sacred.

From this day,
The sacred pipe will stand on the red earth,
And you will send your voices to *Wakan Tanka.*

There are seven circles on the stone
Which represent the seven rites
In which you will use the pipe.

The Buffalo Calf Woman then instructed the people to send runners to the distant bands of the Sioux nation, to bring in the many leaders, the medicine people, and the holy men and holy women. This they did.

When the people gathered, she instructed them in the sacred ceremonies. She told them of the first rite, that of the Keeping of the Soul. She told them that the remaining six rites would be made known to them through visions. As she started to leave, she said:

Remember how sacred the pipe is
And treat it in a sacred manner,
For it will be with you always.
Remember also that in me are four ages.
I shall leave you now,
But shall look upon you in every age
And will return in the end.

The Sioux begged the spirit woman to stay with them; they promised to erect a fine lodge and to give her a fine man to provide for her, but she declined their offer.

No, the Creator above,
The Great Spirit,
Is happy with you,
You, the grandchildren.
You have listened well to my teachings.
Now I must return to the spirit world.

She walked some distance away from them and sat down. When she rose, she had become a white buffalo calf. She walked farther, bowed to the four quarters of the universe, and then disappeared into the distance. Her sacred bundle was left with the people; and to this day, a traditional Sioux family, the "Keepers of the Sacred Bundle," still guards the bundle and its contents on one of the Sioux reservations.

Since the revival of our Sun Dance Ceremony, several Sun Dances have been held close to where the sacred bundle is kept. It is in a place we call Green Grass. Green Grass was where I danced my sixth, and last, Sun Dance. It is a sacred place, and one knows instinctively that something *wakan*, something very holy, is near.

Indian people feel that it is very poor manners to refer to the Buffalo Calf Woman's appearance as a myth or superstition. Indians do not scoff at the story of the Israelites fleeing Egypt when the Red Sea was parted by the Great Spirit in order for the Jewish people to escape the pharaoh's pursuing army. We have been told over and over by Christian missionaries that a man, born of a virgin, died, rose again three days after his death, pushed a big stone back from his tomb, and then ascended into the spirit world. An Indian would consider it poor manners to make fun of this spiritual story, especially if it is a part of a people's spiritual history. Similarly, the Jewish people would be offended if the story of Moses' vision questing on the mountain were called a myth, especially the part where the Great Spirit appeared to Moses and gave him special instructions, or commandments, on living and conduct.

Perhaps it is because our spirit guide happens to be a woman that the male-oriented missionaries find it difficult to grasp. That is very sad. It is their loss. Is it not obvious that women are the peaceful ones? Does not the animal world exhibit this observation? The males fight far more than the females do. Since the dawn of recorded history, it is the men, not the women, who have plunged into war. Womankind is half of the human world, but most importantly, women are the peaceful ones, and in this new era, it is the most peaceful ones who will bring ultimate harmony.

The Great Spirit does many things in balance. The Buffalo Calf Woman is a strong balance to other spirit guides and brings forth a needed harmony. We can hope that communication and knowledge will change the old ways of narrowmindedness among religions. We can hope that spiritual leadership roles will be equally represented among all ways. Reaching such goals presents a strong challenge for spiritual women, both Indian and non-Indian.

The Seven Original Sacred Rites

Seven traditional rites or rituals use the sacred pipe in accordance with the Buffalo Calf Woman's teachings.

The Keeping of the Soul

In the Keeping of the Soul Ceremony, the first rite given by the White Buffalo Calf Woman, the soul of a dead loved one is purified so it can return to the Great Spirit from whom it came. Another part of the ritual is the give-away, a ceremony to release the soul for its journey to the Great Spirit, which may take place a year after death. A current version of this ceremony is giving away the deceased's possessions a year after the funeral—the first anniversary of departure to the spirit world. During the year, the widow or widower makes and procures gifts and assembles the possessions of the deceased and decides what friends to give them to. The possessions are passed on to friends and relatives at a give-away dinner. Such dispossessing is efficient, teaches nonmaterialism, and provides for reuse of the goods. It is also a nice way to remember a departed friend or relative.

Inipi: The Sweat Lodge Ceremony or Rite of Purification

The *Inipi* (Sweat Lodge Ceremony) has been used as a cleansing and a preparatory ceremony. It is like a spiritual sauna; one feels reborn, renewed, and strengthened through the commingling of one's own lifeblood (sweat) with the lifeblood of the planet. These commingled waters are carried forth out of the lodge by the four winds, the four directions. The lodge itself allows a special closeness to Mother Earth. This ceremony is becoming a very popular ceremony for Indian and non-Indian alike. The *Inipi* is described in detail in subsequent chapters.

Hanblecheyapi: Vision Quest

At the center of the individual's quest for closeness to *Wakan Tanka* is the Vision Quest Ceremony. It is an individual ceremony, performed on an isolated mountain top or a badland butte. Some woodsland Indians created platforms high in the trees on which to do their quests. In addition to isolation, the vision seeker also endures a period of fasting and going without water. This ceremony is discussed in detail in chapter 9.

The vision quester prepares himself or herself in the sweat lodge before ascending to the mountain top or isolated area. A Vision Quest can be an important ceremony for young people about to face the challenges of an adult world. It provides a personal time in which they may reflect seriously on their spiritual and occupational paths.

Wiwanyag Wachipi: The Sun Dance Ceremony

The Sun Dance is the annual coming together of the tribe to thank the Great Spirit for all that the Creator has given to the people. Where the Vision Quest is an individual ceremony for inner peace and strength, the Sun Dance exists for tribal unity, peace, and strength through the honor and thanksgiving offered to *Wakan Tanka*.

The Sioux do not worship the sun, but acknowledge that it was placed in the universe by the Great Spirit so that the people might live. Life springs from the fire, the sun. This meaning is also recognized in the Sun Dance, but the overall meaning is an annual tribal thanksgiving to God.

Hunkapi: Making Relatives

The purpose of the *Hunkapi* (Making Relatives) rite is to create between two people a blood bond that is closer than a kinship tie. Sometimes we are fortunate enough to find friends who are generous, sharing, supportive, and loving. This ritual is for friends to adopt one another into a new relationship.

Three ideals of peace form the basis for this ritual. Peace comes to the souls of those who realize their relationship to the universe and to the Great Spirit, who is at the center of the universe. This center is the same for everyone, everywhere. Second, peace between two people recognizes the kinship of all people. Third, peace between nations recognizes that all people are family or kin, and children of the Great Spirit. The entire ritual reflects the spiritual relationship between humanity and *Wakan Tanka*.

The exchange or gift of a peace pipe, a crystal, or a *wotai* stone (a smooth stone that has a significant image or several images within its grain) can symbolize this spiritual blood bond that occurs with the making of a new relative.

Ishnata Awicalowan: Preparing a Girl for Womanhood

The *Ishnata Awicalowan* (Preparing a Girl for Womanhood) ritual recognizes the importance of women as the source of the flowering tree of the Sioux nation. It teaches young girls that they will be as Mother Earth and will bear children, who will be reared in a holy manner. The ceremonial rites are a source of much holiness for the women who participate and for the entire Sioux nation.

The older a woman becomes among the Sioux, the more powerful she is regarded to be, because her acquired wisdom is listened to and respected by all. It is women who sit in the place of honor, holding the sacred pipe in the Spirit-calling Ceremony, because it was, after all, a woman who brought the sacred pipe and the seven ceremonies to the people. It is a woman who will make the first cut on the Sun Dance tree, so that it can be felled later and brought to the dance arena. A woman must also be the first to open the Sun Dance arena. In this day of dangerous atomic weapons, womankind is the peaceful segment of humanity; therefore, women's importance and leadership should advance and be recognized, both spiritually and politically.

Tapa Wanka Yap: Throwing the Ball

The *Tapa Wanka Yap* (Throwing the Ball) ritual, which developed over the years into a game, was originally a rite in which all participants were to have the ball. The ball used was symbolic of *Wakan Tanka* and the universe. In the ceremony, a small girl stands at the center of the circle and throws the ball from the center outward to the four quarters of the universe. This symbolizes that *Wakan Tanka* is everywhere and that, just as the ball descends, so does the Great Spirit's power. The small child represents eternal youth and purity, like *Wakan Tanka*. The ritual establishes the relationship of the people to the universe, or to *Wakan Tanka*, who is everywhere.

Among the Sioux in this day, other ceremonies have supplanted some of the original seven ceremonies taught by the Buffalo Calf Woman. The Sun Dance, Sweat Lodge, and Vision Quest are still major ceremonies that are practiced widely. The Pipe Ceremony itself is now used to open gatherings, meetings, and sweat lodges. The Pipe Ceremony is used in naming ceremonies, in which one is given an Indian name. The pipe is also used in Indian marriage ceremonies.

The *Yuwipi* (Spirit-calling) Ceremony is a powerful event practiced mostly on the reservations, although at times holy men will perform this ceremony before urban or off-reservation gatherings. This ceremony calls in the spirit beings, usually the spirits of our deceased ancestors, to predict, foretell, find, or protect. Wisdom and guidance pertaining to the tribe or the nation are also sought in a *Yuwipi* Ceremony.

The Pipe Ceremony is the most widely practiced ceremony both on and off the reservation, the *Yuwipi* Ceremony the fourth. Sweat Lodge and Vision Quest ceremonies are more readily available because only a few holy men from each reservation are capable of the powerful *Yuwipi* spirit calling. Unlike the Sun Dance Ceremony, the *Yuwipi* Ceremony is often performed off the reservation. In his younger days, Fools Crow, the renowned Oglala holy man and Sun Dance chief, traveled as far as the west coast to perform some highly successful *Yuwipis*.

Some of the original rites have undergone transformation and some have been replaced. In the old days, the "days of plenty," a warrior's favorite horse or horses were killed after his death, and he was buried in his favorite buckskins and clothing along with his weapons. Later, when the Sioux were herded onto the bleak reservations and had to live in poverty, this practice was considered foolish and wasteful.

The Keeping of the Soul Ceremony underwent a transformation toward a greater emphasis on sharing and an outright giving away of many of the belongings of the deceased. The Giveaway Ceremony began as a means of redistribution and a reuse of needed objects and clothing. Horses and hunting equipment were of value, to be kept for the overall good of the living. The give-away, held a year after the death, is now a ceremony in itself and is practiced considerably more than the soul-keeping ceremony.

The Throwing the Ball and the Preparation for Womanhood ceremonies have been replaced by the Pipe Ceremony and *Yuwipi* as major rites. The high emphasis of the woman in all ceremonies has not diminished, however. She always has the place of honor and opens the major ceremonies.

When times change, some of the ceremonies change also. In times of religious persecution, the visible ceremonies had to go underground. Sweat lodges, which were common around most cabins and tipis in the early reservation days, started to disappear when the Christian missionaries began to entrench their power with the governmental authorities. The peace pipe was much easier to conceal. Lakota spirituality thus came to depend more and more for its secret expression on the pipe. Now that Native Americans have successfully fought back for their religious freedom, the Pipe Ceremony remains established.

The Buffalo Calf Woman told the Sioux where to find the sacred red stone to make the peace pipe. In the pipestone quarries in southwestern Minnesota, near the town of Pipestone, the Sioux and all other Indian nations dug for their red stone in peace. They traveled to and from the quarries in peace also. No warfare was allowed. Peace councils were often held in this place, an early example, perhaps, of a United Nations.

Lakota ceremony recognized the forward change of life so, like the two-leggeds, ceremonies adapted also. The Sioux adapted considerably as they migrated from the Carolinas to the Great Plains. The *Yuwipi* Ceremony was highly important back then, and no doubt was a powerful force in warning the people that they had to flee west for survival. The Lakota and Dakota listened, and they survived.

Now our planet is in great danger. Why not turn to ceremony, at least to get the feeling, the message that our planet must live? She is speaking to us quite strongly already. Let her speak also in ceremony. We can gain a special resolve by communicating within the ceremonies. By listening to nature through nature-based ceremonies, we can be like the Sioux. Against what seemed like insurmountable odds, they managed to live. Deforestation, the thinning ozone layer, global warming, and overpopulation present great odds. But we can adapt. We all can live, and our planet can live.

Black Elk's Vision

Most anthropologists who study acculturation assume that all aspects of Native American culture have, or will become, "Americanized" without examining to what extent aspects of Euro-American culture have become "Indianized." The tenacity of Oglala cultural values, however, seems to negate that assumption and affirm the validity of the latter approach.

WILLIAM K. POWERS, Oglala Religion

Visions and foretelling prophecies are not uncommon among my people, the Oglala. The demanding Vision Quest—in which the seeker stays alone, up on an isolated mountain top or badland butte—the Sun Dance ritual, and the powerful *Yuwipi* (Spirit-calling) Ceremony have resulted in strong foretelling power for our holy men and holy women.

Long ago, a holy man called Drinks Water envisioned that the animals, primarily the buffalo, would go back into the earth—that is, they would be killed. He saw that the Sioux would be ruled by a different race of people, who would make the Indians live in square, gray houses on a barren land, and that they would starve. His vision was true. History shows that in the 1890s the Sioux were, indeed, forced to live on reservations in square, gray houses and that many starved to death.

The Sioux had yet to win the Battle of the Little Big Horn, when a young boy, who was destined to be a Lakota holy man, received a vision from the spirit world. Black Elk saw two men descend with flaming spears. They took him, on a cloud, to a great plain. There a bay horse greeted him, accompanied by prancing horses of different colors: black, white, sorrel (red), and buckskin (yellow). (Later, the colors of these horses would represent the four directions.) Leaving the horses, Black

Elk went into a rainbow-covered lodge, the lodge of the Six Grandfathers (the powers of the four quarters, or four directions, of the universe and of Mother Earth and Father Sky).

The first Grandfather, the power of the west, gave Black Elk a cup of water, the power to sustain life. From the black west, thunder beings release the life-giving rain. Then the grandfather handed him a bow and told him he would also have the power to destroy.

The second Grandfather, the power of the north, gave him a white wing and a sacred herb of sage. The wing, like the northern snow, exemplified the power of cleansing, endurance, and courage. The herb provided truth and honesty, strong, healing sustenance for our bodies, Mother Earth, even world governments and leadership.

The third Grandfather, the power of the red dawn rising in the east, gave Black Elk the sacred pipe, the power of peace. The daybreak star appeared, and he was told he would have the power to awaken others. Powerful knowledge would come to this land, and peace would come, through knowledge and wisdom.

The fourth Grandfather, the power of the south, gave him a bright red stick sprouting leaves. The Grandfather said that a tree would grow in the center of the nation. A yellow hoop appeared, symbolizing in its color, growth and physical healing, in its circle, the unity of all things.

The fifth Grandfather, the spirit of the sky, became an eagle. He spoke, saying that all things of the sky—the winged, the winds, and the stars—would be as relatives and would come to Black Elk and help him.

The sixth Grandfather was really Mother Earth, the Earth Spirit. The Earth Spirit took Black Elk outside the lodge and told him the Earth Power would be with him. In time, the two-leggeds would desperately need Mother Earth's help.

Black Elk was instructed to set the red stick in the center of the yellow hoop. There, the tree was to grow, and around it people would gather. In time the tree would bloom.

Black Elk saw the earth becoming sick. The animals, the winged ones, and the four-legged ones grew frightened. All living things became gaunt and poor. The air and the waters dirtied and smelled foul. Below, Black Elk saw a blue man living in and empowering the sickness. The powers of the four directions, represented by four horses, charged the blue man, but were beaten back. The Grandfathers called upon Black Elk. His bow changed into a spear, and he swooped down on the blue man, killing him. When the blue man fell, all life came back upon the earth; all things became fresh and healthy again.

Then Black Elk took the bright red stick and cast it into the center of the earth. The stick became a Sun Dance tree, a *waga chun*, a cottonwood tree. A peace pipe descended to the tree's base, spreading deep peace, and the people sang with delight. The daybreak star rose. Black Elk was told that the star would be as a relative to the people; those who saw it would see much more, because the star represented wisdom.

Black Elk was then shown his people over a great span of time, beginning with the time his people all walked in a sacred manner, following the good red road, camping in a sacred circle. A holy tree stood out sharply within the encampment's center. "Behold, a good nation, walking in a sacred manner, in a good land," the people sang. In time, however, the people broke into little groups and denominations, each group following a different path, and all around them was fighting and war. The sacred tree withered. Black Elk saw miserable, starving faces of people who were sick and dying.

A red man appeared among the people. His transformation into a buffalo indicated a time of plenty. A sacred herb became four flowers, four blossoms on a single stem. The four-rayed herb—red, yellow, black, and white—became the flowering tree. Black Elk heard a song: *A good nation I will make live, this nation above has said, they have given me the power to make over.*

Then Black Elk saw that the sacred hoop of his people was only one of many hoops, all joined together to make one great circle, the great hoop of all peoples. In the center of the great hoop stood a powerful, sheltering, flowering tree, and under it gathered children of all nations.

At the end of Black Elk's vision, two spirit men gave him the daybreak-star herb of understanding. He dropped the herb down to the world below, and it flowered, spreading its power out into the whole world. In time, he was promised, his people would be free and would help spread this power of peace and understanding.

Black Elk lived to be an old man. In his lifetime he witnessed the free spirit of the mystic warriors of the plains become a tethered eagle in a *washichu's*, or white man's, zoo. He and his people became captives of the dark reservation road. Old warriors waited in remoteness, amid poverty and despair, for the promise of yesterday.

Before his passing, the old man ascended Harney Peak (Thunder Being Mountain) in the Black Hills, to lament aloud to *Wakan Tanka*, the Great Spirit of All Powers. He believed his once powerful vision had failed, for there was no Sun Dance tree, no greening leaves, and the flowering herb had failed to bloom. He pleaded, crying piteously for one last bud, a springing leaf, a glowing ember, to signify the return of the Indian spirit, somehow, some way.

Comments on Black Elk's Vision

There was a time of trials and despair, as the Grandfathers predicted. But history has also proved Black Elk's healing vision correct, although the old holy man didn't live to see the return of the Sun Dance, symbolizing the return of the Indian spirit, a few years after his death.

The red stick with the green leaves now has risen in the center of the Sioux nation. The Sun Dance Ceremony, *Wiwanyag wachipi*, is currently being performed annually. The Indian spirit lives, the Sioux have taken up the old beliefs and values. The Indian people had first to regain their spirit, and their ceremonies, before the flowering tree and herb of understanding could bloom for the whole world. The young of our tribe are embracing the return of the good red way, and now some traditionalists are beginning to bring the wisdom of the Native American experience out to the ears of those who will hear it. They would become like flames, Black Elk predicted.

The blue man of Black Elk's vision is seen as a symbol of those who have harmed Mother Earth and all her creatures. The blue man, the great violator, symbolizes greed, corruption, dishonesty, and selfishness. Mother Earth, represented by the four directions, has fought back against the one who has made the grass and animals sick and the streams and air unclean. Mother Earth has natural self-healing powers, but without the help of knowledgeable humans, she cannot set herself right. A reversal of world values, a spiritual concept of the earth as God-created and sacred, is in order before we two-leggeds can be environmentally effective on a global basis. The blue man will meet his death when this comes about.

The bright red stick with the green leaves symbolized that Indian people had to regain their nature-based spirituality. The coatings of bad influences from the selfish ones had to be shed like an unwanted skin before there could be new growth. Old ceremonies have been revived, and those who would inhibit this spiritual rebirth often meet outright resistance.

The stick planted in the center of the nation is symbolic of the Sun Dance tree. Before the tribal Sun Dance begins, a cottonwood tree is selected and cut down, then carried and erected in the center of the Sun

Dance circle. The tribal people gather in tents, trailers, and tipis, creating a surrounding encampment. The people watch the sundancers and pray together as a tribe when the dancers are pierced on the last day, the fourth day. The Sun Dance tree centers their prayers, and like a spiritual wind, the prayers shoot upward to the Great Spirit, *Wakan Tanka*, above. In fulfilling the annual tribal thanksgiving to the Creator of All, the people are also fulfilling a teaching from the Buffalo Calf Woman. It is a powerful time for prayer and beseechment.

The sacred herb, the daybreak star, symbolizes the powerful knowledge and serenity that flow from knowing and applying the ultimate values that only a nature-based value system can provide. Those who become close to nature, and respectful of her, discover these powerful truths. By viewing the world through the clear crystal lens of this kind of value system, one can see the great power of healing, as the Grandfathers promised. It must be remembered, it is God that has created nature. We are learning directly from God's creation. There is no middle person to alter, or confuse, the direct perception of real, God-designed knowledge.

The red man symbolizes a time of plenty, which we all have experienced in recent times. The red man is not the red people, but a symbol of the abundant plenty that flows from this North American land. Native agronomy has aided considerably, however. Corn, potatoes, beans, natural fertilizers, and most of all, a pure land with unpolluted aquifers were great gifts while the Native Americans were in stewardship. Because of this stewardship, the vast majority within this land enjoy freedom from want. This status affords us the time to project knowledge to a higher state of harmony, unity, and growth.

The herb of understanding is imparted to humanity at the end of Black Elk's vision. The great opening of modern communication leaves no question that we are, indeed, at the threshold of this time.

Today, the flowering tree is blooming before many. The bright rainbow, symbolic of the flowering tree, is now blooming among the environmental and spiritual gatherings of enlightened peoples that have begun to flourish throughout the land. The rainbow-covered lodge of the six Grandfathers is a strong symbol of the old holy man's prediction that, someday, the flowering tree would bloom. The blooming has begun and will continue—if only some blue man doesn't push the wrong button.

Pilgrims, Founding Fathers, and the Indians

Mother Earth cannot heal herself alone. She needs our help. We two-leggeds must all come together and form a commonalty of realization, a realization of potentially fatal calamities. Most of our remedies will be to cease, or drastically curtail, what we have been doing. Rising temperatures, vanishing rain forests, overpopulation, pollution of waters, and acid rain can be, and will have to be, addressed by abrupt remedies. Some solutions will be reached through *have* nations sharing and helping *have not* nations. Other solutions will require convincing major corporations that they can no longer pollute, and that they, too, are related to all things.

I am optimistic that workable models of caring and sharing can be reached within this great global undertaking. My optimism stems from knowing that past models did reach out to help others who were in need.

When the Pilgrims came to New England shores they remained aboard ship during the first winter. The several winters following were times of hardship and deprivation. This ordeal would have been fatal had it not been for the sharing and generosity of the Indians, who kept them alive and taught them how to live in this land, how to plant corn, a new form of nourishing food that Indian agronomy had nourished and developed from a Central American weed.

I view with great appreciation that scene of the first time my people looked at white people. Here was a people in its own land, looking on at another people, newcomers with a different color skin and wearing strange clothes, coming and mooring a huge, ocean-going canoe in the natural harbor.

The first act of the Pilgrims after coming ashore was to rob an Indian grain cache. The Pilgrims even admit this in their logs. They came ashore and stole the Indians' grain; the Indians looked on, magnanimously figuring that these new people must have been quite hungry, coming ashore and taking someone else's grain. The Indians didn't protest, didn't send out a war party and demand the return of their goods. They let the Pilgrims keep the grain, and when springtime came they taught the Pilgrims how to plant their own grain, how to fertilize naturally—a practice unheard of in Europe. They kept the Pilgrims alive! Can we imagine the Indians meeting the same degree of hospitality had they decided to build an ocean-going canoe and migrate eastward across the Atlantic and sail up the Thames or the Rhine, picking out land on which to grow their corn, perhaps taking some stored grain? From what I know of European values in that time, I doubt that they would have met such generous hospitality.

Seeing such "noble" conduct by "savages" should encourage us to look at their political and social structures. At the time of the Pilgrims, the Native Americans maintained an advanced governmental system that afforded far more democratic privileges than any existing system in Europe. The Indians, who did not use money or own land (Mother Earth was not for sale), lived in a state of equality and just social conditions unknown to the self-proclaimed "civilized" Europeans who had to migrate from their own portion of Mother Earth because their "civilized" system wasn't working for them. The kind of individual freedom and liberty that we know in America today was practiced long ago by a people who held their spirituality close to nature. Freedom of speech, freedom of speech in council (open assembly), the right of all adult tribal citizens—including women—to vote, the privilege to remove the elected leader, and even the existence of a federal governing system were enjoyed freedoms that were honed from the Natural Way. Because the words *thine* and *mine* were not words of ultimate possession and ownership in their language, greed was prevented from corrupting their political system. Because of this nonmaterialistic value system, the Indians could look on at the Pilgrims stealing their grain and not consider this act thievery. The Indians probably assumed, simplistically, realistically, and by all means humanistically, that the Pilgrims were desperate.

The Pilgrims' knowledge of democracy was mainly theoretical; they came from a land where class privilege and monarchy ruled, whereas the Indians were free from nonelected, unimpeachable rulers and social classes based on ownership of land. No doubt the newcomers were amazed by the personal liberty that the friendly Indians enjoyed, but their self-centered concepts of superiority and their narrow view, fostered in no small part by their religion, prevented them from discovering the high state of civilized advancement the red people had made. The Pilgrims came from a past where the king ruled by "Divine Right" and was succeeded by progeny, not by a ruler chosen by vote in an open assembly. The supreme authority among the Indians rested not in one individual, but in councils elected by the tribe. Chiefs governed only through consensus and could be overruled by the council and impeached. In Europe, under the undisputed sovereignty of the king, nobles and aristocracy controlled the land and the lives of the common people. Most European religious institutions were influenced and even largely controlled by the aristocracy and the royalty.

Unfortunately, Eurocentric ego has often kept these truths out of Western history books. Recently, however, some modern writers—such as Jack Weatherford *(Indian Givers)* and Bruce Johansen *(Forgotten Founders)*—are finding these missing truths from North American history—to the benefit of all.

Jack Weatherford tells of the writings of Baron Lahontan, a French ethnographer who lived with the Huron tribe. The Hurons decried the European obsession with money that compelled European women to sell their bodies to lonely men and compelled European men to sell their lives to the armies of greedy men who used them to enslave yet more people. By contrast, the Hurons lived a life of liberty and equality. According to the Hurons, Europeans lost their freedom in their incessant use of *thine* and *mine*.

One of the Hurons explained to Lahontan, "We are born free and united brothers, each as much a great lord as the other, while you are all the slaves of one sole man. I am the master of my body, I dispose of myself, I do what I wish, I am the first and last of my nation . . . subject only to the Great Spirit."[1] Weatherford goes on to say that Lahontan's writings rested on a solid base of ethnographic fact: the Hurons lived without social classes, without a government separate from their kinship system, and without private property.

The first person to call publicly for a union of the thirteen American colonies was Chief Canassatego, speaking in 1744 to a Pennsylvania assembly negotiating the Treaty of Lancaster. Canassatego spoke for the Hodenosaunee, the Iroquois League, and urged the colonies to follow the example of the Hodenosaunee and unite in a single government with one voice.[2]

Hiawatha and Deganwidah founded the League of the Iroquois sometime between A.D. 1000 and 1450 under a constitution they called the Kaianerekowa or Great Law of Peace. The league was made up of five Indian nations—the Mohawk, Onondaga, Seneca, Oneida, and Cayuga. Each of these nations had a council composed of delegates called sachems who were elected by the tribes of that nation. Benjamin Franklin became a lifelong champion of the Iroquois political structure and advocated its incorporation into the American political structure.[3]

As Pennsylvania's Indian agent, Benjamin Franklin took Canassatego's words seriously at the Albany Congress in 1754 by repeating the call for union. Another signer of the Declaration of Independence, John Hancock, penned a long speech to the Iroquois in which he quoted the advice of Canassatego. When the delegates of the colonies met in July 1776 to proclaim independence, Iroquois representatives attended the meetings as friends and official observers from the Hodenosaunee. After the American colonists won their freedom, Franklin urged the Constitutional Convention to adopt many governmental features directly from the Indians.

Thomas Paine (1737–1809), the first of the early colonials to propose the name "United States of America," was sent to negotiate with the Iroquois during the American Revolution. He sought to learn their language and subsequently used them as models of how society might be organized.

The Founding Fathers adopted aspects of Iroquois federalism. In the Iroquois League, the five (later six) member nations exercised equal voices without respect to size; this became the founding principle for the Continental Congress and eventually for the U.S. Senate. The league also accepted new members on an equal status with old. The Americans copied this tradition, allowing new territories to be admitted as new states rather than exploiting them as subject colonies.

The Indians of the eastern United States gathered frequently with the European settlers in meetings where each person had an equal voice in decisions. The colonists had so little experience with democratic institutions that when they started convening such meetings themselves, they had to adopt the Algonquin word *caucus* to designate this new decision-making procedure. Eventually this grew into a major organizing factor in the Congress and in local town meetings. The caucus still operates today in the American convention system to nominate political candidates, and the influence of the caucus system has spread to institutions as diverse as student councils, city governments, and the annual stock-holders' meetings of public corporations.

Thomas Jefferson, Thomas Paine, and John Adams boasted with pride of the ideas and institutions that they borrowed from the American Indians. In recognition of the uniqueness of American democracy, the architects of the U.S. Capitol building fashioned the columns to resemble stalks of Indian corn and covered the ceiling with carvings of tobacco leaves and flowers.[4] If visitors to the U.S. Capitol today look closely in some of the oldest parts of the building, they can still see some of the original carvings of Indian images and plants showing through the overlay of classical marble. The Indian heritage of America is not lost; it is only ignored.

It would seem to me that after examining the concepts of democracy and the virtues of sharing and generosity as practiced by the Indians, modern citizens will also realize other beneficial attributes of the early tribal Americans. I hope, for the sake of Mother Earth's recovery, that the descendants of the Pilgrims will not blind themselves to the exemplary environmental practices exhibited by the Native Americans.

The Massachusetts tribe taught the Pilgrims to hunt and fish and even taught the Pilgrims about Thanksgiving. Yes, the Indians are largely responsible for that national holiday. Indian tribes throughout North America annually thanked the Great Spirit for all they had been given. The Sioux' annual thanksgiving was the Sun Dance, which was held following the summer buffalo hunts. After the meat was dried for the long winter, it was time to thank the All-Providing One for their lives. In the Southwest, the Navajo and Hopi had their Corn Dance thanksgiving after the summer corn harvest; the Ojibway and northern woodlands tribes held Wild Rice Harvest thanksgivings. It was all part of the great circle of life, and a sacred time within that circle was to give the Creator thanks for being allowed to be here. Europeans celebrated few tribal-related or national gatherings for annual thanksgivings to their concept of the All-Providing One before the time of the Pilgrims.

Unfortunately for the whole world, the Pilgrims were too narrow-minded to recognize the benefits of the Indian Way, even after it had saved their very lives.

The Pilgrims faced crisis and had no choice but to accept help. Today, we all face a great environmental crisis. We will have to reassess our values and look to the natural way for wisdom. The Western world has an enormous defense budget. Not billions, but trillions of dollars are projected for weapons upon weapons. These resources will be needed for the renewal and the beginning of the end of the poisoning of Mother Earth. In the light of global warming and a thinning ozone layer, it could well be an environmental holocaust, not humanity's distrust of one another, that can spell the end of life for us all.

It is time to take the example of the Indians at Plymouth Rock and the Iroquois League. We should have confidence in great global undertakings, because we have real models upon which we can look back. We two-leggeds can approach others, others of completely different cultures and creeds, in peace and support. We must shed our narrow-mindedness; we must stop exploiting one another. We must eliminate wasteful expenditures for weaponry that is useless for reviving our planet. We don't have to be alike to work together for the common world good. We are fortunate that modern technology allows communication with our so-called adversaries who, in reality, want peace as much as you and I do. Communication and universal understanding coupled with generosity and sharing can do more for world peace and the ultimate rehabilitation of Mother Earth than all of the weapons can do. It is time for communication and wisdom to replace false fear, mistrust, and narrow-mindedness.

Red, White, Black, and Yellow

Egalitarian democracy and liberty as we know them today owe little to Europe. They are not Greco-Roman derivatives somehow revived by the French in the eighteenth century. They entered modern Western thought as American Indian notions translated into European language and culture.

The Iroquois abhorred slavery. Thomas Paine, who certainly knew of these Indian values, became one of the first Americans to call for the abolition of slavery. He went to France after the War for Independence to help the French draft their constitution. Later, the French writer Alexis de Tocqueville, writing in the first volume of *Democracy in America*, repeatedly used phrases such as "equal and free." He said that the ancient European republics never showed more love of independence than did the Indians of North America. He compared the social systems and the values of the Indians to those of the ancient European tribes before they became "civilized" and domesticated.[1]

The Spaniards, although in language, custom, religion, and written law descended directly from ancient Rome, brought nothing resembling a democratic tradition with them to the Americas. The French and Dutch, who settled parts of North America, also settled many other parts of the world that did not become democratic. Democracy did not spring up in French-speaking Haiti any more than in South Africa, where the British and Dutch settled about the same time that they settled in North America.

Even the Netherlands and Britain, the two showcases for European democracy, had difficulty grafting democracy onto monarchical and aristocratic systems soaked in the strong traditions of class privilege. During the reign of George III of Great Britain, while the United States was fighting for its independence, only one person in twenty could vote in England. In all of Scotland, only three thousand men could vote, and no Catholic could hold office or vote.[2]

American anglophiles occasionally point to the signing of the Magna Carta by King John on the battlefield of Runnymede in 1215 as the start of civil liberties and democracy in the English-speaking world. This document, however, merely moved slightly away from monarchy and toward oligarchy by increasing the power of the aristocracy. It continued the European vacillation between government by a single strong ruler and by an oligarchic class. An oligarchy is not an incipient democracy, and a step away from monarchy does not necessarily mean a step toward democracy. In the same tradition, the election of the pope by a college of cardinals did not make the Vatican into a democratic institution, nor did the Holy Roman Empire become a democracy merely because a congress of aristocrats elected the emperor.

When the Dutch built colonies in America, power in their homeland rested securely in the hands of the aristocracy and the burghers, who composed only a quarter of the population. A city such as Amsterdam was governed by a council of thirty-six men, none of whom was elected; instead, each council member inherited his office and held it until death.[3]

Henry Steele Commager wrote that during the Enlightenment, Europe was ruled by the wellborn, the rich, the privileged, by those who held their places by divine favor, inheritance, prescription, or purchase. The philosophers and thinkers of the Enlightenment congratulated themselves because the "enlightened despots" such as Catherine of Russia and Frederick of Prussia read widely and showed literary inclinations. But too many of those philosophers became court pets; from their privileged position they believed that Europe was moving toward enlightened democracy. As Commager explains, Europe only imagined the Enlightenment; America enacted it.[4] This Enlightenment grew as much from its roots in Indian culture as from any other source.

When Americans try to trace their democratic heritage back through the writings of French and English political thinkers of the Enlightenment, they often forget that these people's thoughts were heavily shaped by the democratic traditions and the state of nature of the American Indians. The concept of the "noble savage" derived largely from writings about the American Indians, and even though the picture grew romanticized and distorted, the writers were only romanticizing and distorting something that really did exist. The Indians did live in a fairly democratic condition, they were egalitarian, and they did live in greater harmony with nature than did the Europeans.

The modern notions of democracy based on egalitarian principles and a federated government of overlapping powers arose from the unique blend of European and Indian political ideas and institutions that sprang up along the Atlantic coast between 1607 and 1776. Modern democracy as we know it today is as much the legacy of the American Indians, particularly the Iroquois and the Algonquians, as it is of the British settlers, of French political theory, or of all the failed efforts of the Greeks and Romans.[5]

The American Revolution did not stop with the thirteen Atlantic colonies; it soon spread around the world. As Thomas Paine wrote in *The Rights of Man*, "From a small spark, kindled in America, a flame has arisen, not to be extinguished." He went on to say that the flame "winds its progress from nation to nation, and conquers by silent operation."[6]

As the United States moved toward Civil War in the nineteenth century, pride in Indian heritage was obscured. Southern politicians recognized that the practices of Indian liberty were incompatible with the bizarre concept of a slave democracy as practiced in Greece. Rejecting notions of Indian liberty, the slaveholders emphasized instead a mythological American connection to Athens and the ancient city-states of Greece, where democracy was practiced by an elite few while the majority of the population worked in slavery.

These new politicians covered over the original architecture of the Capitol with Greek columns and replaced the tobacco leaves with the Greek acanthus leaves. To dramatize the tie to the classical world, slaveowners gave their horses, their hunting dogs, and even their slaves Greek and Roman names such as Cicero, Pericles, Homer, or Cato. The slaveholders made a fetish of Greek style as they built courthouses, churches, and even their own plantations and gazebos in a mock classical style.[7]

In one of Samuel Goodrich's "Peter Parley" books that I once had but have since lost, Parley invited the reader to stand with him atop a six-story building, one of New York City's tallest at that time. He told the reader to look west from that lofty perch and imagine seeing as far as the Mississippi River. He said that the reader was facing the greatest slave market of all. But, he cautioned, when these healthy and hardy red savages were captured, they would not submit to good, servile Christian work. They would not submit to slavery, even though beaten and chained. They would wait, he claimed, until they could scheme a release from their fetters, then sink a blade into your backside and slink into the forest to rejoin their heathen brothers.

While Parley's racist observations were a bit overblown, he was right about one thing: my people have never been willing to submit to slavery in any form. They were like the Jews of Masada who chose death before submission, and they were not opposed to making a slaveowner pay dearly for his presumption. Captured Indians knew that back in the forest, freedom awaited them. On the other hand, if they had been captured, chained, torn from their homes, and taken across an ocean without hope of return, I'm not sure how well they would have fared. Such a separation from their own portion of Mother Earth probably would have been fatal to their spirits.

If the black people who were brought to this country as slaves had known they had refuge with sympathetic friends, the Indians, they might have attempted escape en masse. Maybe history could have been different. But to keep the blacks isolated and afraid to run away, slavers told them fearful stories about the savagery of the Indians.

Most readers will be familiar with the television series (or the book) *Roots*, by Alex Haley. Haley traced his family's history back to their African home, capture, and dislocation to America as slaves. He told of some slaves' repeated efforts to run away and related how horribly they were punished when they were caught. Some, he told, escaped to the north. But he didn't tell about those who escaped and were befriended by the Indians, and there were many of those. Even today I still see and hear evidence of that group of people; often people of black heritage will come to tell me that their forebears were black and Indian, dating back to slavery days.

The Seminole nation shows a good example of what I have been saying. Chief Osceola had a black wife whom he loved so much that he surrendered himself to her captors to save her life. Seminole warriors resisted invasion of their land so successfully that the United States government couldn't force them to sign a treaty. The federal and state forces that invaded the Florida and Georgia swamplands where they lived were easy targets for Seminole bullets and arrows. This formidable resistance force who fought for their freedom included blacks and Indians fighting side by side. The Seminoles fought for their homes, their freedom, their lives, and the lives of their brothers and sisters, the blacks.

When Indians say that we are all related to all things, we mean that all races have the same Mother, Mother Earth, and we are all brothers and sisters. Humankind and all earth-dwellers are one *tiyospaye* (extended family)—humans, the winged ones, and the four-legged, finned, and planted ones. We are all one family.

A nature-based orientation and life style supports the concept of extended family and discourages prejudice. Perhaps, since Africans and Indians both lived in nature-based cultural systems, they had a ready-made basis for their mutual empathy. Unfortunately, the Europeans who came to claim the Americas had lost touch with the nature-based value system in their history. They had lived too many hundreds of generations under a system of religious and political domination that encouraged human and ecological destructiveness and, thus, prejudice. That prejudice supported and even encouraged slavery; the interhuman violence that had been practiced on their European ancestors now became the model for their treatment of blacks and Indians.

Indians weren't prejudiced, because their religion and cultural system taught them that Mother Earth gave and nourished every particle of their beings. Through her food and water they grew and replenished their bodies. If all things on earth are from Mother Earth, related through her, and sustained from her, there is no basis for prejudice.

In my own tribe there was a black man named Keeawksa sapa. A runaway slave, he had been found by the Oglala, lost and starving, along the banks of the Missouri River. He was taken into my tribe and nourished back to health. He said that the plantation owners had told him that the Indians were all cannibals and would eat the blacks if they ran away.

Keeawksa sapa married into the tribe and had a family. After he learned our language, he became well known as a songwriter and composer of lyrics to many of our old dance songs. He lived out his days in the midst of these people who respected all races as equal.

White men lived with the Indians as well. For example, many of the old mountain men were taken in by different tribes. Denver, Colorado, began with two white men who had Sioux wives. At that time, the Sioux ranged as far south as Colorado. As long as these men were good to their wives and children, the Sioux let them live. A trading post on Cherry Creek was started, and settlers heading west stayed along the banks of Cherry Creek. Denver grew.

I feel good about the value of Mother Earth spirituality when I think about the humanitarianism exhibited toward brothers and sisters of other colors by the red people.

Willard Rosenfelt, in his book *The Last Buffalo*, talks about the travels of the American artist George Catlin (1796–1872) among the American Indians during the middle third of the nineteenth century.

The artist George Catlin, who lived for eight years among 48 North American Plains Indian tribes, said in 1841: "All history of the subject goes to prove that, when first visited by civilized people, the American Indians have been found friendly and hospitable—from the days of

Christopher Columbus to the Lewis and Clark Expedition . . . and so also have a great many other travelers, including myself. Nowhere, to my knowledge, have they stolen a six-pence worth of my property, though in their countries there are no laws to punish for theft. I have visited forty-eight different tribes, and I feel authorized to say that the North American Indian in his native state is honest, faithful, brave . . . and an honorable and religious being."[8]

Rosenfelt also quotes Catlin's creed about American Indians.

I love a people who have always made me welcome to the best they had.

I love a people who are honest without laws, who have no jails and no poorhouses.

I love a people who keep the commandments without ever having read them or heard them preached from the pulpit.

I love a people who never swear, who never take the name of God in vain.

I love a people who love their neighbors as they love themselves!

I love a people who worship God without a Bible, for I believe that God loves them also.

I love a people whose religion is all the same, and who are free from religious animosities.

I love a people who have never raised a hand against me, or stolen my property, where there was no law to punish for either.

I love a people who have never fought a battle with white men, except on their own ground.

I love and don't fear mankind where God has made and left them, for there they are children.

I love a people who live and keep what is their own without locks and keys.

I love all people who do the best they can.

And oh, how I love a people who don't live for the love of money![9]

Catlin's creed tells how highly evolved socially, environmentally, and spiritually the native North American people had become. We two-leggeds in this modern world must take a very serious look at how they could have developed and arrived at such a high plane of living that brought forth a natural flow of fairness, honesty, respect for all things and an ongoing multiplicity of interlocking virtues and values beneficial to the entire planet. We must also realize that they knew how to avoid that which was harmful to all society around them.

Chief Sitting Bull said, "I have advised my people this way: When you find anything good in the white man's road, pick it up. When you find something that is bad, or turns out bad, drop it and leave it alone!"[10]

Modern technology has brought many good things to the two-leggeds. It has given us a great deal of time to sit back and contemplate. We do not have to fear nature as in old times, yet we must always respect nature's requirement that she is to be kept in balance. Otherwise we can be punished severely. When we have taken so much that we are causing harmful pollution it is time to stop our appetite for excess materialism and leave it alone. Modern technology and modern pursuits that harm us, our relatives, and our planet are portrayed as the Blue Man in Black Elk's vision. Communication, whether it is by word of mouth, the media, or scientific exploration, must continually expose that which can bring calamity and disaster. Care must be taken to be truthful, however. False claims and exaggeration will destroy environmental credibility besides circumventing worthwhile projects and exploration.

Why were the Indians so successful?

They lived close to nature. They saw the Great Spirit in nature and believed *Wakan Tanka* was revealed to them through nature. This approach allowed them a very harmonic lifestyle. They had the wisdom to look for wisdom through what and how the Great Spirit created.

The Significance of Four

Four has many important meanings to the Sioux. The Native Americans look for many meanings and signs from the Great Spirit's creation. Non-Indians use the term Mother Nature. Indian people believe that "Mother Nature" can be a living bible from which one can see, hear, touch, feel, and learn a great deal. Nature or Mother Earth was made by the Great Spirit; therefore, there are obviously many revelations that the two-leggeds may learn if they simply have the sense to look. One sign that they have observed is the many examples of four.

There are four faces, or four ages: the face of the child, the face of the adolescent, the face of the adult, the face of the aged.

There are four directions or four winds, four seasons, four quarters of the universe, four races of man and woman—red, yellow, black, and white.

There are four things that breathe: those that crawl, those that fly, those that are two-legged, those that are four-legged.

There are four things above the earth: sun, moon, stars, planets.

There are four parts to the green things: roots, stem, leaves, fruit.

There are four divisions of time: day, night, moon, year.

There are four elements: fire, water, air, earth.

Even the human heart is divided into four compartments.

Since the Creator has made so many things in four, the Indian therefore strives to express, in ceremony and in symbology, a reflection of four: There are four endurances in the Sweat Lodge, four-direction offerings in the Pipe Ceremony, and four-direction facings in the Sun Dance. The vision quester carries four colors and places these four colors in a square within which he or she sits.

Four has a special meaning to me in many ways. Four people led me down my spiritual path: my grandmother, Ben Black Elk, and two Sioux holy men, Fools Crow and Eagle Feather. It was not easy for these four to help keep our culture alive, especially back in the time when traditional Sioux ways were scorned and condemned.

I was fortunate to come from a tribe that kept its native spirituality despite the oppression my four mentors and their traditional peers faced. Even though we were aided in our period of secrecy by the sheer size and remoteness of our reservation, our religious ways had to go underground. The Great Spirit aided us, allowing our tribal preservation against great odds. Not only were we Sioux guided onto the Great Plains, but through ceremony, we were spiritually warned back when we migrated from eastern woodlands, and then from Carolina cornfields, to avoid the white man. Because of our western migration, our culture was prolonged for several added centuries, when most of the eastern tribes that remained were exterminated or reduced to remnants. Our holy men and holy women were our salvation; aided by their visions and foresight, we retained the best of our good way.

Legend has it that the mystic warriors played their part, as well, to preserve tribal ways. The mystic warriors served the chiefs and the holy persons. Not only on the field of combat did they serve, but they accepted and performed spiritual missions at the direction of the seers, the healers, and the foretelling ones—the respected medicine persons of the tribe.

I was doubly blessed in that two powerful holy men, Fools Crow and Eagle Feather, took me under their spiritual wings. Fools Crow was schooled by a holy man named Stirrup and by an old Sun Dance Intercessor named Spotted Crow. He also received some of his knowledge from Nicholas Black Elk. Eagle Feather learned much of his wisdom from Fools Crow. My grandmother and Ben Black Elk led me toward these two holy men. Therefore, I can say four people led me down my red path—four influential people who respected the red way.

It was through the two *wichasha wakan*s (holy men) that I was exposed to our Lakota beliefs and ceremonial manner of beseechment, expression, and thanksgiving. Not only were these men wise in the ways of the spirit, but they were great storehouses of wisdom applicable to everyday living.

I was not born into my traditional Indian knowledge. In my earlier years, I was blinded to the good of our Indian Way, primarily by the Christian missionaries, who dominated our reservation for a long time. They were a strong force on all Indian reservations. The Bureau of Indian

Affairs, a federal agency, worked hand in hand with the missionaries to subvert and destroy native ways. Federal agencies have no right to work with religious denominations to subvert citizens of minority religious faiths, but nevertheless, such cooperation was allowed, and most Indians were brainwashed into believing that the old way, the traditional way, was the work of the devil or, at best, was merely superstition.

One must bear in mind that, in the recent past, the great majority of Indian youth were educated in boarding schools, separated from their parents for most of their developmental years, in the names of education, assimilation, and proselytizing salvation. The missionaries at Pine Ridge and throughout the Dakotas, for example, ran large boarding schools from grades one through twelve. All of my brothers and sisters were sent to Holy Rosary Mission Boarding School, save the last two of us. Indian religion at this institution was regarded as heathen and pagan, with no value relative to one's spiritual growth. Indian youth, used to being very close to not only their parents, but also their grandmothers and grandfathers, aunts and uncles, their *tiyospaye,* were abruptly separated at the age of six from this close relationship and cast into an alien, cold, unnatural institution, devoid of the natural warmth and closeness that the *tiyospaye* provided so well.

My parents were kind and loving. On top of that I also had aunts and uncles and a grandmother of whom I was fond. Although we were poorer and less "modern" than our non-Indian counterparts (neither of my parents ever learned how to drive a car), we didn't know it, because the love in our home made up for everything. My sister Delores and I would have had to suffer the long separation from our parents in the boarding school had not two events spared us from this ordeal. One was the death of my older sister Elsie at the boarding school; the other event was World War II.

Elsie died of pneumonia. Her death was not anyone's "fault"; many children died of pneumonia and tuberculosis; many Indians, adults as well as children, were susceptible to tuberculosis. But my parents were not notified of Elsie's illness until only a few days before her death. My oldest brother, Albert, was informed in class, quite heartlessly, by his teacher, "Albert, your sister Elsie died. They buried her yesterday." It was this attitude toward Indians by boarding school administrators and teachers that was resented; it still lingers as bad memories among many Indian people.

World War II came after Elsie's death, and the northern end of our reservation was designated an Air Force bombing and aerial machine-gun range. My father's ranch was within this range, and all of the Indians in this area had to move out in a short time. My family moved to Rapid City, where my father found employment at the new military air base under construction. He worked on the runways for the airplanes that flew down to the reservation and used his ranch buildings for target practice. Four of my brothers volunteered and served in World War II, seeing combat action throughout the war theaters.

Every autumn, the reservation priests would come to Rapid City and round up Indian youth for the boarding schools. Had we still lived on the reservation, we would have been compelled to attend, but living off the reservation gave us the legal right to attend public schools. I went to public school in Rapid City, where I received a better education than I would have had at the boarding schools. At the boarding schools, both boys and girls spent considerable time not studying, but cleaning—the barns, cattle yards, shops, dormitories, laundry, kitchen—and doing other related chores. At the mission boarding school, academic time was spent on religious education. Students rose early to attend daily morning church services before school began. About half of the academic schedule was spent on labor or religion. When it came time for an Indian student to attend college (and only a very few ever did), he or she was poorly prepared.

In the fall, I was always fearful that my mother would let the reservation priests take me down to the boarding school. She was fearful of the Christian religion but, somehow, managed to hold firm against the priests. "No, Father," she would say. "He can't go down to school this year. He was real sick with pneumonia last winter, and he might not make it down there. Maybe next year," she would promise. I am very thankful that I missed out on the boarding schools and that I wasn't separated from my parents.

I was also fortunate to have the Black Hills, the sacred Paha Sapa (Black Hills), as my childhood playground. I swam in a clear mountain stream, not some square, concrete, adventureless municipal pool. The Paha Sapa afforded trout fishing, camping, and spiritual spaciousness. My taste for adventure was allowed to spawn at an early age, thanks to this wonderful resource. The Sioux legally own the Black Hills through the treaty signed in 1868, which my tribe won in combat under Chief Red Cloud's leadership. All Sioux Indian youth should have had the Black Hills as their playground, but that treaty, though legally binding, was never honored, because of the vast amounts of gold discovered in the Black Hills. Maybe if that gold had not been there, my fellow Sioux would have experienced their youth as I did.

My playground may have been a child's utopia, but my mother made sure that I attended Sunday mass and catechism at the parochial church close to our neighborhood in Rapid City. Being Indians, my sister and I were never socially accepted at this church. We felt like outcasts in our first communion and catechism classes, where we were taught that if we ever missed Sunday church and died unconfessed, we would go straight to hell with a mortal sin. Not being welcomed by our peers, we used to walk across town to feel less conspicuous in what at the time seemed a spacious cathedral. At least, if we died that week, we would not go straight to hell.

Church was a dilemma for us. We were shunned and made fun of by some of the non-Indians, yet we were taught to be fearful and afraid to miss church. I am thankful those days are history and that I now have seen through such fallacy. I am much more comfortable with my own concept of the Great Spirit, but as little children we didn't know any better.

In high school, I found a social outlet in sports. I had few dates, as there were no Indian girls in my class of several hundred students, but I did meet some good friends on the sports field. These friendships still exist.

I also started Indian dancing in my junior and senior years, and this powwow dancing led me down to my spirit path, back to my ancestry and the red way—my finding of the power of the hoop.

Powwow dancing is not a religious or true ceremonial form of dance. It is social dancing and is done simply for fun and enjoyment. It is very different from the serious religious form of dance, as in the Sun Dance, in which the dancer is a praying participant more than a dancer. The powwow regalia and social dance gathering allow natural expression and natural form, which emanate from the dancer. The eagle feathers swivel in bone sockets mounted in a stiff-haired porcupine hair roach (*pay sha*), worn as a headpiece. The *pay sha* accents the dancer's head movements. The shoulder bustle and tail bustle mounted on the dancer's backside accent the shoulder and hip movements. Bells around padded fur anklets help the dancer's feet keep time to the drumbeats. Some tail bustles are in the shape of a butterfly or a bird's wings. The dancer imparts a naturalness to the dance by imitating the flight or actions of the flying ones, gracefully fanning with an owl's or a hawk's wing. Breast plates, bone hairpipe chokers, colored breech cloths that match the plumage of the tail bustles, and beaded armbands accent the dance costumes. The colors are patterned and matching, as exhibited by many of the flying ones and by nature's decorative world.

Women also join in powwow dancing, although their attire is different. When my sister danced, she wore beautiful, beaded buckskin dresses.

Powwow dancing is very individual. One doesn't have to worry about a partner, and the dancer can express himself or herself within the drumbeat as the dancers dance in a circle within the dance arena. Social dancing is a happy time, a relaxing time, for each drumbeat seems to match one's heartbeat. You can dance a long time when you powwow dance. At Pine Ridge, my sister and I would powwow dance long into the night, and then we would watch the Sun Dance Ceremony in the morning.

In the mornings, I was moved deeply by the sun dancers. This ceremony drew me like a magnet. I never thought of being a sun dancer as I watched. I was simply moved spiritually. The Sun Dance, like the Sweat Lodge, has a strong, captivating power. It wasn't until I went off to war and returned safely that I danced my first Sun Dance.

My social dancing, and my grandmother, led to my first observance of the Sun Dance. Bill Eagle Feather, the Rosebud holy man, boldly defied the missionaries and brought our sacred Sun Dance out into the open. I watched as Fools Crow, the Oglala holy man, pierced Bill, the lone sun dancer. There was something in my lineage, something in my past primordial genes, that registered itself forever into my spirit, for I can still vividly recall Bill standing alone beneath the Sun Dance tree and pulling backward, his taut skin stretched, pulling upon his rawhide braided rope. Even his gestures and rhythm of movement I can yet recall clearly. Eagle Feather and Fools Crow would become my spiritual mentors in later years. An event at a summer's Sun Dance would lead me to both men. Through this event, I would also be led back to Ben Black Elk, whose spiritual advice I would heed.

Ben Black Elk, the interpreter for the book *Black Elk Speaks,*[1] named me, as a boy, *Wanblee Hoksila* (Eagle Boy). Later, when I became a fighter pilot and a warrior who returned to dance the Sun Dance, Ben, Bill Eagle Feather, and the Sun Dance chief, Fools Crow, named me *Wanblee Wichasha* (Eagle Man).

My grandmother prepared me for the spiritual knowledge I would gain from these three mentors. At the beginning of this chapter, I pointed out that four has many significant meanings. I am thankful that these four "influencers" led me toward my red path.

My father was a good influence also; although he conveyed little Lakota culture or tradition, he did tell me many stories about life on the reservation, and these stories included many events and happenings among the old-timers who had tasted the freedom of the plains. My father was a kind and gentle man, and I have fond memories of him. He passively resisted the missionaries. I saw him in church only once. He spoke of God through the eyes and ears of the Indian, but told us to do our mother's bidding and go to church. He didn't want any trouble with the priests, for, to us, they were powerful. Eventually, the Jesuits built an Indian Mission in Rapid City, and we felt more comfortable going to church with our own kind.

My grandmother had long braids and always wore ankle-length dresses. She had her own cabin on the reservation, and it was a treat to visit her there. Sometimes in the summer, she would come to stay with us. Actually, in white man terms she was my stepgrandmother, but traditional Siouxs do not use that kind of language. We do not like to use the terms half brothers, stepsisters and other such family designations. In our customs, we consider each other as full brothers and sisters regardless of having a different father or mother. Indian children do not like to be called a half brother or a stepdaughter. My grandmother was a great source of stories, especially when she and my father would sit telling tales of long ago. Ben also visited my family and told of the old ways. My father, Grandma, and Ben cast the memories that sprouted my Indian Spirit alive when I saw Bill Eagle Feather and Fools Crow at the first Sun Dance.

PART TWO

EARTH

The Seven Mother Earth Ceremonies

The Sioux sacred rites have undergone change since the Sioux were forced from their plains freedom to the bleak reservations of despair. The seven Mother Earth ceremonies that have evolved are offered to bridge across to the sacred in the natural world and to foster a regard for our planet as a living relative who must be sustained. Such ceremonies were followed down through time by the successful caretakers, who served well at their stewardship of Mother Earth. Reviving these ceremonies in this time of crisis will, it is hoped, bring forth a new-found perception and respect for the natural elements. I hope that the reader will attempt to do some ceremony in order to carry on that position of stewardship, even if it is a simple holding up of a stone to the rising dawn in recognition of the earth wisdom that comes with each new day.

6

The Natural Way

Global warming is the first major warning from our Mother—Mother Earth. The masses who have kept the blindfolds and earplugs over their environmental eyes and ears have been jolted by the withering climatic conditions. The crop losses resulting from rising temperatures are spreading shock waves throughout the world. Following this decline in food productivity, leading scientists predict deserts advancing into the Great Plains, rising seas, evaporating lakes, and salted aquifers. It is happening.

The generations unborn, our heirs, will curse our generation if we do not seriously heed these first rumbling, ominous warnings. Regardless of philosophical, religious, or theological persuasion, we must begin immediately to meet on some common ground to slow down and eventually halt the polluting and unbalancing causes.

For the sake of agreement, let us begin with this planet. There is, on this earth, an environment, a natural state that we are dependent upon. Even a two-legged (the American Indians' way of saying "human being"), even a two-legged without any spiritual persuasion (an atheist) would agree with the statement that we are totally dependent on this planet. We need not argue this point.

Next, let us cover another aspect that we should avoid arguing and fighting over. Let us discuss the concept of God, the Creator, the Great Spirit, the Great Mystery, or whatever other concept the Life Factor may be called or referred to as, and let us realize that the earth is heating, so that we will not prolong our discussions.

Wars, deaths, fights, break-ups of families, break-ups of tribes, lost loves, and migration have been just some of the dire consequences evolving from man's egocentric attempt to define specifically who or what the Great Creator is. Many different concepts have been formulated. Some insist that their way is the only way, and great conflict has resulted when others disagreed or resisted.

In our resolve to work together to revive the health of our Mother Earth, let us respect our brothers' and sisters' spiritual vision and not argue and fight over the exactness of defining who or what the Great Spirit is. The American Indian deplores arguing over "the exactness" of attempted description of the Great Power that Created All. As many holy ones have advised me, "It is a Mystery, leave it at that; no one can describe such a vast mystery."

North American Indians believe there is a limit to the human brain, at least while a person lives upon this planet. There may be some higher answers in the spirit world where it is believed our spirit travels, but to probe and argue with one another in this lifetime is considered utterly foolish and quite nonspiritual. Traditional Indians believe that attempts to describe to another two-legged an overly definite concept of the mysterious vastness of the Great Provider of All are crude and unmannerly and show lack of humility. When a proselytizer approaches a traditional Indian and attempts to tell the Indian that he or she has the only key to the spirit world beyond and that the Great Mystery can be explained as such and such, usually with hell-fire and damnation thrown in, the Indian at first feels a sense of pity for the proselytizer; in the end, the Indian regards such a one as ignorant. Indians want to be generous with their respect. "Respect your brothers' and sisters' visions," we are always told, but at times we have to draw the line.

I have been very fortunate to meet others of diverse and rich harmonic paths. Recently, I have learned to grow and expand through my observations and contact with the good of other visions outside my Native American world, other visions of deep spiritual wisdom, yet these enlightened ones never held up their knowledge as the sole source of truth. I spoke with my good friend Thunder Owl, a fellow traditional Sioux who lives close by on a Sioux reservation. He too was moved by the harmonic wisdom that emanated from these open-minded non-Indians.

I had been locked into my own way for a long time, but I have been awakened to the realization that spiritual and philosophical knowledge outside one's own culture can be deeply rewarding. Age-old superstitious taboos and nonharmonic customs can be thrown off. The borrowing and implementing of just some small facet can make a ceremony more spiritually rewarding. For example, several churches that I have attended have the custom of holding hands as a symbol of unity during the last prayer or song. Now, holding hands for the last prayer in the

Sweat Lodge Ceremony is not Native American custom. Most Indians do not do this at present, but it won't take them long to implement it into their ceremony if they find it provides or allows for more spiritual expression. Within the sweat ceremony, it is a unifying expression, especially during the last prayer, the last chant. This expression I have borrowed from outside the Native American culture.

My non-Indian spiritual friends encouraged me to put down in writing my experiences and knowledge gleaned from the wisdom of my mentors and visions and experiences within and related to the ceremonies. They said this knowledge was needed. Thunder Owl agreed. These new friends are spiritual and equally, profoundly environmental. They have asked me to teach and speak in their gatherings, churches, and conferences. Not one of them has ever approached either Thunder Owl or me to adopt his or her way, for they all respect the good within the many visions. Their open-mindedness is growing at a phenomenal rate; to me, as a Native American, this growth of open-mindedness is very encouraging. As people evolve spiritually in this modern age, with its great gift of communication, more and more of the deeper-thinking ones of all walks of life and all races are realizing and agreeing and meeting together without the age-old religious narrow-mindedness that held back spiritual and environmental progression. The end result will be harmony for all.

So let us look at the natural view and perception followed down through time by the successful caretakers of this portion of our planet— the red brother and sister caretakers of the North American tribes. These successful ones perfected ceremonies that brought them very close to Mother Earth and the related Powers. They were able to unify their being with all of *Wakan Tanka*'s creation. In this modern age, you, too, can participate in and be a part of these enriching and fulfilling ceremonies that rewarded the former inhabitants of this land for thousands of years.

Sharing and generosity were exemplary values common to the North American tribes. *Tiyospaye* and *mitakuye oyasin* formed the basis for their closeness to the beginning Mother—Mother Earth.

It will surprise many, no doubt, that North American tribes had a commonality of beliefs and values. Many ceremonies were similar, and the meanings behind the ceremonies were also closely related. Indians were great borrowers of spiritual customs. When something or some way proved more spiritually enhancing, they simply adopted what they considered as an improvement. They didn't let pride or ego get in their way when it came to spiritual or religious concepts. They were not held back by an organized hierarchy of religious leaders, either. Their religion was not for sale or "customerized." An organized hierarchy and the resultant commercialism of spirituality is as fatal to the fresh, clean spirit as pouring chemicals into a clear mountain stream is to a water supply.

A sweat lodge is an excellent example of the noncommercialism of the Indian way. It costs only a ball of string to build this beautiful temple that will leave a spiritual impact no cathedral can match. Building plans and funding drives are unnecessary, and the lodge can be used in but a few hours. If you wish to get very close to Mother Earth, spiritually, environmentally, or both, enter a sweat lodge, my friend, and you will find her.

The Sioux are a representative North American Indian tribe. Their ceremonies are reflective of those of most tribes, especially the Sweat Lodge *(Inipi)* and the Vision Quest *(Hanblecheyapi)* ceremonies. The Sun Dance *(Wiwanyag wachipi)* and the Spirit-calling *(Yuwipi)* ceremonies are reflective in that these ceremonies have the same meaning as other related ceremonies held by other tribes. Most tribes had annual thanksgivings to the Great Spirit. These were held in the open upon the great amphitheater of Mother Earth. After the summer buffalo hunts, the Sioux had their annual Sun Dance thanksgiving to *Wakan Tanka*. Other tribes had similar ceremonies, usually after a time of plenty—the corn harvest or a wild rice harvest—in which they paid homage to the All-Providing One. A key ingredient toward their fulfillment of inner peace was to be thankful to the higher powers, the created forces, and of course, *Wakan Tanka*. The spirit-calling ceremonies were conducted in similar fashion but had different names. Ancestors were beseeched and ancestors answered the calling whether the ceremony was called *Yuwipi, Kiva,* Shaking Tent, or Longhouse.

The Sweat Lodge Ceremony is held by most major North American tribes. The lodges themselves are of similar construction and have similar purposes. The facing of the lodge opening, the different tribal colors, whether one smokes a pipe within or outside the lodge, or whether or not a woman should be the first to open the lodge—these dissimilarities would be considered petty by most Indians and would certainly not be a bar to participation should a member of another tribe of differing customs be invited. At a gathering of holy men and holy women of differing tribes, I noted with pride the refusal of the spiritual leadership to get "hung up" on petty differences. Traditional, pipe-bearing Indians abhor arguing over religion. That is a good custom worth following.

Before the Sioux came out onto the Great Plains, their medicine pipes were mostly made of clay brought with them in their long migration from the Carolinas. Then, the Buffalo Calf Woman gave them the red peace pipe, quarried from the pipestone of southwestern Minnesota, which evolved into a beautiful, powerful altar that is the clear wellspring of Indian ceremonies, the ceremonies that kept the Indians closely related to the earth and *Wakan Tanka* above and everywhere. Ceremony, to the Indian, is a realization, an experiencing realization of the spirituality that surrounds all. Ceremony brings forth that profound, deeply powerful realization from beyond into the world of the two-leggeds.

After the red peace pipe was introduced by the Buffalo Calf Woman, Black Elk, as a young boy, had his powerful vision. The Buffalo Calf Woman introduced the power of the pipe into the ceremonies, and Black Elk reinforced the incorporation of the natural forces, or powers, under the Great Spirit. The six forces—consisting of the four directions, or four winds, Mother Earth, and Father Sky—were strongly symbolized in Black Elk's vision. The red peace pipe was also reinforced as a strong spiritual symbol along with the annual thanksgiving, the Sun Dance. Black Elk's vision and prophecies have been very accurate. The Indian spirit was predicted to undergo some trying times, dying down to a bare ember, but it was also predicted to burn brightly again. Its nature-based wisdom would be very helpful in later times, not only for the Indian, but for all two-leggeds. It must be respected that Black Elk's vision came directly from the six powerful forces of this universe. A flowering tree and a rainbow were the most symbolic of Black Elk's prophecies. The flowering tree, from the herb of understanding, is beginning to bloom now. I believe that the highly evolved, harmoniously spiritual, and environmentally respecting people of this time are the leaves of this flowering tree.

The rainbow is a symbol of the Great Spirit and the many colors, ways, and races unifying. Black Elk said that the rainbow people would become the spreading flames for a unifying force of good. Many people already have rainbows in their purses or pockets, the little crystals many people wear or carry. A crystal can contain a rainbow when you hold it up to the light. The new Rainbow Tribe is coming into being!

If Mother Earth were to judge, I believe she would say that the Indian Way has been proved to be a good way. Now that it has been largely supplanted, she has issued powerful warning signs. However, despite the track record of the red way, there will be no proselytizing or conversion from the red people. A traditional Native American realizes the limitation of a two-legged's brain. He or she does not proselytize or convert. There is no conversion ceremony in our seven ceremonies given to us by the Great Spirit through the Buffalo Calf Woman. There is no formal conversion or membership sought through the seven Mother Earth ceremonies that have evolved and adapted since the Sioux had to give up their natural freedom. The seven Mother Earth ceremonies have a much higher purpose.

After these pages, I hope you will keep your present vision and simply go on. Go on your own path, strengthened in a deeper respect and understanding for our Mother Earth and the perceptive natural view, which was followed down through time by the successful caretakers who served well their stewardship of this western hemisphere of Mother Earth.

7

The Peace Pipe Ceremony and the Crystal

Those who desire to benefit their spiritual path by learning Native American knowledge and wisdom, some of which will come through the ceremonies, are recommended to get a peace pipe. The peace pipe is not restricted to only one race or one culture. It has been jealously guarded by Indian people, however, and rightfully so because many are fearful that the pipe may be used disrespectfully by non-Indian people.

I believe that a powerful good for all things can emanate from the respectful use of the pipe, but it must be deeply regarded as a spiritual instrument by the pipe holder, whatever his or her lineage or color happens to be. The pipe can become a strong catalyst to import a powerful feeling for our Mother Earth and all living things.

Black Elk predicted that we would go forth in numbers as flames to bring forth beneficial change in this generation. The pipe, and the respectful pipe holder, will be a needed force to disseminate a spiritual basis for the goal being sought throughout this nation. There are far too few Native American pipe holders to accomplish all of this alone.

Even some Indian people must be reminded of our four cardinal principles: respect for *Wakan Tanka*, respect for Mother Earth, respect for our fellow man and woman, and respect for individual freedom. And I have met many good and understanding non-Indian brothers and sisters who deeply respect the knowledge and wisdom that emanates from the red way. Under the old regime, we did suffer severely from those that came upon our red path only to convert, destroy, and replace it. Those of this new era seek to help, not to destroy. They are open-minded, not narrow-minded. We Indian people should allow these people insight; together we will all join forces to make a better and a more peaceful world.

The ceremonial use of the peace pipe is a simple ritual. The peace pipe serves as a portable altar. It is loaded with tobacco, and only tobacco, or a tobacco variation called *kinnic kinnick,* which is the bark of the red willow and nonhallucinatory. The bark of the red willow has a pleasing aroma, very similar to tobacco, and served principally in the old days as a substitute, since tobacco was a scarce commodity on the Great Plains. No form of mind-altering substance whatsoever is condoned or recommended by true Native American religion traditionalists. Unfortunately, the use of peyote, a mind-altering cactus bud brought up from Mexico and not native to the present-day United States and Canada, is wrongfully associated with traditional Native American religion and ceremony. The peyote religion blends Christianity, peyote, and semblances of traditional Native American culture. It is unfortunate that true, historical Native American religion has been wrongfully distracted from by such inaccurate association. True Native American Way finds the Great Spirit through "our own juices" (fasting, knowledge and observance of God's creation, and the Sun Dance, Vision Quest, and Sweat Lodge ceremonies). We do not need or use hallucinating substances.

The Pipe Ceremony begins with loading tobacco, a natural substance, into a pipe and then acknowledging the four directions, Mother Earth, and Father Sky; it culminates with the final offering to the Great Spirit. The pipe is held firmly by the bowl in the palm of the hand with the stem pointed outward. The last step of the pipe offering is the holding up of the pipe with its stem pointed straight upward, out into the center of the universe. Although the Indian readily admits that God is everywhere, in ceremony, *Wakan Tanka* is regarded as above.

A Sioux pipe holder may begin with the east direction for the first acknowledgment, but there is no such requirement. I prefer the east because the sun rises in the east, and it is the beginning of a new day for each of us, so the following description begins with an east-facing celebrant.

The pipe holder stands to face the east, holding the pipe with its stem pointed eastward in one hand, a pinch of tobacco in the other, and sprinkles some tobacco upon the ground before inserting the tobacco into the bowl of the pipe. By sprinkling a portion upon the ground, the pipe holder is recognizing that we must always give back to Mother Earth part of what we have taken. The sprinkling also demonstrates to the onlooking spirit world that a portion of the tobacco is for the powers from the east.

The pipeholder may say,

> Red is the east;
> It is where the daybreak star, the star of knowledge appears.
> Red is the rising sun
> Bringing us a new day
> New experiences.

> We thank you, Great Spirit, for each new day
> That we are allowed to live upon
> Our Mother Earth.

> From knowledge springs wisdom and goodness
> And we are thankful, oh *Wakan Tanka*,
> For the morning star that rises in the east.
> Knowledge shall become the beginning
> For ultimate peace throughout this world.

This is an example of an Indian prayer beginning with the east.

Onlooking participants will also face east while the pipe is loaded in such a manner.

The pipeholder turns to the south and points the pipe stem in that direction. A new pinch of tobacco is held slightly above eye level in a southerly direction. Onlooking participants face south.

> The south is yellow.
> Our Mother Earth gives us our growth,
> Gives us all that sustains us,
> The herbs that heal us.

> She brings forth the bounty of springtime
> From the warm south wind
> and the yellow hoop.

> We think of strength, growth, and physical healing
> And a time for planting our energies,
> My friends, while we load this pipe.

After such acknowledgment, the pinch of tobacco is put into the pipe bowl.

The pipe holder then faces west.

> Black is the color of the west
> Where the sun goes down.
> Black is darkness, release, spirit protection.
> In the darkness, the spirit beings come to us.

The spirit beings warn us,
Protect us, foretell for us, release for us.
They are the spirit helpers to *Wakan Tanka*.

Black is the cup of water;
The life-giving rains come from the west,
Where the thunder beings live.
Water is life.

Black stands for the spirit world
Which we shall all enter someday.
What we do or do not do upon this earth,
We shall carry with us over into that spirit world.
We shall all join together and either be
Ashamed or proud of how we treated one another,
How we respected or disrespected our Mother Earth,
How we respected or disrespected all living things
That are made by the Great Creator,
Wakan Tanka.

We will see each other
And yet know each other in the spirit world.
Those we have harmed,
They will remind us for eternity.
Those we have helped,
They will be thankful for eternity.
Therefore, we must walk the path of truth
With one another.

The west
Is where our spiritual wisdom comes from,
If we care to seek it.

The pipe holder sprinkles tobacco upon Mother Earth and puts some tobacco into the pipe bowl.

Every time the pipe holder faces a direction, all onlookers face that direction also and listen to the speaker's words intently.

The last of the four directions is north.

White is for the north.
Waziya ouye—the north power
Waziya ahtah—the white giant from the north.

Strength, endurance, purity, truth
Stand for the north.
The north covers our Mother Earth
With the white blanket of cleansing snow.

The snow prevents many sicknesses
Found in places without snow.

After the winter snows
Our Mother Earth wakes refreshed
To bring forth the bounty of springtime.

For us two-leggeds,
It is the time of long contemplation.
We must think of when we will have
The face of the old.
We will want to look back upon our lifetime
And hope that we stood for the straight road
In our relationship to all things.

It is also a time to do small things,
Crafts and creative works,
In order that we may pass through
And enjoy our long winter's wait.

Courage and endurance,
These strengths we seek
And wish to be blessed with
As we stand here facing north.

The tobacco is sprinkled to the north and then inserted into the bowl.

A note regarding prayer or acknowledgment: Indian people memorize very few prayers or acknowledgments. Rote prayers are not recommended. The Our Father, common to Christians, would be considered too lengthy a recital to be memorized by traditional Indian laypeople. Sioux holy men, holy women, and medicine people do chant lengthy songs and prayers in a prescribed manner for certain ceremonies, especially in the Spirit-calling and Sun Dance ceremonies. But, by and large, Indian prayers, beseechments, and acknowledgments flow from the heart. A prescribed symbology is followed, especially in regard to the four directions. Knowledge in relationship to the east, growth from the south, and so forth, are included, but rote prayers are not generally followed.

A note on the colors of the four directions: the red, yellow, black, and white, beginning with red for the east and following clockwise to the south, is in accordance with Black Elk. Some medicine people interpret the four direction colors as depicted. Many Sioux people, especially those who have not read *Black Elk Speaks*, however, use other color arrangements; blue is often substituted for black.

Traditional Indians do not quibble over the colors, however. Rarely, if ever, do arguments spawn over such trivialities. Indian people consider it disrespectful to argue over the Great Mystery's mystery. Acknowledge, respect, and do not harm one another or interfere with one another's spiritual visions are cardinal traditional Indian principles.

After acknowledging the four directions, the pipe holder touches the pipe bowl to the ground.

> Green is the color for Mother Earth.
> Every particle of us comes from her
> Through the food we take from her daily.
>
> We all start out as tiny seeds.
> We have grown to our present state and status
> Through what she provides.
>
> She is truly our Mother
> And must be acknowledged and respected.

Tobacco is sprinkled upon Mother Earth and the pipe is loaded.

The pipe is then pointed at an angle toward the sky. We usually point our pipe toward the sun; if it is evening, we point it toward the moon, to acknowledge Father Sky.

> Father Sky gives us energy from the sun.
> Father Sky provides the fire that
> Fuels our homes and lodges
> And the energy that moves our bodies.
>
> Father Sky has daily communion with our Mother.
> Together, they are our true parents.

Some tobacco is sprinkled on the ground, and the major portion is loaded into the pipe.

The pipe receives a portion of tobacco one last time, and then the pipe is held almost straight up into the sky.

> *Wakan Tanka,*
> Great Spirit, Creator of us all
> Creator of the four directions,
> Creator of our Mother Earth and Father Sky
> And all related things,
> We offer this pipe.

If the Pipe Ceremony is preceding a Sweat Lodge Ceremony, the address may be as follows:

> Oh, Great Spirit,
> We now offer this pipe to begin
> Our *Inipi* (Sweat Lodge) Ceremony tonight.

The pipe tobacco in the bowl is then capped, or temporarily covered, with a piece of sage (flat leaves of cedar or other natural material may be used in place of sage for capping the pipe), which will be removed when the pipe is ready to be smoked. After the sage is inserted, the pipe is placed on a pipe rack to await the completion of the particular ceremony that will follow. (Many pipe bowls, especially on ceremonial pipes, have a pointed tip. The pointed end is inserted into the ground with the stem usually pointed toward the sun or the moon. In the Sun Dance Ceremony and during an evening Sweat Lodge, pipe stems generally face the west.) If a pipe is to be smoked immediately after loading, there is no need for capping.

In a Sweat Lodge Ceremony, the pipe is smoked following the actual ceremony, after the participants emerge from the lodge. The ceremony culminates in the smoking of the peace pipe. Usually the participants will change into a dry set of clothing, in order to be comfortable, before they gather in a circle to smoke the peace pipe. After this last ritual, the participants can then partake of a meal, which is a general custom following an evening sweat that is not a preparatory ceremony for a Vision Quest or the Sun Dance.

The smoke from the pipe represents the participants' visible breath and stands for truth: truthful words, truthful actions, and a truthful spirit. In regard to the actual smoking, most participants do not inhale the tobacco.

Nonsmokers simply hold the pipe momentarily and then pass it on to the next person.

If there is still some unburned tobacco remaining within the bowl after the pipe has made its journey around the circle, one who smokes will generally be asked to smoke out all the tobacco loaded in the pipe; the ashes will be cleaned from the pipe and sprinkled upon Mother Earth. The Pipe Ceremony is then regarded as being finished.

The pipe is disassembled. Its bowl, generally, resides within a red cloth sack within a pipe carrier's buckskin or animal-hide pipe bag. The stem is also stored within the pipe bag. A cloth pipe bag may be used in place of a hide.

When a peace pipe is loaded indoors, a woman will usually serve as acceptor for the tobacco that is normally sprinkled onto Mother Earth. The woman represents the Buffalo Calf Woman and will take the accumulation of tobacco offered to the four directions, Mother Earth, Father Sky, and the Great Spirit outside at some later time and sprinkle the tobacco upon the earth.

The Crystal

Many people now have crystals in their possession. Some wear them, or carry them in their pockets or purses, or have them in their homes. There are, no doubt, as many misconceptions of the crystal as there are misconceptions of the peace pipe.

I regard a crystal in much the same respectful spiritual perspective as I do a peace pipe or my own personal *wotai* stone, which I found after my second Sun Dance. My *wotai* stone is an agate with a rainbow rim and a crystalline center. There are many strong images within this stone, and it came to me in a very powerful, spiritual manner, indicating to my Native American perspective that it was *lelah wah ste wakan* (very holy and spiritual).

A crystal is obviously very special and *lelah wakan*. Hold it up to the light. It reflects the rainbow. This is a very powerful, God-made symbol. What do we see after the life-giving, refreshing, nourishing rains? The rainbow, the beautiful rainbow of all colors. Yet this powerful symbol is compacted within the clear, clean, rain-resembling crystal. I need not elaborate further about the specialness of this Great Spirit–designed unique stone. It can be regarded as spirit rain, with a refreshing rainbow.

For the sake of practicality, I will be the first to admit that I do not foresee a mass of people going to Pipestone and purchasing peace pipes despite the deep and powerful meaning of the Pipe Ceremony. Some pipe holders will come forth, and that will be good, but the majority will continue on their journeys.

I believe that the crystal can help with relating to this new knowledge from the Native American world. Simply take the crystal and beseech the four directions, Mother Earth, Father Sky, and *Wakan Tanka* (or one's respectful concept of the Great Spirit) with the crystal in the same respectful manner as one would use a peace pipe. We as Mother Earth–concerned people desire to have a relationship with all living things. The Pipe Ceremony provides this avenue; so can the crystal.

The Sweat Lodge Ceremony

Sweat lodges are easily constructed structures made of saplings bent together and tied with twine to form a half sphere. A pit is dug in the center for heated rocks. The structure is covered with a tarp or blankets. In the old days, hides or buffalo robes covered the sapling frame. The earthern floor is strewn with sage, flat cedar, flowers, grass, or reeds. Participants gather within the darkened interior to endure the steam generated by dippers of water poured over the hot stones. *Inipi* is the Sioux term for sweat lodge.

While the sweat lodge itself is simple to describe, it is beyond any mortal writer's ability to adequately convey the ultimate culmination of spiritual, mystical, and psychic expression of the Sweat Lodge Ceremony. Everyone that I have seen experience a Native American *Inipi* agrees wholeheartedly: the Sweat Lodge Ceremony is impossible to describe fully. You have to experience it to truly realize its fullness and depth.

The average-sized lodge is approximately eight feet by twelve feet. A group can get together on a remote or semiremote area and build its own "little church" in a few hours. I personally prefer a lodge of eight to sixteen people, but there are times when larger lodges must be built.

In the past, participants visited the sweat lodge before engaging in the Vision Quest, Sun Dance, and occasionally the Spirit-calling ceremonies. Traditional people held these main ceremonies to meet the spiritual needs of the tribe, group, or individual. In the "old days," the sweat lodge "got them ready" for a higher, deeper plane or dimension. Before the Sun Dance, sun dance pledgers cleansed themselves physically and spiritually within the steamy mist of the sweat lodge. Then the Sun Dance chief or assisting holy man would conduct the *Inipi* in the early morning hours, before or while the sun rested on the horizon. Vision questers would usually cleanse and prepare themselves in the sweat lodge before ascending a lonely hilltop or badland butte or before the long climb to the top of Spirit Mountain (Bear Butte) in the Black Hills.[1]

In this day and age, however, the cleansing experience is fast becoming a major ceremony for those of all races, creeds, and nationalities who seek natural, nature-based, Mother Earth–based expression. Even among Native Americans, for whom it was once only a preparation, the sweat lodge experience is becoming a major ceremony, especially among urban Indians, who have limited access to other tribal ceremonies.

Once the lodge is covered and the ceremony is under way, the participants find a deep connection back into a past. A tribal closeness to the Natural Way unfolds like a budding blossom. A natural bonding begins within the misty, generative womb of Mother Earth—a bonding to one's own concept of God, the Creator, and the created Mother, upon which we all thrive daily. The spiritual bond is likened to an attachment to Mother Earth as one sits within her warm womb. It can be a key function in the search for a spiritual link to God's creation—nature, the environment.

I personally equate the *Inipi* as the ceremony that "intermingles and conveys the lifeblood of the world." Water is the lifeblood of this ecosystem of fire, water, air, and earth—the four elements. Although the Pipe Ceremony precedes a Sweat Lodge Ceremony, the peace pipe is not smoked until after the participants have endured the Sweat Lodge Ceremony. The Pipe Ceremony honors and brings forth universal truth, but first the lifeblood of water must come forth from the participants.

The four directions are called upon within the lodge. The misty, fire-heated steam covers you, bringing forth your own mist (your sweat). Your universal lifeblood comes forth and intermingles with the misty waters of your brothers and sisters around you. The waters of the world (the bucket of water), which have been brought into the lodge, join and mix with the air of the four directions when the dipper of water is ladled onto the hot stones, making steam. The four winds will carry the life blood out of the lodge to the four quarters of our planet. A part of your lifeblood will seep back into our Mother Earth.

The peace pipe is smoked after the four endurances of the Sweat Lodge. The participants are refreshed; their lifeblood is traveling through the ecosystem; and their visible breath, symbolizing truth, will be carried throughout the universe. The sweat lodge, in conjunction with the peace pipe, makes for very powerful ceremonies.

As in a *Yuwipi* Ceremony, the Sweat Lodge Ceremony recreates time and space, at least in the Indian sense. Powers wrote very perceptively in *Oglala Religion*, "The placing of tobacco representing the four winds, zenith, nadir, and Spotted Eagle in a sacred pipe renders the pipe powerful because it contains the entire universe. When it is lighted, life and breath are invested in the universe; and when it is smoked, the universe passes through one's own body and is sent back to *Wakan Tanka*."[2] The universe stands for truth. It is, after all, Great Spirit's ultimate creation, and all universal things work synchronistically, harmoniously, in accord with the ultimate truth of the Great Mystery Creator. All traditional Indians are very careful regarding what they say while holding the pipe. Their visible breath of their words must be truth, otherwise they would be very disrespectful of the universe and of the Creator's ultimate power, which was passed through the pipe.

The Ceremony

Some Indians prefer males only in *Inipi* ceremonies; others do not differentiate, or mind mixed male and female participation within the same lodge. My mentor, Chief Eagle Feather, never minded both sexes attending together in his *Inipis*, and, as time moves on, mixed lodges are becoming more prevalent. Personally, I cannot understand why there should be much differentiation, as we are all creations of the Great Spirit, all equal, all holy, especially in the spiritual sense. What differences there are between man and woman are special, due to the Creator. It is a special relationship, in practical respects, but on a spiritual level there is an equal sameness.

Bill Eagle Feather was a powerful and good *wichasha wakan*. What was good for Bill is good by me. I guess I could sum it up simply by that.

An *Inipi* usually starts with the loading and offering of the peace pipe, as described above. As in the majority of Sioux ceremonies, the woman's role reflects her position of honor. A woman, representative of the Buffalo Calf Maiden, will take tobacco and circle clockwise around the fireplace, trailing some particles of tobacco. She will then leave a trail from the fireplace to the sweat lodge opening. She enters the lodge with her remaining portion of tobacco and circles the stone pit with a light sprinkling. The sweat lodge is now considered open, and the participants may proceed to undress for the lodge.

Tennis shorts or swimming trunks are preferred for the men, shorts and a halter or T-shirt for the women. Participants may wear, or carry in their pockets, special stones, crystals, or other significant objects. Once the ceremony group has entered and is seated around the stone pit, the ceremony leader enters, sitting slightly to the side of the doorway. If the leader has an assistant or a singer, that person sits on the opposite side of the doorway. A fire tender is stationed outside and may serve as a doorkeeper and water tender as well. I find it more convenient to have a separate fire tender and doorkeeper, if there are enough volunteers available.

The lodge leader calls upon the doorkeeper to drop the flap, usually a thick blanket, covering the lodge opening. The lodge becomes black, and at this point the lodge leader asks for a short, contemplative silence. Many holy men or lodge leaders bring the red-hot rocks into the lodge immediately after the participants are gathered within. I prefer to give newcomers, especially "first timers," a while to adjust to the confines of the lodge before introducing the glowing stones, which seem to cause some apprehension among new participants.

After the brief silence the flap is raised, and the leader calls upon the fire tender to bring in the stones. Before a ceremony, a fire tender should be briefed on the safe handling of the stones. A pitchfork is preferred to a shovel for bringing the stones into the lodge as it prevents glowing coals, which create discomforting smoke within the lodge, from being carried along. A shovel is preferred for fire tending at the fireplace site, especially when glowing coals have to be kept over the rocks or stones to keep them hot for a second ceremony. In the old days, elk horns or deer horns were used for pitchforks and shovels.

The lodge leader and his or her assistant usually have a short, stout stick and greet the entering stone. *"Hau kola"* (Hello, friend), they say to the stone. After four stones have been brought in, the flap is closed.

The lodge is dark, quiet. The participants see only the glowing red-orange stones within this dome-shaped, sapling-framed lodge. Some may see within those stones images that have waited since time immemorial. Energized by Father Sky, energized by the fire, which, in turn, was from the trees, and they, in turn, gave of themselves, they whose life energy came from the Sun, the Sun a part of Father Sky—all creation part of the great Oneness. Long, long ago, those rocks were created by the One, and the images reflected from them were placed purposely by the Creator, specifically for the participants' perception at this particular moment in time. Purposely, specially, and powerfully! A Sweat Lodge Ceremony thus begins with deep, meaningful, refreshing power.

Before the first dipper of water is poured on the rocks, the leader should assure all within the lodge that anyone is free to leave at any time. Anyone who becomes frightened or fearful should try to endure or try to summon courage to stay, but at times there are some who cannot take a Sweat Lodge Ceremony. If this is the case, the participant should simply call out, and the ceremony will be halted temporarily so that person can carefully leave through the doorway.

The following is the way I begin a ceremony while the participants are looking for symbols within the cooling stones.

First Endurance: *Wiyopeyata* (West)

The recognition of the spirit world is symbolic of the First Endurance. For some, it is a time to ask the Almighty for a spirit guide.

> In Black Elk's vision, the First Grandfather was from the west. This Grandfather held a cup of water and said that water was the power to make live.
>
> In the west, in the black, we believe the spirit beings live. Someday, if we have lived a good life, we too will be among the spirit beings and will be looking down upon this world and our relatives and friends.
>
> In this ceremony we are going to ask those above, who are looking down upon this tiny lodge, to hear the prayers that shall come from the lodge.
>
> Black Elk spoke of the powers of the four directions; we will call upon these powers in our four prayers, our four endurances tonight [today].

At this point, a dipper of water will be poured upon the rocks. Steam will shoot upward.

> This water is from the four quarters of the universe. It shall be carried to the four quarters of our planet by Father Sky, who promised his powers would be with us when we pray in the spirit of peace, knowledge, wisdom, and healing. Mother Earth has provided this water, and she too has promised to help us, for there will be many troubles, and we will need her power.

Three more dippers will be poured onto the rocks.

> My friends, we will contemplate and pray to the Great Spirit above, *Wakan Tanka*, thanking the All-Providing One for the life-giving rains which this water symbolizes. We shall ask that our spiritual lives become strong and healthy. Let this ceremony, with its lifeblood of water, cleanse

our spirit and refresh us. We will be mindful that the four directions shall enter here tonight, and our lifeblood of water that we give up from our bodies shall be carried to the four quarters of this planet. We therefore shall pray sincerely, because of the power of this ceremony. We shall ask the helpers of the Great Spirit to enter into our lodge, and to give encouragement to the prayers and beseechments that we will make here tonight.

A drum may be sounded at length, an eagle-bone whistle blown, or a song sung. Depending upon the temperature, a few more dippers of water may be applied to the stones, because it usually takes more than the first endurance to adequately heat the lodge. Use caution, however.[3] After the drumming or song, the lodge leader will call out a prayer.

> Oh, *Wakan Tanka*,
> Oh, Great Spirit above,
> We are gathered here below
> In our pitiful little lodge
> Made upon our Mother, Mother Earth.
>
> We shall call upon the four powers
> The four quarters
> The four directions
> The four Grandfathers of Black Elk's vision.
>
> Father Sky said he would help us;
> Mother Earth said she would help us;
> The Buffalo Calf Woman has instructed us;
> And our relatives shall be looking on while we pray.
>
> Oh, *Wakan Tanka*,
> Oh, All-Providing One,
> Oh, Creator of All,
> We shall beseech you
> Through the Powers you have created for us.
>
> *Mitakuye oyasin* [literally, for all my relatives]
> *Ho. Hetch etu aloh* [It is so, indeed.].

At this time, those within the lodge may introduce themselves to the Spirit World, beginning with the person to the left of the lodge leader.

"Oh, forces that come among us within this womb of our Mother, I am Red Pipe Woman, and I am most pleased to be here tonight. *Hetch etu aloh.*"

The introductions help to allow a more personal perspective within this powerful group beseechment. After the introductions, the fire tender or doorkeeper will be called, and the cool air will be allowed to refresh the participants for a few minutes before the second endurance begins.

The leader may comment while the flap door is held open:

>Appreciate the lifegiving air.
>We must be aware.
>Someday, each of us will take our last breath.
>This cool air rushing inward
>Reminds us to appreciate
>Our Breath
>Our Life.

More rocks may be called for, although if an "easy" approach was followed in the first endurance, there is usually enough heat in the stones for the second endurance without the need for additional stones.

Second Endurance: *Waziya* (North)

The flap is closed and the second endurance begins. The cleansing steam and the recognition of courage symbolizes the second endurance.

>We will now call upon the power
>From the white north
>Let us think about the Great White Giant, *Waziya,*
>Or *Way-ah-zahtah.*
>The one who puts our Mother Earth to sleep
>Under the winter's mantle of snow
>Endurance, strength, cleanliness, honesty.

A dipper of water is poured upon the rocks. Enough dippers are poured to bring forth the steam throughout the lodge.

>Endurance, cleanliness, strength, purity
>Will keep our lives straight
>Our actions only for a good purpose.
>Our words will be truth.
>Only honesty shall come from our interaction
>With all things.
>I shall give up some of my waters.
>I shall endure this ceremony to send my prayers.

The drum may be sounded for a time, while the participants endure and contemplate.

> The Second Grandfather
> Held an herb of power in his hand.
> The black horse, the horse of the spirit
> Was gaunt and sick.
> The black horse took the herb and
> Became strong and healthy.
>
> Oh, powers of the universe,
> I will take this herb
> To become strong and healthy to endure.

At this time, the leader may pass out sage to the participants to hold or chew. The sage represents the healing herb, the fortifying herb, the herb that can help overcome the bad things of the world.

Since from the north comes the great, white, cleansing wing, the leader can take a wing, or several feathers, and fan the air.

> The thunder nation is appearing.
> Behold.
> The white goose nation is appearing.
> Behold.
>
> Let this cleansing wing
> And the sage you have upon you
> Give strength and courage to endure this ceremony.

If the heat subsides, more steam may be generated by applying more water.

The second endurance comes to an end after a period of contemplation. By this time, all the participants should be sweating. The fire tender or doorkeeper is then called upon to lift the flap. As the flap is raised and held open, the leader asks the participants how they are feeling. Most usually respond enthusiastically at this stage. A dipper of water may be passed to those participants who desire to pour the water over their heads. *Minne mitak oyasin* (water for all my relatives) may be called out, meaning that the water shall take their water (sweat) into all parts of the earth and to all their relatives.

Third Endurance: *Wiyoheyapa* (East)

Usually more rocks and a new bucket of water are needed before the third endurance. After the new stones have entered, the flap is closed. The recognition of knowledge and praying individually out loud symbolize the third endurance. All within look upon the stones in silence, viewing images upon and within the red glow. After a while, water is poured upon the rocks, and the leader begins.

> Red is the color of the east. The third Grandfather, the Grandfather of the daybreak star, appeared to Black Elk. The daybreak star symbolizes an awakening. From awakening can come knowledge and wisdom for all races to overcome the ignorance, the destructive and wasteful, consuming fears that detour our resources. This morning we began a new day. New knowledge came with this day, as evidenced by the knowledge of the red way that is before us here. The red peace pipe was presented by the third Grandfather. The pipe is spiritual. With spirit and knowledge the world can be made well.

The drum is sounded for a few moments. The leader continues:

> Brothers and Sisters
> Each of you is asked to pray:
> Pray for what you desire in this life,
> Pray for a loved one or a relative,
> Pray for better leadership in this world,
> Better religious leadership,
> Better political leadership,
> Pray for our Mother Earth.
> Any and all of these ways you may pray for.
> End your prayer with HETCH ETU
> When you are finished, so that your brother or sister
> Next to you may begin his or her prayer.
> My sister or brother sitting next to me,
> Please begin your prayer.

This prayer indicates the beginning of the individual prayers. The participant sitting to the left of the leader prays first. The rest follow with their prayers in a clockwise or sunwise manner.

> Oh, Great Spirit,
> I thank you for this experience tonight.
> I pray that all ways, all hoops
> Come together in understanding.
> I pray that the world leaderships come together
> To end the needless waste of war spendings.
> I pray that the ways of the Indian people live on.
> I pray that our environment
> Becomes cleaner and less polluted.
> I thank you again, Great Spirit, for this ceremony.
> HETCH ETU ALOH.

This prayer or versions thereof are common in a Sweat Lodge Ceremony.

After all have prayed, the leader calls for the fire tender or doorkeeper to raise the flap.

Mitakuye oyasin is called out as the flap is raised.

The dipper of water may be passed around again to those who wish the water to be poured over their heads to refresh and help cool themselves and to facilitate the mixing of their lifeblood of water with Mother Earth.

Fourth Endurance: *Itokaga* (South)

The last endurance centers on healing. *"Yupayo!"* (Close the door) the fire tender is commanded, and the last endurance prayer may begin.

The south stands for healing and growth. Black Elk spoke of south, from whence comes the power to grow. The bright red stick with green leaves in Black Elk's vision was given by the south Grandfather. The stick grew into a great shading tree that stood in the center of the nation's circle. From knowledge (the east) comes growth (the south), and from growth can come healing.

> Let us think of Mother Earth, her rich bounty that will result from springtime, the golden corn and the seeds of harvest, all grown strong from Mother Earth, the spring rains, and the energy of Father Sky. It is time to consider healing: healing of ourselves, healing of a loved one, healing of adversaries for peace among nations, and healing of the harms done to Mother Earth. There are four concepts of healing, my friends, For you to contemplate to the Great Spirit above While I sing this song [or play the drum].

The leader will then pour four dippers of water onto the rocks, and the steam will build. The drum is played and/or a song is sung while the participants contemplate.

The leader may call out a short reminder for the benefit of the participants' contemplation; for example:

> Oh, Great Spirit,
> I pray for myself in order that I may be healed.
> Oh, Great Spirit,

I pray for my close friend who is sick and needs help.
Oh, Great Spirit,
I pray for this world so that all these atomic weapons
And other bad things that we point at each other
Will someday soon all be destroyed.
I pray that adversaries will communicate
And all of the mistrust will be healed.
Oh, Great Spirit,
I pray for the environment.
I pray for its cleansing
And the renewal of our Mother Earth.

The leader may even point out some specific areas and ask for the Great Spirit's wisdom regarding them.

When the steam has subsided, the leader will usually offer a summarizing prayer, or one or several of the participants may pray out loud in respect to a particular area of healing. Usually the leader will have briefed certain individuals regarding preparing, to some degree, a prayer regarding healing; or the individuals are free to request time to voice their healing prayer.

The leader concludes the ritual with a short final prayer—a prayer of thanksgiving for a successful Sweat Lodge Ceremony. It is not traditional to hold hands in this ceremony, but in this modern era this is a good new custom that can be adopted. All may join hands and repeat a short, meaningful prayer.

The light of the Great Spirit surrounds us.
The love of *Wakan Tanka* enfolds us.
The power of the Creator protects us.
The presence of God watches over us.
Wherever I am, the Great Spirit is!

The fire tender or doorkeeper is called and the participants leave the lodge one by one in a clockwise manner, beginning with the first person to the right of the entrance.

The participants will usually change into a dry set of clothes to be comfortable when they gather once again to smoke the peace pipe that was loaded earlier. The pipe will be smoked in the same manner as described in the Pipe Ceremony chapter.

After the pipe has been smoked, there might be a supper. The hot coals are excellent for metal boiling pots loaded with vegetarian or non-vegetarian stews, which are cooking while the ceremony is in progress.

Coolers of juice, mineral water, sodas, or colas are consumed in quantity by thirsty participants after the ceremony. Garbage sacks are brought to take out all that has been brought in. A plate of food is placed at a distance from the lodge as an offering to all the spirits that entered the ceremony.

The ceremony is very refreshing. Many participants will linger to sit around the fire in peace and serenity, appreciating and remembering their moving spiritual experience.

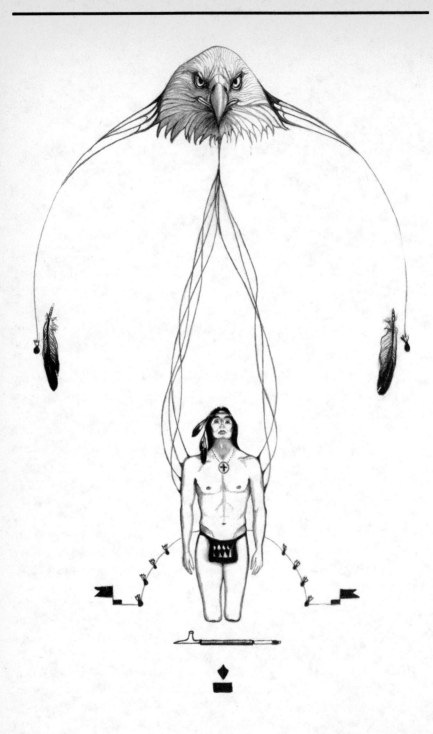

Crying for a Vision

The Vision Quest Ceremony *(Hanblecheyapi)* puts you alone before the Great Mystery. Compared with other ceremonies, *Hanblecheya* (Crying for a Vision) needs little else but yourself and an isolated setting. A Sweat Lodge Ceremony needs a structure, fire, and water. A Sun Dance needs the centering tree, an arena, and the tribal gathering. *Hanblecheya* needs only you and four twigs with pieces of colored cloth, representing the four directions, tied to them.

For some, an isolated space may not be readily available, especially if you live in a major city. But there will be space if you really set your mind to it. There are always local places in which you can get away and be alone if you look carefully. Being alone, out somewhere in a remote or semiremote spot on Mother Earth, is the main ingredient of a Vision Quest Ceremony. It will no doubt work for you even if you forget the twigs and the four colored pieces of cloth to mark off your protected area. But I doubt that it will work as well if you don't find yourself some isolated spot where you can be free from interruptions.

We all have dreams. In our dreams we may feel we are alone—alone with our concept of God, the Great Spirit, a Higher Force—but we are not conscious in our dreams. In the Vision Quest, we start out alert, conscious, watchful, ready to make contact with the Higher Power that is out there, all around us or within. The vastness of life around us helps eliminate self-centeredness. We are not doing the Vision Quest to make ourselves feel important or to be interesting to our friends but to realize the vastness of the universe and our oneness with it.

Why should someone cry for a vision? Should we not spend a day and evening, all night, or several days and nights in serious contemplation of the Creator who allows us to be here? Why not spend at least a day and night of serious, uninterrupted prayer and communication with the powers of the universe in the greatest temple of all—out in God's created nature under God's vast heavens. No church or building can give such visualization of the Great Mystery's magnitude.

In the old days, when people were stronger physically, they sometimes vision quested for as long as four days without food and water. But for your first Vision Quest, I would recommend one day and night or two days and nights at most. You should fast all the time that you are "on the mountain," which means while you are isolated. You may take a couple of small bottles of mineral water, but most vision questers seldom drink anything unless they are fasting for several days.

The Vision Quest offers more than a vision or meaningful dreams while you sleep and observe upon a mountain. It is a special opportunity to observe nature as well. It is a rare time free of the pressures so prevalent in modern living.

If you know of a high hill or an isolated spot, go to it. Sit quietly and stay into the evening. Watch the sun lower over the western horizon. Notice the birds and animals who share your space while you wait for the sun to set. Notice even the little crawling ones near you and around you. Watch the industry of an ant hill or the gathering of bees who happen to be nearby. Watch the activity of all moving beings change as night begins to fall.

There is no exact time to begin a vision quest, but it is practical to find your place on a mountain before nightfall if you are unfamiliar with your surroundings or you do not have a guide or sponsor that is taking you to a place he or she is familiar with. It is entertaining to watch the change in animal activity as the daylight draws to a close. Observe the appearance of the night beings, the owls, night hawks, or evening swallows feeding on insects. Rabbits will begin to appear while the squirrels and chipmunks will be retiring for the night. If you are sitting on a high hill, you will be able to watch the deer coming out into the meadows below for their evening browsing. The animals—the winged and even the small crawling ones—remind us that we are all related, all part of the created whole. When we observe nature, our egos can be dispelled, and we learn to make our requests in humility and need. The great vastness projects its immensity and lets us know that we are but a tiny speck in vast, indescribable, ultimate space. That alone teaches us humility and brings us down to size.

Look up at the cloud people while the sun sets. Note the colors and their changing hues as the rays of energy create new colors tinted with silver and gold. A totally new projection of earth, sky, nature, and space takes place at sunset. Be in on it. Observe and receive this special blessing for the beginning of your Vision Quest. Express your appreciation that you have had the opportunity to spend one more day upon Mother Earth.

The moon will be welcome. If it is a full moon, its light will seem like a blessing. You might drowse. Dreams may come and go. In time, the stars in all their multitudes will canopy the sky. You will have many new and profound insights as you immerse yourself in the Oneness of it all.

Look up and stare at the great vast space. Millions, billions of other suns are out there. Millions, billions of other planets revolving around those star-suns. Other planets, other worlds. Other life? Other lives of their own? Parallel universes? Feel yourself part of it all.

I usually think about Black Elk's dream journey up into the spirit world when I sit alone on Spirit Mountain in South Dakota (my own preferred vision-questing location). This nine-year-old boy had a powerful vision while his people camped near a place they called the Greasy Grass. Two spirit beings led the Oglala boy into the spirit world, where he was welcomed into the rainbow-covered lodge. This is the lodge of the six powers of the universe. His journey seems quite plausible as I look out into space, out there where exists galaxy upon galaxy, unending light-years of space and mystery. The Creator of all that vastness is far beyond any form of human comprehension. That is why the Native Americans aptly named it *Wakan Tanka*, the Great Mystery.

It is too much of a mystery for us to describe fully, yet I can identify with the onlooking six powers. There is a west power where the sun sets. I can hear, see, feel, and touch the life-giving rains that come from the west, *Wiyopeyata*, where the sun sets. I am dependent upon the life-giving rains. Thunder and lightning are powerful tools that the Great Spirit lets me see and hear. The west, the first power of Black Elk's vision, is a real, actual, life-giving power on which I depend while I am here on this earth journey.

The second power of Black Elk's vision is also very concrete. I can feel the cold and see the white blanket of winter snow that *Waziya*, the north power, draws down upon Mother Earth to let her rest through the long winter. Truth, endurance, honesty, courage, and cleanliness are all characteristics received from the north.

Wiyoheyapa, the rising sun, is the power of the east. Red is the color of the new dawn. The morning star awakens. With each new day come knowledge, new experiences, new journeys, new associations, new communication, and the wisdom that springs from these. These gifts from the east are all real experiences that can raise me up to a higher plane of understanding.

The fourth power is *Itokaga*, the yellow south. The sun will reach its highest point as summer approaches. The days will become longer. Mother Earth will blossom forth the bounty of spring into food, medicines, and timber for shelter. The great forests will leaf out and once again begin to make our air clean and breathable. Growth, healing, medicine, strength, and shelter are received from this fourth power of the rainbow-covered lodge. It is at its strongest every summer quarter of the annual cycle.

Mother Earth and Father Sky are the fifth and sixth powers. I live upon one of these two powers. Every particle of my being is a part of her, and my physical entity is fueled by the energy from the sun, which is the heart of Father Sky. I do not need any special book to tell me that it is all made by an ultimate power beyond the six powers. I am satisfied that *Shakopeh Ouye Wowanyanke Hehaka Sapa*, the six powers of Black Elk's sacred vision, are very real and much more understandable than the entities that the white missionaries have put before me. They pray to entities that I cannot see and who have never appeared in my visions or upon my earth journey. I do not object to what they do for themselves. I object to their attempts to stop me from doing what I believe is good for me.

A Vision Quest is done for the purpose of self-improvement. It is done for a deeper insight into the why of our being here. All purposes in the Lakota ceremonies are for the good of the people, for right living, for the improvement of oneself, or for good health. Now, we seek to have the great powers enlighten all peoples, to have the masses of people begin a spiritual journey and wake up to the wisdom of Mother Earth knowledge so that our planet may live.

When something is asked for and is received, a payment of something back to the spirit world is expected. In your Vision Quest, seek self-improvement besides asking for what you desire. Strive to give something back in return. Promise that you will work for the improvement of Mother Earth or some other worthy cause.

In Fools Crow's *Yuwipi* Ceremony, held for me before I left to be a pilot in Vietnam, I asked to return safely from combat. This was a beseechment to the spirit world. I believed in my heart that I had more things to do with my life than go up in a Phantom jet and bore holes in the sky. Flying was losing its thrill and adventure for me, and I was realizing that it held little meaning. In addition, I believed that my people's ways were good ways and that the missionaries were destroying the power of our ways. Most tribes were going into cultural oblivion, and I wanted to keep my people's ways alive. I promised that if I lived, I would dance in the Sun Dance. I fulfilled that promise after I returned from flying 110 combat missions. Something was asked. It was granted. I paid back in return by enduring the Sun Dance.

Most Sioux vision questers will go to a holy man or a holy woman with a peace pipe and make it known that they desire to vision quest, although it is not necessary to go to a holy person before a Vision Quest. Some off-reservation Sioux or reservation Indians with no spiritual leaders close by go directly to the mountain, hill, or butte. An individual can expect a strong Vision Quest, providing, of course, that ego is dispensed with and heartfelt sincerity is demonstrated during the vision-questing period.

For sun dancers, the Sun Dance chief will recommend that the dancer who intends to return for an additional Sun Dance should vision quest before that time. Both ceremonies intertwine and are highly complementary. A sincere Vision Quest will usually result in a meaningful Sun Dance and helpful vision during the piercing time.

A Sweat Lodge Ceremony is performed before the Vision Quest. The purification of the sweat lodge thins down the "spiritual veil." Within a sweat lodge, during the length of the ceremony and most intensely during the third and fourth endurances, profound spiritual activity takes place. One can feel the spirit world strongly within the lodge and can often see manifestations in colors or lights. The vision quester is cleansed in mind, in spirit, and in body by the lodge. This occurs because of both the steam and the penetrating spiritual atmosphere.

The Sweat Lodge Ceremony, when held for vision quests, centers on the endurance of the east because the red east signifies knowledge, wisdom, and understanding. The east also represents seeking, the seeking of spiritual insight to allow grace to accompany the benefits of knowledge, wisdom, and understanding.

After the vision questers come out of the sweat lodge, they towel their bodies dry, dress, and go up the mountain, carrying their pipes and colored flags. The group may start up the path together, but they will split up later, each to find his or her own isolated space.

Some vision questers will make tobacco offerings before the Sweat Lodge Ceremony takes place. Pinches of tobacco are placed on one-inch or two-inch squares of cloth which are folded up to keep the tobacco inside. A string is wrapped and tied around the cloth to form a small bundle. Four or seven of these bundles are usually made and tied together. Some vision questers may make up to 405 of these little bundles and tie them together to form the boundaries of the vision quest area once the beseecher reaches her or his spot on the mountain.

Which of the four colors is selected for the cloth is the vision quester's choice. Some bundles may be red for knowledge and understanding. White may be used for endurance and courage or to forget a bad episode from the past. The long, white winter can help erase some aspects of a past that needs to be left behind; therefore, white will be used for the beseeching bundles. Yellow may be used to ask for spiritual healing for a particular ailment, injury, or disease. Orange may be selected for the healing of an addiction, since this would require both knowledge and understanding from the east (red) and the alignment and attunement of the physical body from the south (yellow). When you see black offerings, they may have been made with the desire to be a holy man or holy woman or a medicine person. Black also can be a beseechment to the powers of the west for the life-giving rains, especially in time of drought.

You do not need a peace pipe to vision quest. It is nice to have one, and I am so culturally immersed in using mine that I would feel almost alone without it. But I have many friends who have had meaningful quests without the pipe. A crystal or special stone is a good substitute for the pipe. If you do not have a special stone, simply find your stone while you walk the path on the way to your isolated space. Everyone has a special stone. Your stone will beckon to you. Pick it up and use it to beseech the six powers while you are up on your mountain. If you do not yet have a special stone, seek one. Several weeks before your quest, take some solitary journeys near creek beds or streams. The rocks in these areas are worn smooth and carry an assortment of colors and pictures. Your special stone with its special images may be waiting for you.

In cooler weather or at higher elevations, carry a blanket or even a sleeping bag. A backpack is handy for carrying warmer clothes that you may need when you cool down from the sweat lodge and your hike. Higher elevations bring cool or cold nights even in the summertime, and extra warmth will be appreciated. If you get too cold, you may have to come off the mountain in the middle of your quest, so it is best to be prepared. Do not be overdressed for your uphill hike, however. The exercise, especially with pack and sleeping bag, will keep you warm enough without need for heavy clothing as you climb upward.

Recently, since I came to know the rainbow people, I have made an annual journey with them to Spirit Mountain for a Vision Quest. I will tell about our trip, and in that way some questions pertaining to vision questing may be cleared up.

Our trip is rather unusual in that our path takes us through the pipestone quarries, where we camp overnight. We usually stop to view ancient petroglyphs carved on slabs of rock before we reach Pipestone. The carvings go back many hundreds, perhaps thousands of years. Some of the old carvings have the four directions symbol inscribed on the long, flat, stone outcropping projecting out of the earth. No doubt, ancient inhabitants sat and carved the symbols while they followed the herds of game across the great grasslands of what are now the Dakotas and Great Lakes states.

Four or five cars travel from the city on a Friday afternoon, meeting at the petroglyphs in southern Minnesota. After viewing the ancient symbols, we feel that we have connected way back into the past. There seems to be a welcoming kind of feeling as we gather. Maybe the spirits of those long gone by are pleased that a group of rainbow people *(wig-munke oyate)* are going to go to the Black Hills to commune with nature and the Great Spirit as they used to do centuries ago.

At Pipestone, we tour the quarries. Usually, we are met by a Sioux from the area, from whom some of the vision questers will purchase a sacred pipe. As I said earlier, not everyone has a peace pipe for vision questing, but it is not surprising that many want to purchase one at Pipestone. These pipes will experience a sweat lodge and the mountain almost immediately after they have been purchased and will not become just an unused decoration hanging on a wall.

The Pipestone quarries are situated in an extraordinary, aesthetic setting as should be expected. Standing rock slabs resembling stone grandfathers and grandmothers are parted by a trickling stream. Oaks, elders, cottonwood, shrubs, grasses, and prairie plants border the tumbling waters.[1] Beneath the ground, Indian people still dig for the red stone that will be honed into portable altars.

After camping overnight nearby, the group assembles to drive west to the Black Hills. Usually another car or two joins the caravan in the morning.

The drive into the Dakotas is a little monotonous until we reach the broad Missouri, where the land changes abruptly from farmland to wide open plains. We rest at an overlook above the Missouri. The water is stopped by a dam, and it reaches back widely for miles.

The next stop is one of the highlights of the trip. As the Black Hills come into view, the highway drops down to another river considerably smaller than the Missouri. The erosion of time has carved out a long descent to the river bottom. The cars are parked at a rest stop, and the group climbs through barbed-wire fences to reach the river. In the heat of the summer, most plunge into the river to cool themselves before they begin their search for their *wotai* stones.

The trip becomes almost a treasure hunt at this point. There are squeals of delight as people call out their special finds. These "finds" are simply rounded, smoothed stones that have tumbled through time out of the Black Hills, yet the sounds of joy rival someone finding lost treasure. There are many images within the stones and many colors to pick from. Most of the rainbow people leave with a few extra special stones whose images bear a particular personal symbolism.

It is difficult to leave the Cheyenne River, but we drive onward. At Rapid City, we stop at a hardware store and purchase a black construction tarp for the sweat lodge. The tarp costs less than twenty dollars, and one dollar per person more than covers both the tarp and a ball of twine.

Finally, we arrive at Spirit Mountain, where lodge frames have been constructed in the park. In the grasslands below the parking lot, we pick some sage to use in the sweat lodge and while sitting on the mountain that night. Buffalo move behind the spacious enclosure that allows them to graze at the base of the mountain. Bull buffalo stare at us, seeming to know that we are reaching back into a Mother Earth past that once held them in huge herds throughout the grasslands.

A sweat lodge frame is selected, and the tarp is unrolled over the sapling frame and tied down with the twine. Rocks are placed on a stack of wood in the fire pit, and kindling is lit. Several water pails are filled from a faucet close to the parking lot. A dipper is not available, so a coffee cup is substituted. While the fire heats the rocks, a group of vision questers sits on a spread-out blanket and cuts colored cloth to make their tobacco offerings. Some make sage wreaths or tie sprigs of sage together to wear in the sweat lodge. When the rocks reach a red glow, some elk horns are brought out along with an old pitchfork to transfer the rocks into the lodge. The participants file into the lodge.

All Sweat Lodge ceremonies are highly spiritual and quite moving. Comparing them is like comparing mountain peaks, waterfalls, whales, eagles, or mountain lions. They are all impressive, but the sweat ceremonies held at Spirit Mountain seem to have a heightened power. After the ceremony, the participants towel themselves dry and dress in their hiking clothes, then retrieve their peace pipes from the ceremonial altar beside the fire. Carrying their packs and pipes or crystals, they ascend the trails leading to various places on the mountain. They also carry the four colors representing the four directions tied firmly to hardwood sticks.

When they reach their places on the mountain, each is separate and alone. With the aid of a jackknife, each digs down into the hard, dry mountain and sets out four flags in the form of a square or rectangle. This will be the vision quest area. Each quester will also wear a piece of sage or a circular sage wreath while vision questing.

The night will be spent in contemplation, some sleep, and, it is hoped, some dreams. The experience of each upon the mountain top will be unique and memorable. Dawn will finally break, but most will stay on the mountain until late in the morning; then they will gather down below. Some may choose to remain upon the mountain for another night.

In the end, the quest is very personal. It is you and your thoughts and your prayers to the Great Spirit. There is no blueprint for vision questing, no checklist of do's and don'ts. Just you, the powers, and isolation. If you vision quest only once in your life, at least you took time out. This is *time out* to sit down and contemplate and seek communication with the Creator as to why you are here. Afterward, you, the vision quester, will be better prepared to use the special gifts with which the Great Spirit has endowed you to join with those concerned ones who seek to help this planet.

The Sioux Sun Dance

While the Vision Quest is a lone beseechment, an individual ceremony, the Sun Dance is a tribal gathering, a tribal beseechment and an expression of thanksgiving. The Sioux Sun Dance Ceremony lasts four days. In times gone by, it was held after the summer buffalo hunts, when the buffalo meat was cured and dried for winter provisions. It was a time of celebration and plenty. The Sun Dance of today is usually held in late July or early August. It is started on a Thursday in order that the fourth day will be a Sunday, a day that most people do not have to work.

The Sun Dance chief (Intercessor) arrives early in the week to set up his campsite and supervise the raising of the large ceremonial tipi where the sun dancers will dress and prepare. Sweat lodges will be built. Firewood and heating stones will be gathered. *Intercessor* is also a term used to designate the most responsible person. I prefer the term *Sun Dance chief*.

The Sun Dance chief is responsible for the ceremonial activities that take place and makes most major decisions during the four days of the event. He is usually the most respected holy man among the medicine people and, of course, very knowledgeable in the ways and traditions of the Sioux. In the six Sun Dance ceremonies in which I was a participant, Fools Crow was always the Sun Dance chief. The devout, powerful, and goodly man was a great spiritual anchor for all of us who danced *Wiwanyag Wachipi*.

On the day before the first ceremony day, a felling party goes out to a cottonwood tree, and a woman, representative of the Buffalo Calf Woman, takes the first cut on the tree with an axe. She speaks to the tree and tells it that her people are sorry to have to take the tree's life but the ceremony is necessary because it will be the *Wiwanyag Wachipi*, a ceremony in which the people dance, gazing at the sun. It is a ceremony, she explains "highly important, for by doing it, the people will live."

Ropes are attached to the tree and it is cut down. The felling party is careful that it does not fall upon the ground but is supported by short poles across the shoulders of the people. Many of its branches are pruned, and it is carried back to the Sun Dance arena, a large circle bordered by a shading bower made of poles and cut pine boughs under which the people will gather and pray together as they watch the Sun Dance. On the way to the arena, the carrying party sets the tree down and rests four times.

The cottonwood tree is planted in the center of the arena. Before the tree is raised, a peace pipe is placed in a hole dug for the tree trunk. In the old days, buffalo tallow was also placed in the hole to acknowledge the rich provisions given by the buffalo to the people.

Cloth banners in the colors of the four directions are tied to the branches with green and blue banners for Mother Earth and Father Sky. Above the long bolts of cloth, a rawhide cutout of a buffalo is tied with a rawhide cutout of a human image. Twelve chokecherry branches are tied crosswise beneath the buffalo and the human images. The branches symbolize the twelve moons, the twelve months of the year. The cutouts represent thankfulness. The people are thankful for their lives. The buffalo represents provisions that were placed on the plains by the Almighty, *Wakan Tanka*.

The tree is finally raised, and the camp area springs to life with new arrivals coming not only from the Oglalas, but the Hunkpapas, Brules, Yanktons, Minnecoujous, and all the rest of the Lakota tribes and bands. While the Sioux nation gathers, other preparations are made by the traditionals who will be responsible for the ongoing activities of the Sun Dance.

The evening of the tree moving, a Sweat Lodge ceremony is held for the Sun Dance pledgers. In these pledges, one promises to undergo the piercing pain of the Sun Dance ceremony. Those who pledge usually take their vow the preceding year and live their lives accordingly, keeping in mind that they will be dancing the ceremony before the people, the spirit world, and ultimately before the six powers of the universe and *Wakan Tanka*.

The pledged dancers seek to avoid disharmony and strive to conduct themselves in an appropriate manner. The Sweat Lodge Ceremony usually brings forth a restatement of the pledgers to pierce on the fourth day. Within the lodge, anyone who believes that one who has pledged has not conducted himself in a respectful manner is bound by honor to speak out. After deliberation by the Sun Dance chief and assisting holy men and senior sun dancers, that individual may be prevented from piercing. Even so, he usually will be allowed to dance within the ceremony as a way of atonement, unless his offense against society was very grave.

Because of my closeness to war and violence—I was recently back from Vietnam, where I had flown 110 combat missions—I was not allowed to pierce in my first Sun Dance even though I had taken the vow in Fools Crow's *Yuwipi* more than a year before. I was pierced for the first time in my second Sun Dance.

There is another reason for not piercing a first-time sun dancer. In older times, the holy men wanted to study a first-time dancer and test his sincerity. They would observe the way he conducted himself in his first Sun Dance. If the dancer came back the second year, his return would be taken as a positive indication and a sign of sincerity.

I never questioned the decisions of Fools Crow, Eagle Feather, or John Fire (Lame Deer), the holy men who were in charge of the Sun Dance. I had experienced the power of these men in the Sweat Lodge and *Yuwipi* ceremonies. When you have seen how close to God's nature these men are and have seen the acknowledging power backed by the six Grandmothers/Grandfathers of the rainbow-covered lodge, you never doubt their wisdom.

My first Sun Dance, I danced with a small boy, mostly off to the eastern side of the dance circle. It was a fairly simple ceremony for me and the boy and yet, during the fourth day, I received a very profound vision, a deeper vision than any that I had when I was pierced and leaning back from my rope. I saw the Buffalo Calf Woman quite clearly up in the clouds. It gave me strength and a deep realization of the significance of the red way as the spiritual path that I would follow.

The first day of the Sun Dance begins in the early morning with a Sweat Lodge Ceremony for the male dancers. For those who have not been purified in the lodge the night before, the morning sweat will get the later-arriving dancers ready. Female sun dancers have their own sweat lodge in the morning. After the Sweat Lodge Ceremony, the dancers towel themselves dry and dress in the ceremonial tipi.

The men wear a kilt skirt secured by a belt around the waist. Many dancers simply use a woman's shawl as a dance skirt or kilt. Sage wreaths circle the dancers' wrists and ankles, and a more elaborate wreath with a pair of upright eagle feathers is placed on the head like a crown. As a necklace, many dancers wear a rawhide cutout of a sunflower, painted yellow with a black center. All dancers carry eagle-bone or wooden whistles and a peace pipe. If a dancer does not own a pipe, there is always a pipe available from the onlooking crowd or from visiting holy men.

The dancer's chest receives a symbol from the holy man, usually painted in red. Before a dancer is pierced on the fourth day, the holy men also paint a symbol on the dancer's back. The symbol upon my chest was a petroglyph-like eagle. On the fourth day, Bill Eagle Feather and Fools Crow drew four lines zigzagging up and down my back. Once, when we had many young, new pledgers, Fools Crow had John Fire draw on the symbols.

After all are dressed, the men file out of the tipi and join the waiting women sun dancers. The women wear plain white dresses made of cloth or buckskin. The elaborate beadwork often found on buckskin dresses is absent on these dresses. At most, simple beadwork in a symbolic design or in the colors of the four directions—red, yellow, black, and white—adorn the dress. In modern times, the more comfortable cotton or monk's cloth dresses are worn since buckskin can become quite hot under a July or August sun. (At one Sun Dance, a very old woman danced with us. I hesitate to guess her age, but I would estimate that she was in her late seventies or early eighties. This woman stayed with us the entire time in the hot sun.)

In the five Sun Dances that I participated in at Pine Ridge Reservation, the same man carried a buffalo skull and led the line of dancers behind the leading holy men and the sun dance chief. George Gap, an Oglala who lived in Ogallala, Nebraska, was the bearer of the skull. Like many of the spiritual leaders of my tribe—Fools Crow, Eagle Feather, Lame Deer, Pete Catches, Buddy Red Bow, and Mary Louise Defender—George was an open traditionalist who was not afraid to stand up for our religion at a time when even local Indians put down the revival of Indian spirituality. It was also a time in which many Indians held back, and although they were not openly critical of our ceremony, they did not join us to support it. Their feelings are easy to understand because the missionary boarding schools had done a thorough job of convincing them that all the old ways were bad. Many people are like sheep. It takes quite a few of them to make a move before the rest will follow. Fortunately, the young of our nation rose up almost overnight and supported us strongly. They were called militants by some; I call them mystic warriors. After their support, the criticism of our traditional way and the ridicule of the holy men diminished.

When I was a sun dancer, a reservation missionary took strong exception to our religious expression. The crowds had been growing each year for our Sun Dances, and each had been more successful than the last. The people themselves were hungry for the revived native spirituality that they found in the Sun Dance. The missionary interpreted this success as a threat to his more structured institution and Christian spirituality. The reservation mission was well staffed and well supported by donors from off the reservation, so the missionary had ample funds to use to fight the Sun Dance. The mission was also the largest landowner on the reservation, partially because elderly people often willed over their lands at the time that the mission's last rites were conducted. The mission had power, and it was used on the tribal council to combat the Sun Dance.

When I was on leave from the military, I had come to watch the Sun Dance, but instead I watched the missionary drive his pickup into the arena and stop the dance so that he could celebrate Mass at the base of the Sun Dance tree. Although he held Mass in the church fifty-two weeks of the year, on this occasion he felt that he had to impose his ceremony over ours. His portable altar was unloaded, and I had to watch a non-Indian ceremony take precedence over our people's ceremony right on my own reservation.

There are several reasons that I want to describe the overzealousness of the missionary. First, I do not want anyone to think that we had an easy time bringing our traditional ways back. We were up against more than one fanatic. I wish to emphasize how destructive it is for people to attempt to impugn a proven culture in order to impose their own religious practices. It is especially inconsiderate when they pick on people who have been beaten down and defeated. I saw this happen on my own reservation. These are hard things to hear and hard to share, but I do not want our early battles to be forgotten.

This same missionary had been successful over the years in replacing our ceremonies with his own, and he was going to try again the third year that I was a sun dancer. His ultimate plan was to stop the Sun Dance altogether if he could. The tribal council, stacked with his church members, had decreed that the Sun Dance would last only three days, Thursday, Friday, and Saturday. Saturday would be the piercing day. On Sunday, the missionary would say his Mass at the base of the Sun Dance tree. A Sun Dance committee was even formed to take away the power of the Sun Dance chief.

The dancers and holy men were too afraid to challenge the authority of both the priest and the tribal council. All pierced on the third day. I did not. I had been in the Marines and had flown combat in Vietnam.

My warrior's blood was up, and I was not afraid of the missionary. He shook his fist at me and told me that I must put his God into our ceremony. When I would not relent, he claimed to have some special knowledge or power to predict that my spirit would not go to a good place. I felt that he was making preposterous statements and told him so. He alluded again to his special powers and suggested that I was possessed by the devil. I was glad that I was a traditional Sioux; since we do not have a concept of the devil, he was not able to use that age-old tactic to scare me into submission.

As he was ranting and raving at me, I was moved to accept the role of the mystic warriors of the past. He threatened me, and I felt the need of strong spiritual armor. These mystic warriors were like knights of old. They were the spiritual helpers to the holy men and holy women, and they were fighters to protect the spiritual ways. The mystic warriors would also participate in all the difficult spiritual tasks that the holy men performed, such as fasting alone on the mountain. Because of this, the people would have more confidence in the traditional ways. And the holy men would not have total power to frighten the people with bad spirits to keep them under control.

I was too stubborn for the priest. On the fourth day, I was the lone sun dancer. Fools Crow pierced me, and an old man named Loon stood beside me with a cane. He was half-blind and half-crippled, but he threatened to hit anybody who attempted to stop the piercing. I had challenged a lot of authority and caused a great deal of commotion, but the Sun Dance that year went the full four days.

The next year, the missionary made one last-ditch effort to change our ceremony. But at that point, the young people of the tribe rose up. They surrounded the priest when he tried to force his way onto the Sun Dance grounds. The young people warned him to leave us alone or else he would face some serious trouble. Since that time, our Sun Dance has gone on for the full four days, and the young ones have come forward in large numbers to pierce and take part.

I recall many scenes from that time of spiritual revival. I can see Bill Eagle Feather leaning back against his Sun Dance rope, Fools Crow kneeling over Buddy Red Bow and Red Bow not flinching as Fools Crow pierced him. I remember Pete Catches dancing against his rope with the eagle feathers sewn to his skin fluttering with his movement. I see John Fire standing beside a sun dancer who elected to be pierced while standing instead of while lying down on the bed of sage as is usually done. I see Mary Louise Defender, dressed as the Buffalo Calf Woman, accepting the pipes from the dancers. I also vividly recall George Gap holding the buffalo skull as we waited together for Fools Crow to give the signal to move the procession to the Sun Dance circle.

There is no rehearsal for a Sun Dance. It is a ceremonial prayer, and like all Indian prayers is spontaneous. Although the ceremony is certainly dramatic, the traditional Indians are not putting on a show or trying to impress onlookers, especially outsiders. The Sun Dance is simply an annual prayer of thanksgiving to the Great Spirit and to all of the powers between the breathing ones and *Wakan Tanka*.

But even in this spontaneous prayer, certain forms are followed. A woman is selected from among the dancers, and she is the first to enter the dance arena. This may be the same woman who accepts the pipes or she may be one of the women sun dancers. This woman dances alone and makes a full circle around the cottonwood tree, dancing to the beat of the drums. As she rejoins the waiting participants, the entering song is sung by the singers who are stationed around the barrel-sized drums situated at the four directional points on the periphery of the circle. The dancers then enter from the east and proceed sunwise (clockwise), shuffling around the arena to a slow drumbeat. When the line of dancers comes full circle, they are stopped on the eastern side by the Sun Dance chief. At that time, the sun has risen from the plains. Each day, the sun is considered as a helper to bring new knowledge into our lives. Beseechment songs are sung to the powers and blessings of the east. When the songs are finished, the dancers are directed to the south, and songs recognizing all that is good and needed from the south for the two-leggeds are sung. The line of dancers is then moved to the west and finally to the north, and the honoring songs are sung to each of those powers to complete the greetings to the four directions.

The dancers are next taken to a bower where they rest on shaded benches while a holy man or holy woman addresses the crowd. The address usually tells of the way of the Sun Dance and imparts a message on morals and values for the tribe. After the address, the dancers are summoned to present their pipes to the woman or man who accepts them. If there are many dancers, the Sun Dance chief will usually split the dancers into four groups, each one facing a cardinal direction. Each dancer is then brought before the acceptors, a woman flanked by two holy men. The drums beat out their rhythm while each dancer parades around the circle, led by the Sun Dance chief or one of the holy men. If there are a considerable number of dancers, this portion of the ceremony may be broken by another rest and another address by one of the holy men.

As each pipe is accepted, it is placed beyond the buffalo skull resting on the ground. The buffalo skull, with its curved horns, is placed in front of a pipe rack for the sacred pipes. The rack is made of two forked sticks inserted into the ground with a connecting cross-stick. (See the illustration on page 84.) Almost all ceremonial pipes have a pointed end beyond the bowl because this design allows the pipe to be lodged in Mother Earth for support while it rests against the pipe rack. In this way, the stem is left pointed at *Wiyo*, the sun mate of our Mother, or, as in the Sun Dance, toward the spirit of the west.

A few pipes have an axe blade projecting downward below the pipe bowl. These are warriors' pipes. The bearer is a traditional, respecting warrior who is going off to war or has returned from war or is fighting for a cause. I no longer have a pipe of this design. But at the time when the missionaries and their critical sheep were attempting to subvert and degrade our native spirituality, my warrior's pipe was a powerful symbol for me. It signified that they were in for a good fight.

Elbow pipes are squared-off pipes without projecting axe blades or projections beyond the bowl. These pipes cannot be inserted into Mother Earth and so are less useful in ceremonies. Many elbow pipes are made by pipe makers to economize since they require smaller amounts of pipe-stone. They are equally popular with tourists who are not using them for ceremony.

After all the pipes have been presented, the dancers rest while the Sun Dance chief makes a stirring address on spiritual values. The dancers then go before the four directions to prepare themselves. They face each direction to the beat of the drum as they contemplate that direction's blessings. While facing east, the dancer will consider knowledge, wisdom, peace and harmony, or related values that are part of increasing experience or truth. Some dancers may consider communication, for it is the great messenger that can remove the ignorance, fear, and egocentricity that hold back enlightenment and wisdom.

The third day of the Sun Dance is little different from the second day, except that the crowd and the ring of tents and campers grow larger. The manner in which the sun dancers enter the arena in the morning and in which they offer their pipes to the four directions is the same. Clockwise the four directions are beseeched, beginning with the east,

If it is not the piercing day, the dancers will usually be led from the arena after facing the four directions and the pipe offering. Their pipes will be returned to them before they leave the arena. Some of them will have been smoked by the singers and drummers or the traditionalists within the onlooking crowd. The ceremony is over within the morning hours, and the dancers are free to rest and fast in their tents while they wait for the following dawn.

In addition to being a religious ceremony, the Sun Dance is also a social event. In the afternoon, some fancy dancing or powwow dancing will take place. In the evening, especially on the evening preceding the final Sun Dance day, many colorful powwow dancers in their traditional dance costumes will fill the Sun Dance arena. These dances are quite energetic and are danced to a much faster beat than the Sun Dance. The happy heartbeat of a people expressing in rhythm their traditional ways goes on long into the night.

Because four has a special meaning in Sioux spirituality, the fourth and final day of the Sun Dance brings the culmination of the ceremony— the piercing. Those who have pledged to be pierced now give of themselves. They will give something that money or position cannot buy so that the people, the way, may live.

Because Sioux religion recognizes woman as having already given of her pain for the people when she gives birth, the women in the Sun Dance do not pierce in this special portion of the ceremony. Woman's pain is regarded as more than the pain of a sun dancer because childbirth may bring death to some women, and certainly the facing of death is considered the greatest challenge. It is said that a sun dancer has understood more fully a woman's pain by doing the Sun Dance. I have been pierced four times, and I certainly agree with that saying.

On this final day, after the four directions have been faced and the dancer has seriously contemplated the six powers of the universe, he is led to a bed of sage at the base of the cottonwood tree. The following is a recollection of my own moments of piercing.

You lie down on the bed of sage. Your tribe is looking on. When the holy man pierces you with his blade or sharp skewer, you don't want to quiver or move a muscle. The old warrior lineage is still in you. You are an Oglala, and you will show that you can take pain. You won't grimace or move.

You look straight up. The tree with its wide ribbons of color fluttering in the breeze, the holy cottonwood tree that is the center of the nation is above you like a protecting umbrella. "The piercing will only be short-lived," you say to yourself as you see the holy man kneeling over you.

It is painful for the holy man who is going to pierce you. His way of life is to help remove the "hurts" of life through his medicine way. This is a contrary experience for him to have to hurt someone. You know that when he sets his jaw, he will make the two parallel cuts on your chest, then thrust the awl into the first cut and out the second. (The skin of the chest is pierced, but not the muscle or connective tissue. Skin is extremely strong, and there is no need to pierce deeply.)

You hold up the hard wooden peg to show him. An experienced sun dancer will make sure that the peg is sanded smooth so that it slides in easily. It is sharp on only one end. You show the peg to let him know that you are ready. You focus on the great cottonwood spreading its limbs out to the world. It does what the Great Spirit has all trees do. They take out the gases we emit and replace them with oxygen. Without the trees, we will all perish, so the tree is a beneficial relative.

The cloth banners of the six powers flutter above. You know the six powers will flow their medicine strongly through you during the piercing time. Right now they are watching and they are listening for your thoughts. The cuts are made, and the pain begins when the awl is tunneled through. You are giving your pain so that the people may live. "Peg, *chanwi*," the holy man calls out. You give him the peg that you have been squeezing in the palm of your hand.

You look up at the tree of life. It is comforting.

You appreciate lying on the bed of sage, for you have been on your feet in the hot sun. You think of these things for distraction because you know that the inserting of the peg across the cut in your chest will be more painful than the pushing in of the awl. It feels like hot fire when the peg is inserted. Most men never face the pain of the Sun Dance piercing, and of those who do, most never come back for a second time.

An assistant hands the end of a coiled rope to the holy man who wraps a leather thong around the projecting ends of the peg once it is in place and ties the thong to the rope.

You rise somewhat shakily from the bed of sage, carefully holding the attached rope. You become aware that you are now attached to your mother, Mother Earth. The holy man and his assistant support you momentarily while the steadiness comes back into your legs. You hold the weight of the dangling rope in your hand, not yet letting it increase the pain searing across your chest.

The assistant places the sage wreath with its pair of spiked eagle feathers onto your head. With your free hand, you reach up and adjust the wreath. You recognize and appreciate more fully the symbolism of the sage wreath as a badge of honor, with its eagle-wing feathers standing up like spiritual antennae.

The drums in the background are beating. Your tribe is looking on. Another sun dancer is brought to the bed of sage. You hold your rope and move carefully back to your position on the Sun Dance circle. Slowly, you ease the weight of the rope onto the pain in your chest as you begin to dance, shuffling slowly to the beat of the drums, tethered to the Sun Dance tree.

In time, all the dancers will be pierced and all will take their positions. The ropes hanging down are their umbilicals to the Earth Mother. The bone whistles screech in unison. The drums pulse louder. It is time to dance inward to touch the tree of life, the great cottonwood tree. The dancers shuffle inward holding their ropes aside so as not to step on them. The drums throb, the whistles grow shrill as the dancers extend their palms to the tree. They lean against the trunk as they blow their whistles hard. The Sun Dance chief calls out and they back away slowly, shuffling with the drumbeat to the end of their tethered connection. Four times you come in and touch the tree. At the last touching, the tree itself sounds as if it is shrilling back like a huge Sun Dance whistle.

The gathered tribe is deep in prayer at this powerful moment. The tribe's prayers are like a spiritual wind sweeping in over the backs of the sun dancers and hitting the tree. The tree itself is a great absorbing funnel, taking in the prayers and sending them upward to the ultimate powers of the universe and to *Wakan Tanka*.

After the fourth touching of the tree, the dancers lean back against the ropes. Now they are free to seek their own Sun Dance vision. The gathered crowd is seeking their vision. All gathered that day are concentrating once again as a nation up to the Ultimate and out to the relationship of all that is upon the Mother. This is a profound power of the Sun Dance. After a while, the dancers lean back to break the umbilical with the Mother. Sometimes they have to lean very hard. The peg tears through the skin, and this part is not as painful as most people imagine. Sometimes the pegs will shoot across the arena when they come loose. Surprisingly for most pledgers, there is very little bleeding if the Intercessor is skillful when he pierces.

The piercing and the breaking free should not be focused upon, however, when the essence of the Sun Dance Ceremony is being fathomed. It is the gathered tribe, the band, the gathered *Tiyospaye*, acknowledging the spiritual and physical relationship to all that is the *cante*, the heart of the Sun Dance. When all the dancers have ended their connection to the tree of life, the Sun Dance chief gathers them into a line and they leave the circle. The Sun Dance is over.[1]

I recall vividly the people standing in a long line to shake the hands of the sun dancers and the holy men. I remember the looks of satisfaction and appreciation on their faces, especially on the old faces. They looked at us with great hope, saying with their eyes that it was strengthening to see us bringing back a powerful ceremony that had been stamped out, asking us not to give in to those who would stop its return. Their faces conveyed a lasting message.

Now our Sun Dance flourishes on many reservations. But there was a time when we had to fight to be able to bring it back. It is a good ceremony and it has a powerful significance. I am thankful it has returned.

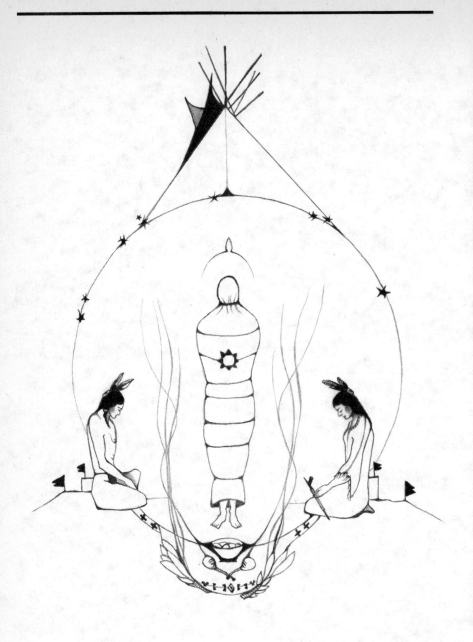

The *Yuwipi* or Spirit-Calling Ceremony

Yuwipi means "they tie him up." The holy man who conducts the ceremony serves as the medium to call in the spirit world. He is literally tied up with a special blanket draped over him and lies in the center of a square within a darkened room or enclosure. Calling songs are sung out to the beat of a drum. The onlooking participants sit around the periphery, and if they are all of one spiritual mind, the spirit beings enter in the form of blue or blue-green lights that whirl through the room, winking on and off to the drumbeat.

It is quite phenomenal. Numerous anthropologists and even Catholic priests have attested to the ceremony and have written books describing it. One booklet, written by William Stoltzman, S.J., is entitled *How to Take Part in Lakota Ceremonies*. William K. Powers's *Yuwipi* is a detailed book on the ceremony. It is academic yet quite personal, and warmly supportive of our Sioux spirituality.[1]

The *Yuwipi* is a special ceremony, usually held for an individual. My first *Yuwipi* experience was at Fools Crow's cabin. The Oglala holy man had called for me to come down to the reservation, and his ceremony prepared me for going to Vietnam. His spirit helper was Big Road, a renowned holy man of the past. A small stone figured in the ceremony; I wore it in a buckskin pouch during my combat missions and flew my fighter plane with confidence. All the predictions made at that ceremony later came true.

Many *Yuwipi* ceremonies are held for healing. Others are to find missing persons. A *Yuwipi* can also be held for thanksgiving, especially when one has been healed of a supposedly incurable disease. In the following pages I describe a *Yuwipi* ceremony used to minister to non-Indians.

To have a *Yuwipi* Ceremony, you must first have a holy man or holy woman who has the power to conduct it. A *yuwipi* holy one keeps his or her power by leading a virtuous life. It is also a life of sacrifices.

I do not know of any strongly empowered *yuwipi* men or women who drank alcohol. If they did, they did not keep their power long because the spirits who make their presence known in the ceremony do not like alcohol. Some of the spirits are no doubt from the times back when there was no alcohol or peyote. These spirits have seen the destruction such chemicals have worked on our people and consequently avoid a ceremony if participants have taken alcohol prior to attending.

Yuwipi-empowered persons hone their power by occasional Vision Quests and fasting. I was fortunate to assist both Fools Crow and Bill Eagle Feather, two powerful *yuwipi* holy men. Both were nondrinkers and never touched drugs or peyote. Bill vision quested on badland buttes. Fools Crow preferred Spirit Mountain in the Black Hills. Both were unselfish and devoted and brave. They demonstrated their courage by bringing back the Sun Dance to our reservation soon after the death of Nicholas Black Elk, who predicted the return of the annual ceremony in *Black Elk Speaks*. Eagle Feather was the first to pierce in a public Sun Dance and Fools Crow was the Sun Dance chief. Their courage and convictions were important ingredients in their successful conducting of the *Yuwipi* Ceremony. Not all *yuwipi* holy men participate in the Sun Dance, but a significant percentage do. The Sun Dance, like the Vision Quest, is a giving up of one's self to the spirit world.

Fools Crow and Eagle Feather conducted some very powerful *Yuwipi* ceremonies. It was not only their vision questing that helped maintain their communication with the spirit world; their steadfast participation in the annual Sun Dance was rewarded with the great foretelling power that was evident in their *Yuwipi*s.

Like the Sun Dance, the *Yuwipi* Ceremony is mostly confined to the reservation. Some holy men and holy women do occasionally travel off the reservation to do a ceremony. Privacy and freedom from distraction are critical to the success of the ceremony.

In previous chapters regarding the traditional ceremonies, the open-minded and respectful non-Indian, especially a rainbow tribe person, soon discovers that the ancient ways of the native peoples can be opened. Sweat Lodge, Vision Quest, beseechment with the pipe or stone can be experienced and even performed by all who seek communication with the here and now of Mother Earth and the six powers. Beseechment, acknowledgment, and thanksgiving to *Wakan Tanka* can be performed through these ceremonies by all respectful two-legged beings. Native Americans are reminded that we all live on this planet together. If the practice of some of our ceremonies by non-Indians helps them to become more conscious of our Mother Earth, then we all benefit. We certainly do not progress toward the halting of pollution and the healing of the earth by keeping fruitful knowledge and ceremonies a secret. The Sun Dance is an annual coming together around a ceremonial centering tree and is a spiritual function unique to a tribe. In time, the rainbow tribe will no doubt have related annual gatherings. Already, like-minded beings have gathered worldwide in their quest for peace, harmony, and environmental consciousness. Some aspects of the Sioux Sun Dance will surely influence some harmonic gatherings and serve to fulfill Black Elk's vision.

The *Yuwipi* Ceremony is a unique spiritual calling. Whether or not this ceremony will ever come fully off the Indian reservations no one can say. Those who seek a sincere reach into the spirit world should follow the example of the devout and selfless holy persons who maintain their *yuwipi* power to serve their people. To achieve this communication, model yourself after the ways and lives of the *yuwipi* persons who have conducted these ceremonies for generations. Men, especially white men, you must learn to subdue your egos if you want to ever come close to becoming a natural shaman. You must also develop and respect your feminine side and learn to balance your skills and knowledge with the female. Correspondingly, woman must learn to develop her masculine side and dispel all hatred of or antagonism for the male, regardless of past sufferings at his hands.

The beseechment of the spirit world is not restricted to the *Yuwipi* Ceremony alone. There are other paths of spiritual connection. Non-Indian people should consider the high degree of contact with nature that occurs in Sioux ceremony. The use of natural objects and the understanding of their meaning plays a powerful role for those who seek direction and foretelling power from the spirits, who are beyond us in the world that we will one day enter.

What are the spirits that are called in for the *yuwipi*? Who are they?

In a way, that question could be analogous to wondering what a grasshopper knows about a locomotive that goes whizzing by. No doubt the grasshopper might ask if it had the means or intellect to speak. No doubt the locomotive would be discovered to go quite beyond the grasp and comprehension of the crawling one who has but one summer's life span.

Basing my belief on *Yuwipi* ceremonies I experienced, I believe that *yuwipi* entering spirits are Native American two-leggeds that have gone on into the spirit world. In the Sioux ceremonies, they appear to be Sioux spirits who were once familiar with the ceremonies when they were on their earth journey. I don't know about you, but I prefer to believe that I will go on some day and remain a viable entity in the spirit world that lies beyond. Familiarity, courage, knowledge, participation, and respect for the Natural Way all seem to go together relative to having successful spirit entry ceremony and/or related, communicative progress. Maybe, in time, as generations pass on, rainbow spirits will enter ceremony. At this point, I feel it is appropriate to remind that life and spiritual power within ceremony are mysteries and my thoughts are mere two-legged supposition; however, these beliefs do afford me considerable confidence and perspective while I am here. I do appreciate the high amount of adventure that has seemed to accompany my quest.

Indian people take their signs from what they observe. The Great Spirit Creator has made so many things and ways in the form of a circle. The circle is an indicator that points toward an unending, circular spirit life. It is a comforting belief.

Indian people also believe that the animals, the flying ones, and the elements are all in concert with each other and with creation. In other words, they follow their right paths. This is why Indians seek to have Indian names. As a child I was named Eagle Boy. After flying in combat and returning to dance the Sun Dance, I was renamed Eagle Man. I am happy with that name, since it connects me with all the beings and with the six powers of the universe.

It seems that some of the spirits that enter a ceremony, especially a spirit helper to a holy man, will come into the spirit area of the *Yuwipi* in the form of the animal or object for which it is named. For example, Grey Weasel was Bill Eagle Feather's spirit helper when Bill conducted the *Yuwipi* Ceremony. A chattering weasel could be heard conversing with Bill during the ceremony. There is widespread belief among traditional Native Americans that the spirits come in many forms. I feel no contradiction in that. Despite the form or forms, it seems from what I have observed and experienced myself that the spirit was at one time a known and respected two-legged.

I certainly wouldn't mind being an eagle in the next life, and this is one of the reasons that I like my natural name. If I were ever called into a ceremony from the spirit world, I would probably brush a few heads with my wing tips. Indian names, or natural names, are being sought after by more and more non-Indians. These people are seeking a natural identity to become more aligned and related to the natural forces that flow in harmony.

The limitations of space and time prevent us from comprehending with any certainty the nature of the spirits who come to us. In the end, we can only surmise their nature and purpose, although it is my belief that basing our assumptions on natural evidence is the best way.

Plato's allegory of the cave offers an explanation of human limitation as related to the afterlife. He set a scene of some slaves, fettered as prisoners within a cave. They were forced to sit in such a way that they always faced a high wall on which shadows were reflected. They spent their lifetimes, from birth to death, within the cave, facing the wall.

A roadway passed before the entrance to the cave. Across the roadway was a fire large enough to cast on the wall the shadows of all things that moved along the roadway. As travelers passed by on the roadway, their shadows appeared on the wall. Some walked by alone, others in large groups, still others in families with children and relations and their pack animals. Sometimes a chariot would rumble by, casting a different kind of shadow. Or a rider would come along the road and his shadow would appear on the cave wall.

The slaves sat through their entire lives unable to see themselves or each other, able only to see the shadows that were cast on the wall. This was their only understanding of reality, and their concept of life was based only on what they could see. They could have no comprehension of the true or complete reality.

If these slaves were once released from their captivity and taken to the entrance to the cave, they could look at the real-life figures on the roadway and through this new knowledge realize that their vision had been limited by what they could interpret from the shadows on the wall. The released slaves could look down at the city where the road led, and they would begin to learn much more about the world.

Plato said that life today is but a mere shadow on the wall compared to the complete reality that lies beyond. This does not mean that we should not study and reflect while we are here. By all means, we should be tugging and twisting ourselves against the darkness around us so that we can be free enough to get a glimpse of the higher plane. But when we become spirit, we will learn immeasurably more than we can comprehend now.

An airplane crashed on the plains during a blizzard when I was attending law school. I was then working part time as the assistant director of the University of South Dakota Indian Studies Department. I had decided to attend law school after I returned from Vietnam. In fact, I was sitting in my first-year law class only eight days after my last combat mission. I had retained my pilot's license and was also employed as a pilot for flying university professors at the time of the crash. Because of this, I became involved in the search for the downed plane, and that search ultimately led me to a *Yuwipi* Ceremony conducted by Bill Eagle Feather, the Rosebud holy man. (This was a special time, as I was actively participating in the Sun Dance over a span of six years. The Sun Dance brought me into a number of *Yuwipi*, Sweat Lodge, and Vision Quest ceremonies. My contact with both my spiritual mentors, Frank Fools Crow and Bill Eagle Feather, was rich and deep, and it was a turning point in my life.)

The blizzard and several following storms buried the airplane, a Piper Cherokee Six, under deep snow. Numerous search parties had failed to find the plane, which had carried five students and the pilot, a professor from a college about sixty miles north of the university. After about a month of fruitless searching for the bodies, I was called by the director of the Indian Studies Department and asked if I could contact one of the two holy men. The president of the college where the students were enrolled had called the university. The man was almost at his wits' end, being besieged by phone calls about the missing plane and its passengers. As a last resort, he called the university and asked if they could contact a Sioux holy man.

Fools Crow could not come, so I contacted Bill Eagle Feather. At that time, when you called the real holy men on the reservation, you had to call the reservation police department. A holy man does not usually have a telephone, so the reservation police would send a squad car out to contact him. The university call was considered important, so they sent someone out for Bill.

After a while, my mentor, with whom I had traveled that summer, assisting in Sweat Lodge and *Yuwipi* ceremonies, was on the other end of the telephone line. Having been a traveling companion with Bill, I had been exposed to his intuitive powers. I was not at all amazed when he said "Nephew, I bet I know why you are looking for me. I bet you want me to come down and find that airplane that got lost."

Bill had received this information from a Sweat Lodge ceremony performed the previous evening. His spirit helpers told him how his nephew, Eagle Man, would be calling for him. Bill is not my blood lineage uncle, but he always called me his nephew after I assisted him in his ceremonies. I had also brought him down to the university several times to speak at cultural workshops and presentations. He was almost as fluent in English as he was in Lakota. (Frank Fools Crow also came to the university on many occasions. When he spoke, we used an interpreter, because he spoke only Lakota at the university presentations.)

Bill arrived the following day with a singer who also served as his driver. At that time, Dr. James Howard was the curator for the University Museum, and arrangements were made with him to have the *Yuwipi* Ceremony in a darkened room within the museum. Eagle Feather didn't seem to be bothered that the *Yuwipi* was to be held in a building other than a house or a reservation cabin.

"Doc" Howard was one of the nicest, most knowledgeable, and most respectful professors at the university and was delighted to be of assistance. He knew a lot about Sioux customs and history, yet was not paternalistic when he communicated with Indian people. This virtue is rare among educated white men who have studied the Native American culture. Most cannot control their egocentricity when talking with Indians, particularly Native Americans who practice traditional ways. Dr. Howard did not have this flaw in his character. I flew him many times in one of the university airplanes to workshops and extension classes and received a valuable education as we winged our way across the plains. Yet he was never paternalistic in the manner in which he presented his vast store of knowledge to me or to other Indian people.

Eagle Feather had met the professor years before while Doc was dancing at powwows and celebrations and liked him. Doc had some beautiful dance costumes and danced well. His two adopted sons were Indian, and he strongly respected our religious practices. From the Indian point of view, it is important for the success of the ceremony that a harmonious relationship exist between the holy man and the one who is responsible for the dwelling in which the ceremony will be held.

A ceremony is to beseech and to pray. Spirit people from the spirit world are called on in the *Yuwipi*. They have a higher realm much freer from the constraints of time and space than that in which we dwell. Therefore, they can be of help to us if properly beseeched.

Some *yuwipi* men have taboos regarding the *Yuwipi*. These taboos are usually in the form of restrictions on some people attending the ceremony or the indication of bad spirits possibly being present. Some publications, especially those put out by missionaries, seem to want to play up all of these negative indications. Bill Eagle Feather seldom dwelled on taboos or on so-called bad spirits. "Everything that the Great Spirit created is good," I learned from him.

There is no such thing as a bad waterfall, a bad stream, a bad rain, a bad owl, or a bad eagle, wolf, buffalo, or tree. Bill said nothing but good is created in nature. He did not have such things as bad spirits or particular taboos invading his ceremonies. He said, "It is only man that can make something be used as bad." Therefore, I do not put much stock in the taboos and fears cooked up by some holy men and played up by anthropologists.

Being respectful in a *Yuwipi* Ceremony and abiding by a certain format for the ceremony is another matter, however. Everyone of any dignity appreciates respect; and in ceremony, where one is before a powerful spirit world, it is beneficial for the participant to exhibit utmost respect. Preparation to attend means coming with a clean mind. You don't want to be sitting in a *Yuwipi* pumped up with ego and be seen to be looking down on the ceremony. *Yuwipi* holy men can pick out those who are attending the ceremony in disharmony or disbelief. Their minds and thoughts are in conflict with the aligned flow of the group as a whole, and the ceremony will be stopped and those not in tune will be told to leave.

Before the ceremony, Eagle Feather asked to look at a map showing the airplane's planned flight path. A friend of mine, a woman pilot, showed Bill an aerial map in which she had traced a line from the airplane's take-off point to its intended destination. Bill was a good-sized man. I can still see him bent over the map spread on a long table, seriously conversing with the blonde pilot who flew the university's airplanes part time. Her name was Carol, and we sat next to each other at the ceremony.

The *Yuwipi* Ceremony was planned for the evening on the second day after Bill arrived at the university. Carol and I secured a thick rug for Bill to lie on from Dr. Howard and placed it on the floor in the room that we would be using. All furniture except for a few chairs was moved out of the room. Most of the participants, students and professors, would sit on the floor. The students who attended were an even mix of Indian and non-Indian. Several of the professors and college faculty were of Indian descent. The university president's wife, a very lovely, intelligent woman, also attended. She was a strong advocate for the Indian Studies Department and helped the department on several occasions.

Eagle Feather brought five coffee cans into the room. Four of the cans were partially filled with dirt. A stick bearing a piece of cloth for each color of the four directions was placed in each can. The cans were arranged in a rectangular pattern about seven feet long and about six feet wide. Some 405 tobacco offerings were strung by two women around the cans to form the barriers of the *yuwipi* area, while Eagle Feather formed his dirt altar just outside the western boundary of the spirit area.

The fifth can held special dirt taken from a prairie dog mound. This earth is pushed to the surface by an animal relative; therefore it is considered to have a special quality. Woodchuck, mole, or gopher mound dirt is also used for altars. These animals are holy and never go against the Great Spirit's wishes. Therefore, this dirt is reflective of harmony and obedience to the ultimate good of nature.

Bill then took the empty can and patted the earth smooth to form a mound with a flattened, elongated crest. He placed six dots on the patted surface and drew a straight line through them. I assume that the six dots were for the six occupants of the plane and the straight line was for the airplane's flight path. Next he drew a hooded head with only a pair of eyes and an oval mouth for features. This figure had also been drawn on the mound of altar dirt at the previous *Yuwipi* in which I assisted him. I believe that this figure was representative of Bill's *yuwipi* spirit helper. He then drew four wavy lines on the altar top. This symbol, I presume, represented the seeking of help from the four directions. (Although I had traveled with Bill and we were close friends, there were many things that I never asked him. It is considered impolite to ask holy ones too many questions. They will tell you what is important for you to know when the right time comes about. Some things they may never tell you unless you go into special training for the spiritual way.)

When the altar designs were finished, Bill reached into his medicine bundle and placed on the altar a power of the hoop symbol: a porcupine quilled circle with two intersecting lines representing the four directions. Two buckskin rattles without handles, about the size of grapefruit, were then placed beside the altar.

*Yuwipi*s are held in complete darkness, and Bill had Dr. Howard turn out the overhead light momentarily to make sure the room would be dark enough. It was pitch black. Dr. Howard was assigned to guard the light switch after the lights were turned back on. Bill's singer sat outside the boundary near the southeast corner with his drum. Bill took his green jade pipe from its buckskin pipe bag, assembled it, and loaded it with tobacco. Sage was passed out to the onlookers who were gathering and sitting on the floor outside the string of the 405 tobacco offerings that formed the rectangle. Most of the Indian participants placed a sprig of sage behind each ear. The remaining sage was placed beside the altar.

Bill removed his shoes and stood in the center of the rectangle, waiting to be tied. While he was being tied, a braid of sweet grass was lit and carried around the room. The pleasant smell dispelled the musty odor of the room. Eagle Feather placed his hands behind him, and I tied his wrists and hands with a long leather cord. His *yuwipi* blanket was then draped over him. This was a light, quilted blanket with an eagle feather sewn to it. The feather was positioned so that it dropped back from Bill's head.

I tied him again, outside the blanket, making seven ties beginning with a noose around his neck and then wrapping him six more times down to his ankles. The singer and Dr. Howard helped me lay his bulky frame face down on the rug. The lights were turned out. The singer began the initial calling song to the spirit world. The audience waited for the appearance of the bluish sparks signifying the entrance of the spirits. The calling song was sung again and nothing happened.

Bill coughed. His muffled voice spoke out through the blanket. "Ho, there is one here tonight who thinks this ceremony is a sham. He is sitting to my right and back toward my feet. He is a professor and he thinks that I am some old trickster that has untied myself and I'm ready to jump around making sparks. Ho. Dr. Howard, turn on the light."

Dr. Howard turned on the light. Bill called out the professor's name. The professor was startled but begged to be allowed to stay, stating that he respected the ceremony and would put aside all disruptive thoughts.

Eagle Feather acquiesced and ordered the lights again to be turned out. The calling song was sung again, and the blue-green lights entered with a flourish. They were accompanied by the pair of rattles that swished through the rectangular spirit area. The electric blue of the lights winked like stars dotted across the room, bringing several gasps from the audience. The singer beat out a faster beat, and the lights and rattles increased their tempo. The drumming stopped, and the lights seemed to vanish into thin air. The rattles stirred close by the dirt altar.

After a brief period of silence, Eagle Feather spoke out. As was his custom, he didn't mince words and got immediately to the point. "Ho, we are gathered here because an airplane took off from here and went to a big city further west. When it came back, it got caught in *Waziya*, the power of the north. Now it is beneath the ice and snow. It never made it back to this fine college." No one corrected Eagle Feather's version. Actually the airplane was from a different college, sixty miles north, but judging from the results of the ceremony, the spirit world was satisfied with this description as well.

"Ho, I am going to call on my helper, Grey Weasel. Ho, *wana olowanpi* [sing now]," he instructed the singer. Once again the lights made their appearance, only this time their flashing lasted for but a brief period. They vanished when a squeaking noise came from the middle of the square. The drum stopped beating, and in the silence, a purring squeak, somewhat like the chattering of a squirrel could be heard, with the pattering of tiny feet shuffling on the floor.

"Ho, Grey Weasel. Ho, Grey Weasel is here," Bill called out. The little animal could be heard purring and chattering excitedly, and sounded as if it were running back and forth on the smooth stone floor. Eagle Feather began conversing in Lakota with the animal. Grey Weasel would chatter back and Eagle Feather would answer. After a while, Eagle Feather explained the conversation. "Ho, Grey Weasel says he will help us find the lost airplane, but first he wants to hear us pray for success. He wants us to pray hard to the spirit world. Let them know we are all sincere and respect the Indian Way."

The singer was the first to pray out loud. He ended his prayer with *Hetch etu*. The first person sitting to his left prayed next. All the prayers asked for a successful finding of the airplane. A dance song was struck at the end of the prayers. The rattles flew around the room at the end of the prayers as well, but this time there were no lights. During the song, I heard a sharp crack come from the floor as if something heavy had been dropped. Something came sliding toward me, and I felt an object touch my outstretched leg. I quickly jumped back, almost sitting myself in the lap of the president's wife, who was sitting to my other side.

The song ended and Eagle Feather spoke out, "Ho, Eagle Man, reach out in front of you and pick up a big rock that has come into our ceremony. It is about the size of a muskmelon." The weasel chattered furiously for several minutes. Eagle Feather interrupted at times with the exclamation "*Hau.*"

The chattering stopped, and after a few minutes, Bill raised his voice to address the audience. "Ho. Upon this big rock we will have seven signs that will help us find the airplane, and then all who are concerned can get on with their lives.

"The airplane is out by two creeks of the same name.

"You will send an airplane out from here with two of you who are like the *zintkala oyate* [the winged people]. These two, one a man, the other a woman, will fly together, and you will follow where the animals point you.

"The animals, the *wamakaskan oyate,* will point you toward a town. After you come across this town, look for other animals to point to the airplane.

"The airplane will be close by, but you will be forced to the ground. Not right away, and do not be afraid, because I see the two pilots looking back with a smile on their faces. They are safe and their airplane is safe.

"There is one of the six who will not be with the rest. She fell out on the way down. She is a girl with big glasses. Her face will be upon this ice-colored rock.

"The next day or two, two who are not looking for the plane will be led to it by another animal, different from the first animals that will be pointing.

"The tail will be sticking out. That which will make you give up your search will make the tail stick out.

"Ho, Grey Weasel has spoken. Ho, *wana olowanpi,*" Bill directed.

The untying song was sung. The rattles and lights flourished, and when the lights vanished and the rattles were almost still, Bill's blanket whirled through the air and landed in a heap on the professor who had had the initial doubts. Bill called for the lights, and Dr. Howard responded. Bill was sitting up in the square, untied. His two tying ropes were wrapped in tight balls and resting near the altar along with the pair of rattles.

The stone was inspected by the audience. Eagle Feather pointed out the face of the girl within the grain. Two lines that intersected represented South Loop Creek and Middle Loop Creek. Deer images could be seen clearly, and a coyote. The coyote image was looking back, and it was close to a T-shaped object that looked like the tail of a plane sticking up. Eagle Feather lit the pipe and passed it around for all to smoke.

The next day, Carol and I flew a Cessna 180 that was assigned to the Indian Studies Program. At South and Middle Loop creeks, we came across herds of deer that stood out in the clear areas rather than within the protective covering of the cedar breaks. They all pointed toward a tiny town with a distinctive water tower. The overcast ceilings were lowering as we approached the town. Rain droplets sprayed across the windshield. Another herd of deer pointed us in another direction after we had crossed the town and flown for several miles.

The rain turned to fog, and we had to fly closer to the ground, eventually circling while we discussed whether to proceed. The weather worsened and we had to turn back, racing the weather back to the university airport close by the Missouri river bottoms. We landed safely and put the airplane in its hangar. As we drove up the hill to the university, the fog rolled in and we looked back at the hangar with smiles, relieved that we had made it back.

Two days later, a pair of hunters followed coyote tracks that led them across the exposed tail of the missing Cherokee Six. The fog had brought the warming temperatures that melted the snow and exposed the tail. Five passengers were found together. The girl described in the ceremony was separate from the others. Apparently her seat belt had broken or unlatched when they went into a high G-spin. She was thrown through the fuselage of the airplane and landed separate from the others. All seven of the predictions made in Eagle Feather's *Yuwipi* held true.

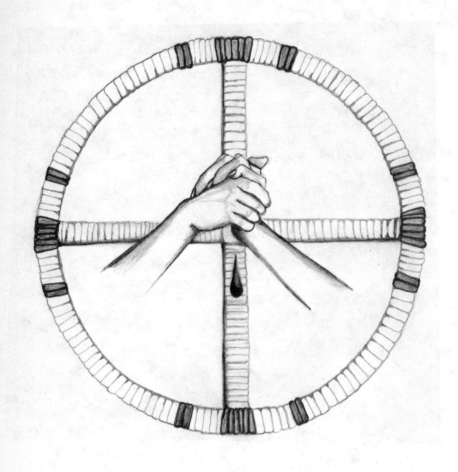

12

The Making of Relatives

Rainbow Crystal Woman, a Lakota Sioux, is my blood relative. Although we came into this world from different mothers and had different fathers, she is now my blood sister and I am her blood brother in the Indian Way. Midnight Song, Jamie Sams, is also my blood sister. She is from the Seneca-Choctaw people. I am also blood brother to *Wakinyan Cetan*, Thunder Hawk, of the rainbow tribe. I am related to each of these people as a blood brother, and they have Oglala blood flowing through them. I have Seneca-Choctaw blood as well as rainbow tribe blood, and each of these friends is now closer because we have been related in accordance with tribal custom.

The concept of making blood relatives is widely known. In this chapter, I will share with you how a modern-day version of the traditional Sioux ceremony is performed.

Rainbow Crystal Woman (Tayja Wiger) was blind for most of her life, starting in her early childhood. She even had a seeing-eye dog. I met Tayja after she had regained her eyesight in a ceremony several years before. This wonderful event happened at a spiritual conference on the same college campus where we were first introduced. We were both invited to the college as speakers on Native American spirituality.

We built a sweat lodge together for the conference being held that year. It was built of willow saplings on an island on the edge of the campus. This island was a beautiful setting for a sweat lodge. A curved oriental bridge reached over to the island, which was in the middle of a gentle stream. While we were working together on the lodge, we became close friends. I felt as if I had already known her for quite some time.

I had been conducting Sweat Lodge ceremonies at the home of Cynthia Bend, who with Tayja had authored the book *Birth of a Modern Shaman*, the story of Tayja's difficult life both as a child and during the period of her blindness.[1] However, Tayja persevered, and her spirituality worked within a healing ceremony to bring back her vision. She is now a spiritual leader, a modern shaman. It was she who encouraged me to appreciate and use spiritual healing powers based on the steady infusion of knowledge that I was receiving from Black Elk's vision, my education by Eagle Feather and Fools Crow, and, of course, my participation in ceremonies. I was content to be a warrior and a teacher, but Tayja took me further down my spiritual path and further into *pejuta makah wakan*, the medicine world. Our friendship has been strong, and our blood line from the Oglalas seems to be a strong bond. We decided to be *hunka*, relatives. We would become blood brother and sister to each other.

The making of relatives is not a complicated ceremony, although I would recommend some alteration in the way that Tayja and I conducted it. Our friends, mostly rainbow tribe people, were happy to hear that we were planning to do a traditional version of the ceremony received from Buffalo Calf Woman. *Hunkapi* is the Sioux name for this ceremony.

In the old days, horse tails were a key item used for the ceremony. We did not have any, but if we could have, we would have used them. In the old days, the ceremony was begun by waving horse tails over the two who were to be related. Horses are free in spirit, especially those who have the freedom of the wide open plains. It is good to be a relative, but the horse tails remind us to remain free and flowing and not to hold each other back.

We chose to become relatives on the island before the evening sweat lodge was conducted. We used my peace pipe for the ceremony. Sage and sweet grass were lit, and their fragrance could be smelled in the still, evening air. Many friends were there who were attending the conference. The peace pipe was offered to the four directions, and as each direction was beseeched, special mention of relationship was made in the ceremony.

The east was first beseeched, and as we held the pipe facing eastward, we asked that we help each other as brother and sister in our quest for knowledge and wisdom while we were on our earth path. From the south, we asked for healthy bodies and promised to recommend to each other healthy foods and abstinence where needed. We also thanked the powers for the regaining of Tayja's eyesight. To the west, we welcomed the presence of the spirit world and said that we had a common path, the red way, and were thankful for our Sioux lineage. We spoke to all ancestors of the Sioux people that had gone on and promised that we would always strive to keep what we knew of the old ways alive. Tayja promised that she would build a sweat lodge within a year's time on land in Wisconsin. I promised the ancestors that I would go there to help build it when she decided on the right time. To the north, we placed tobacco in the pipe and asked that our friendship, through our blood relationship, last for our whole lives.

We then took out a sharp knife. Tayja made a small cut on the heel of her palm with the knife. She handed the knife to me and I cut my hand likewise. We placed our palms together and danced around the sweat lodge fire in a slow shuffle four times, while Thunder Owl, my Mdewakanton friend, played the drum.

The cutting of oneself signifies the seriousness of the two adopters (those who seek to adopt each other). It is not to be a whimsical act, the adopting of another to make a relative. Like the piercing in the Sun Dance, which effectively screens out those who are not deeply serious about their spiritual concerns, the cutting of oneself takes some courage. Actually, the thought and anticipation are more painful than the actual cut, but it serves its purpose. One doesn't make everyone a blood relative.

The Sioux believe that we are all relatives, *Mitak oyasin*, and it is good to meet those that you find on your path who have a special relationship with you. I believe that the cutting aspect of the ceremony must be carefully weighed by the modern world. There are many aspects of modern life that the Sioux consider weak or "wimpy." The lack of courage even seems to be commended and admired by many modern people. This is a difficult thing for the Sioux to understand. I know that the cutting portion of the ceremony will be too much for a lot of non-Indians, even rainbow tribe people. If that is the case, they should not undertake the ceremony. If there is a strong reason to make someone a relative, I suggest that they use some other means to demonstrate seriousness of intention and to screen out whimsical or fleeting intentions. Perhaps fasting for a period or some related form of sacrifice could be offered. Perhaps the giving away of some prized material possession would be more painful than any cutting and could be a worthy sacrifice. The old *Hunkapi* Ceremony bound the adopters together with a light rope. This version could be used as a substitute for cutting. In the old way, there was also a giving away of gifts. A promise to do something for the other may be considered as a gift in this tradition.

If one wishes to be a blood relative in the literal sense, then be careful to use only the shallow point of the knife so that the cut will not be deep. The heel of the hand is the safest place to cut. I recommend also that you do not touch the cut parts but place your hands together so that the cut part of one is on the uncut part of the other. It is a shame that today's diseases make us so precautionary, but that is the way it will have to be.

Also, be sure to use separate cutting instruments and sterilize them to red hot in a flame and then allow them to cool before using.

It was a proud moment knowing that Tayja was my blood sister. She encouraged a powerful gift to come to me within a few days. She gave me the inspiration and confidence to move on into the healing aspect of spirituality. Formerly, I had been content to be a warrior for the way. I fought back at those who would stop our Sun Dance and who ridiculed our other ceremonies and our holy men. I had become a teacher after I had learned from Bill Eagle Feather and Fools Crow. Tayja was the catalyst to move this knowledge on into a holistic realm. Because of my relationship with her, Tayja taught me a remarkable sage healing ceremony, which has proven very beneficial. Since that time, we fulfilled our promise and built the sweat lodge in Wisconsin where she lives.

I also did a similar ceremony with Jamie Sams in her home near Santa Fe. Like Tayja, she is a very strong-minded woman. I feel especially close to the Seneca blood that I received from Midnight Song, *Hancoka Olowanpi* in Sioux.

Jamie has a very large tipi in her yard, and while I was staying there, I built a sweat lodge for her. She drove me out to a canyon where we cut the saplings for the frame. I feel as close to Jamie as I do to Tayja, for they are both my sisters. Jamie has remembered well the teachings from her grandmothers and from her many adventures and experiences. Some of her quests required extreme courage and endurance. Her memory and knowledge are remarkable and equally fascinating.

We brushed each other with an eagle feather during the ceremony. This act symbolized that we believe in the Great Spirit, but as eagles we are very independent and can still have the freedom to agree and disagree with each other.

There is a powerful spirit area where Jamie lives. It was there that I learned a strong ceremony that uses *Wakan Tanka*'s gift within certain stones. Again I found that I was rewarded by new blood even though I was not seeking any reward or gift. Maybe it was the Seneca spirit ancestors, with whom I feel connected because long ago the Sioux people are originally from the same area before we fled from the powerful Iroquois to become peaceful corn planters in North Carolina. The Seneca were our relations way back in time. They are very matriarchal, and our Sioux ways have carried on that value through the centuries. They were highly democratic as well as spiritual. We Sioux reflect those values also.

My last *Hunkapi* Ceremony was with Thunder Hawk. His white name is Tim Ryan. Now he has Oglala blood and is of the rainbow tribe. I was deeply impressed with his sincerity and genuine hunger for the good of the old ways. He led me to a powerful bull buffalo that gave me a strong message. I will tell of that buffalo in a later chapter, but right now I will briefly describe how we conducted our *Hunkapi* Ceremony.

Tim had always wanted to be an Indian. He is still young and strong but is now reaching the prime of his life. Back several years ago, he was at the Greasy Grass, the same area where Black Elk had his vision. This area is now called the Custer Battlefield or the place where the Battle of the Little Big Horn was fought. The Sioux wiped out Custer's command there after he attacked them.

Tim prayed hard at the Greasy Grass when he was still in his teens. He admits that he wept while he was out in the open on the prairie. In the distance, he could see a thunderstorm approaching, yet he remained where he was on the plain. He prayed hard and asked the Great Spirit to help him become an Indian. Most of all he wanted to be an Oglala, because he was close to what that good man John Neihardt had transcribed from the old Oglala prophet Black Elk. Tim said that he also felt a certain pride in the Sioux destruction of Custer. Although he was a white man, Tim could not identify with the cavalry under Custer. He felt a closeness only to the Sioux, who were led by Crazy Horse and Sitting Bull.

When the storm was almost upon him, Tim cried openly. This is a strong man who could do most people a great deal of damage in a karate ring. He trains many hours and is truly a warrior. Yet he is not afraid to show a strong, feminine side in ceremony. He is truly a balanced being.

Two lightning bolts struck near him on the prairie, and when the storm had passed over, two hawks flew up to him and circled over his drenched body. He was told to contact Black Elk and he did. He wrote a letter to Black Elk and mailed it to the Pine Ridge Reservation, not knowing that the old holy man had been dead for several decades. His letter was answered in the Indian way, however. He was led to a class that I was teaching, and we became good friends. As I got to know him, I was pleased to discover his many virtues. He is a handsome young white man, educated and well traveled, and yet he has very little ego. He is a younger version of Dr. Howard, whom I described in the chapter on *Yuwipi*. From all indications, Tim is not one to misuse Indian medicine. The absence of ego and his sincere humility will protect him.

His letter to Black Elk was answered, and I found in my class someone who had read John Neihardt's book even more times than I had. In time, after we had participated in several Sweat Lodge ceremonies together,

I decided that Black Elk probably wouldn't mind if Tim should also become an Oglala.

Tim's *Hunka* blood ceremony took place in a sweat lodge. Many rainbow tribe friends were there, including my Mdewakanton friend, Thunder Owl. It was a little difficult cutting ourselves in the darkness of the lodge, and impossible to tell our blood from the steam and sweat that covers everything. We made several attempts with the knife, and the sting of sweat in the darkness let us know that we had finally succeeded. I do not recommend doing this ceremony in the darkness, but at the time we were committed to our intentions and therefore pressed on as originally planned.

We held our cut palms together while Thunder Owl drummed, and chanted four times:

> *Hunka, hunka* [We are relatives, we are relatives]
> *Hunkapi hunkapi* [In this relative ceremony]
> *Hey hey heyyyy*
> *Oglala wigmunke* [We are Oglala and Rainbow]
> *Oglala wigmunke* [We are Oglala and Rainbow]

Thunder Owl sang a song, and Tim was given the name Thunder Hawk, *Wakinyan Cetan*. Thunder Owl told him that he would be a powerful messenger between both worlds, the Oglala and the Rainbow. It would be his duty and that would be his road. We placed portions of food for the spirit world out in the woods, then smoked the pipe and had a good meal around the campfire.

13

The Giveaway Ceremony

The forerunner of the *Otuha* or giveaway was the ceremony for the Keeping of the Soul. The Keeping of the Soul rite was prohibited by the government in 1890, and the government, under the influence of the missionaries, added the extraordinary requirement that all souls being kept by the Sioux must be released on a certain day established by law. Later, one of the original sacred rites, the Sun Dance, would also be banned by governmental decree. The Sun Dance survived, but the soul rite was transformed into the Giveaway Ceremony.

In the times of plenty, before reservation days, the tipi lodges held a rich store of dried buffalo meat for winter provisions. Horses were sleek and fat from endless grasslands. And the clothing of the people was deerskin, buffalo robes, and elk hide. Game was plentiful, and some of the clothing was richly decorated. Few possessions were needed in comparison to modern-day living. Therefore, an Indian in the past had no need to accumulate possessions, which in any event would be bothersome during the many moves the nomadic tribes would be making.

But horses were indispensable and regarded as great wealth. Nevertheless, these creatures would be sacrificed at the death of the owner. It was not unusual for a departed warrior to be placed on a death scaffold with a piece of his favorite horse. It was believed that the horse would want to go on into the spirit world with its owner and the two could be together.

After the tribes were confined on the reservation, however, horses became too important for survival to be sacrificed. When government rations were disbursed, horses were needed to distribute the provisions to outlying camps. What game still existed to supplement government rations required horses for hunting. The tribe's survival was at stake, and the sacrifice of a horse or even a hunter's weapons had to be stopped.

The dire poverty resulting from reservation conditions led to the need to keep for redistribution what little wealth was left over from the deceased tribe member. Thus, necessity gave birth to the *Otuha* Ceremony.

Indian people by nature are extremely generous, sometimes to a fault. This is a personal characteristic that is taught to children very young. They are expected to take care of others, and selfishness is shamed. Many Indians do not like to ask for money even when they have performed services for others. When they make artistic items for sale, they often feel uncomfortable during the selling process. Non-Indians have taken advantage of this characteristic, and many stories exist of how Indian people have been exploited by those who value possessions over the welfare of the people.

The pattern of materialism and overacquisition by the dominant race is beginning to come full circle, however. Mother Earth is beginning to heat up because of the pollutants that we have placed in the skies. A good many of these pollutants are the result of simple greed or insensitivity. If the earth continues to overheat, the two-leggeds will have no choice but to cut down on consumption. Humans will have to learn to live with less and perhaps to enjoy life more with less.

I have seen more genuine laughter among tribal people and spiritual people who had a sense of belonging when they got together than in the uptight charades of well-to-do people who are trying to impress one another. The Giveaway Ceremony should be practiced by the whole human race, for the sake of the preservation of Mother Earth. The death of a relative is not the only time that this should occur. We should find opportunities to share our possessions with each other.

When my brother-in-law died, my sister held a big dinner after the funeral. He was a big, strong white man in his day and was a devoted husband to my sister. She invited not only family members to the dinner but close friends as well. These were people whom she believed she could count on to help her get things ready for the traditional *Otuha* that is held a year after a loved one's death.

For a year, my sister gathered up her husband's possessions. Tools, hunting equipment, clothes, jewelry, and even building materials were earmarked for distribution to Ralph's friends and relations. Since these were mostly "men's" items, she also had star quilts and baby quilts made, and purchased various household items for the women.

On a weekend almost a year after Ralph had gone on to the spirit world, a big dinner was held at a community hall. Most of the presents were distributed to those who attended. Some tools and building materials were picked up by the beneficiaries at a later time. Good things were said of my brother-in-law by the people who came to receive their gifts.

Many Indian people were at the giveaway, for they remembered Ralph as a man who was always at powwows and at the Sun Dance looking after my sister while she danced. He always had his pickup available to get a load of firewood or had a welcoming cup of coffee for visitors who stopped by while their camper trailer was parked at its usual place during the Sun Dance. He was as devoted to my parents as he was to my sister and respected our customs and religion more than the one he had been brought up in. When I was dancing the Sun Dance and taking criticism from some of my own family members, it was he who encouraged me to go on with the Indian Way.

He was commemorated and remembered by his family and friends in this very special way after his death. His soul had gone on to the spirit world, but his memory survived. Goods were distributed so that they could be reused by people he cared for. His example was remembered by friends and relations so that they could learn from it. This is the *Otuha* Ceremony.

In a number of Sweat Lodge and Vision Quest ceremonies that I have held lately, we have unfolded a giveaway blanket after the ceremony; those who have participated are free to give away possessions to the blanket. Everyone is also free to reach in and take a gift from the blanket. Any items that remain on the blanket will be exchanged, sold, or bartered for tree seedlings to plant in honor of Earth Day. Many of the rainbow people donate substantial gifts, and these will be turned directly into help for our Mother, Earth.

A friend has another version of the giveaway blanket. She carries it to all the ceremonies in which she participates. After the ceremony, when everyone is enjoying the closeness from the ceremony, she opens the blanket. Anyone is free to take something from it. They may give something in exchange or simply give something to it. In this way, the gifts of each group go on to the next group and are shared with all who need them.

After a recent Vision Quest, when all were down from the mountain, she opened the blanket and invited everyone to bring a gift and take a gift. She also asked the group of Indians who were there preparing for their own Vision Quest to take a gift from the blanket. Their holy man selected a beautiful and ornate silver bracelet and said that he would give it to his wife. Although she usually does not know the history of the items on the blanket, in this case she knew that it had come from Bangkok. So somewhere on the Rosebud reservation is a Sioux woman wearing a bracelet from Asia. The blanket is another way in which we show that we are all relatives.

She tells me that being the presenter of this blanket has been a strong teaching experience to her. Although you might think that people would be greedy and take everything just because it is free and available, that is not the case. Many people put quite personal items in it, such as jewelry or special stones. Those who take gifts from the blanket have no one to thank except the six powers and *Wakan Tanka*, since no one owns the blanket and its contents. She says that for herself and for all who take from the blanket, it is a constant lesson in the abundance of the world.

In both these cases, we have adapted the traditional giveaway to the new spiritual needs of the rainbow people. There is no charge for a Sweat Lodge or for the Vision Quest. Our spiritual path is not for sale. But the giveaway blanket has a twofold purpose. We are able to help the cause for Mother Earth and we help ceremony participants learn how to break the habit of accumulation and materialism.

14

Sioux Ceremonial History

The old ceremonies, the seven sacred rites, had to go underground when the Sioux people moved to the reservations. Later, the seven Mother Earth ceremonies evolved.

The Buffalo Calf Woman taught the importance of the pipe. It was to be used in all the seven rites. No doubt she and/or the Power she represented knew the struggle the people would be enduring within but a few generations. In time, the Pipe Ceremony would be the only concealable way in which the Sioux could do ceremony. The pipe could be dismantled, separated into stem and pipe bowl, and hidden from the watchful eyes of the cavalry and the searching zeal of the missionaries. By using this portable altar in all ceremonies while they were yet free on the plains, the Sioux were being prepared for their spiritual survival. When it became the time of great despair and tribulation within the bleak captivity of the reservation, the sacred pipe held the memory, "the looking inside power," generated by the ceremonies. The Pipe Ceremony kept our *Mitakuye oyasin* (we are related) philosophy alive, tucked mysteriously and safely within the seed of the flowering tree of Black Elk's vision.

The flame of the red path died down to a smoldering ember. Its spiritual power was the sleep of a grizzly bear through a long winter. While the buffalo herds were exterminated, the government went about its own path to force the Sioux into its own cultural concept of man's unchecked dominion over nature, its own woefully mistaken belief that the North American continent was a land of unlimited resources, ripe for the raping, by an unrespectful industrial society.

Boarding schools were built to confine the young Sioux for nine months of each year and to teach them to assimilate the white man's way. Through education and confinement away from the tribal *tiyospaye* (the tribal family), new generations of Sioux were programmed for cultural elimination. Missionaries were allowed on the reservations to speed up the process. The initial goal of the missionaries was eradication and outright destruction of Sioux spirituality. Ceremonial participation, reverence of observable God-made nature, and the legend of the historic appearance of the Buffalo Calf Woman were regarded as major obstacles that had to be erased from the new generations. Missionaries were allowed their own boarding schools, and the young Sioux were forced to kneel to the white man's concept of God within enclosed churches, where it was not possible to conceive of, much less commune with the six powers of the universe. Sweat lodges alongside tipis and the square new dwellings called cabins were dismantled under the insistence of the new and foreign spiritual leadership. Peace pipes and sacred bundles were ordered to be gathered up and placed in piles to be burned. The Sioux dared not protest to a vengeful cavalry that killed women and children in cold blood at Wounded Knee and now did the missionaries' bidding. Black Elk himself was interfered with. An overzealous missionary broke into the midst of a curing ceremony and threw sacred objects upon the ground and destroyed them. Black Elk's patient recovered. The Jesuit priest, Father Bosch, died soon after from being thrown by a horse.

In time, Sioux ceremony was explicitly forbidden despite a document called the Constitution, which guarantees religious freedom. A world war came, and Sioux men patriotically volunteered for military service and were sent overseas to fight in the trenches of France. When they returned from their loyal endeavor, they were greeted with a specific governmental decree that banned the Sun Dance and all related forms of Native American worship. Warriors could risk their lives and limbs for the new nation, but their own religion was forbidden. The missionaries became firmly entrenched and began to control tribal government and economics. On my reservation, not unlike Hawaii, one missionary group became the largest individual landholder.

All along, a few old, traditional families would not give in to the reservation authorities. When W. K. Powers speaks of Oglala tenacity in his writings, I think of these families that clung to their family pipes and refused to give up their spiritual concepts from thousands of years of proven past. They suffered. Their children suffered, especially in the boarding schools. These old-way families were never in line for government jobs and positions, nor did their children ever receive scholarships or education grants. Even in my time, I was known among the Bureau of Indian Affairs circles as one who would not deny traditions and never received a dime's worth of available Indian educational grants for either my undergraduate or law degrees, and this was years later. I have no reason to lament, however, compared to the old-time traditionals who wore the secret power of the hoop sign made of porcupine quills. Those old traditionals suffered far more than I ever did. I was allowed to fight back. Back in their time, their children suffered dearly in the boarding schools.

The traditionals went back into the badlands, back into the buttes and hills. The Oglala reservation was spacious. The Hunkpapa and Mini-counjou reservations also afforded hidden valleys and meadows to conceal a Sun Dance. The old traditionals and some of their offspring braved the authorities and held the ceremony that was deemed so vital to their well-being. Precautions were taken. To avoid detection, the ceremonial tree was much shorter, and the dance arena did not have a shading bowery. Other precautions were taken as well to avoid discovery, and secret piercings took place. Sioux tenacity! Indeed, it had its spiritual resolve.

Two white men totally opposite from the missionaries came onto the Sioux reservation. These two men were writers and were unlike the historians who came to record combat deeds of the chiefs and warriors. These writers sought to listen to Indian spirituality and record what they had to say.[1] These men were also beyond the control of the agency heads and the missionaries.

The first to visit Black Elk was John Neihardt. It was late in the summer when they first met, and Black Elk instructed the writer to return the following spring to hear his story of the powerful vision. Black Elk sensed that Neihardt was a special person with a special mission. "There is so much to teach you. What I know was given to me for men, and it is true and it is beautiful. Soon I shall be under the grass and it will be lost. You were sent to save it, and you must come back so that I can teach you." Black Elk was so pleased with Neihardt that the following summer he adopted him and gave him an Indian name, Flaming Rainbow. Later, the other writer came to the Oglala reservation. This white man, Joseph Epes Brown, lived for some time at Black Elk's cabin. Later, he wrote a book called *The Sacred Pipe;* like Neihardt, he too was believed to have "been sent" to preserve the truth and the meaning of the sacred hoop.

Black Elk's story was preserved, recorded, and eventually published through *Pta Wigmunke* (Flaming Rainbow). The story of the powerful vision was like a sleeping bear, however. The new nation's nature spirituality took time to develop. *Black Elk Speaks* slept for a while on bookstore shelves before it began its awakening of the nation.

Some writers have attempted to erroneously claim that the old holy man gave up his Indian spirituality. Black Elk told his story to Neihardt away from the missionaries, and Neihardt refused to allow the priests permission to edit the truth of the old visionary's words. The missionaries chastised Black Elk for not clearing the Neihardt interviews through them, but the old man would not alter a word. Later, both men climbed to the top of Harney Peak for a Pipe Ceremony of beseechment to the six powers of the great vision. How anyone can interpret these actions as a man giving up his native spirituality indicates to me that those writers who are attempting to claim that Black Elk gave up his Indian faith are more interested in pleasing their nontraditional readers than telling and observing the truth of Black Elk's actions.

Neihardt took Black Elk to Thunder Being Mountain (Harney Peak) where the old holy man held forth his pipe and lamented his pitiful beseechment upon the mountain. As they climbed toward the summit, the old man predicted the thunder beings would acknowledge when he would send up his voice.

Another world war came, and Sioux men along with those from other Native American tribes became the highest ratioed volunteer ethnic group into the armed forces. Combat infantry, Marine Corps, paratroops, and other related front-line units were their preferences and assignments. Many of these volunteers spent four to five years in military units living together and working closely with servicemen from throughout the nation. When these Sioux soldiers, sailors, and marines returned in victory, a slow change began upon the reservations.

Some of these warriors, swept with the euphoria of victory, underwent pipe ceremonies of thanksgiving. The government agents and the missionaries looked askance. Families were thankful their sons had returned safely from long years of war. The image of the vanished tribal paradise was once again reinforced and beckoned by the pipe. The once magical existence within the harmony of nature reasserted itself in these early ceremonies. The earth called out, warning the Sioux to question the newcomers' claim of inalienable dominion over Mother Nature. Vast herds of game had vanished, the dust bowls of the thirties had eroded the Great Plains, and the warriors had seen first-hand the ravages and destruction of modern war. Probably these warriors recognized the absence of harmony, simplicity, and closeness to nature in the outer world. The return to the ceremonies had begun.

But even during the war years, the pipe appeared, especially in the remote conclaves upon the reservations. The people were very concerned about their many warriors seeing combat throughout the globe, and they sought spiritual protection through the old way. A sick person or a dying traditionalist would also call out for the pipe in a remote village or an isolated cabin. An elderly holy man would administer to the dying person's wishes. The traditionals came out openly after the return of the world-traveled warriors. A sweat lodge was built here and there. Thanksgiving *Yuwipi* ceremonies were held.

Those who controlled and manipulated were lulled into their own slumber. They seemed unconcerned about the return of the pipe. No doubt they were so within their paternalism and ego that they could not conceive of the idea that Native American spirituality would ever begin to take root, emerge, bloom, and blossom. Besides, the peace pipe was a harmless looking item. The Sweat Lodge and *Yuwipi* ceremonies were frowned upon, but suspicion and detracting rumor could be spread against those who practiced the return of these ceremonies. In the minds of the missionaries, these smaller ceremonies could be "dealt with," but a Sun Dance, a "real ceremony" that could draw the participation of the tribe in numbers, that would have been an alarming matter.

It happened. Not long after Black Elk's departure for the spirit world, a Sioux holy man challenged the governmental authorities and the missionaries. Bill Eagle Feather, the Brule/Sichangu holy man, danced the Sun Dance, and Fools Crow pierced him.

Another seed, a related seed in the non-Indian world was sprouting ever so slowly during this time. Brave new pioneers were beginning to stir and plant the roots of modern ecology and environmentalism. Brave new thinkers and independent spirits out in the non-Indian world were reading the tale of environmental destruction that was in progress. Leading-edge white men and white women were questioning the archaic structures that were damaging the earth and humankind. Strange new challenges called out in a time when artificial values and suppression of nature was the characterization of the industrial nations which the rest of the world looked up to. The vanishing of certain species and near extermination of others jolted many. Wanblee, the eagle, became endangered. This threat to the national symbol made many reach down into their environmental roots. Old values, old hunting practices were questioned. Environmentalists were born from all walks and all positions. Back before World War II, the drought and the Great Depression helped to bring forth some of these pioneers as leaders that answered to the national crisis. Bringing back the land had been a major federal priority. Shelter belts of trees were planted across the continent. Federal work projects shored up soil erosion and flood damage resulting from the harmful practices of the timber, mining, and agricultural interests. Crisis brought forth a strange, new, transformational process. Exemplary men and women scattered throughout the nation projected new visions to begin the change.

Advancing modern communication was a God-given tool that expedited this new enlightenment. New values divergent from past values, new respects backed up by nonmaterial endeavors were the trademarks of these early environmental pioneers—trademarks reflected as respect and care for nature. Humankind was not dominant over nature. Men and women were dependent on nature, after all, and for some there grew the beginning of the belief held by the Indians—nature was a living entity.

The Sun Dance struggled. It was slow but steady in its revival. Civil rights, especially in the South, made a push for racial equality. Men and women of all colors began their stand for equal freedom. The Indians made their push during this opening time for the right to have their religious expressions and ceremonies of old return. The Sun Dance became the focal ceremony. The missionaries made an all-out effort to stop it but could no longer turn to the government agents to do their bidding. The bureaucrats were fearful of the newspaper reporters and the advance of the black brothers and sisters who were finding their freedoms being granted in the courtrooms and from the marches for freedom. The reservation youth rose up, and the annual ceremony returned to tribal throngs of spiritually hungry Sioux. Sweat lodges began to dot the reservations. *Yuwipi* ceremonies were held. Pipe carriers no longer had to remain underground.

What the future may hold for the ceremonies, only time will tell. Will my tribe return to all of the original seven ceremonies? Some tribal members will claim that the original seven are present and being practiced. If that is the case, then it is merely a question of semantics. It is rare that the Throwing of the Ball Ceremony is ever held. Certainly, the *Yuwipi* and the Pipe Ceremony are far, far more popular, and it should be remembered that these two ceremonies, as distinct, separate ceremonies, were not of the original seven. I will leave the arguing for the academics and the detractors, however, for my past and present is of the warrior. Fighting for our Sun Dance until the young could rise up and protect it and now fighting for a harmed Mother Earth are more appealing than sitting around and lazily bickering like a bunch of jealous hang-around-the-tents.

Maybe the Mother Earth ceremonies are for those who must get out and fight for the well-being of our Mother, but if that is the case then it looks like that means all of us who live on the planet. So let's save the negative squabbling for the next life where petty trivialities probably evaporate when they reach that higher plane. We have no choice but to think positively. Mother Earth is all too important, and she needs our total energy and concern.

In honor of those tenacious traditionals who persevered and preserved the Indian Way, let us hear the words of Black Elk.

Black Elk's Prayer upon Thunder Being Mountain

Hey-a-a-hey! Hey-a-a-hey! Hey-a-a-hey! Hey-a-a-hey! Grandfather, Great Spirit, once more behold me on earth and lean to hear my feeble voice. You lived first, and you are older than all need, older than all prayer. All things belong to you—the two-leggeds, the four-leggeds, the wings of the air and all green things that live. You have set the powers of the four quarters to cross each other. The good road and the road of difficulties you have made to cross; and where they cross, the place is holy. Day in and day out, forever, you are the life of things.

Therefore I am sending a voice, Great Spirit, my Grandfather, forgetting nothing you have made, the stars of the universe and the grasses of the earth.

You have said to me, when I was still young and could hope, that in difficulty I should send a voice four times, once for each quarter of the earth, and you would hear me.

Today I send a voice for a people in despair.

You have given me a sacred pipe, and through this I should make my offering. You see it now.

From the west, you have given me the cup of living water and the sacred bow, the power to make live and to destroy. You have given me a sacred wind and the herb from where the white giant lives—the cleansing power and the healing. The daybreak star and the pipe, you have given from the east; and from the south, the nation's sacred hoop and the tree that was to bloom. To the center of the world you have taken me and showed the goodness and the beauty and the strangeness of the greening earth, the only mother—and there the spirit shapes of things, as they should be, you have shown to me and I have seen. At the center of this sacred hoop you have said that I should make the tree to bloom.

With tears running, O Great Spirit, Great Spirit, my Grandfather—with running tears I must say now that the tree has never bloomed. A pitiful old man, you see me here, and I have fallen away and have done nothing. Here at the center of the world, where you took me when I was young and taught me; here, old, I stand, and the tree is withered, Grandfather, my Grandfather!

Again, and maybe the last time on this earth, I recall the great vision you sent me. It may be that some little root of the sacred tree still lives. Nourish it then, that it may leaf and bloom and fill with singing birds. Hear me, not for myself, but for my people; I am old. Hear me that they may once more go back into the sacred hoop and find the good red road, the shielding tree![2]

That good man and adopted relative of my tribe, Flaming Rainbow, stated,

We who listened now noted that thin clouds had gathered about us. A scant, chill rain began to fall, and there was low, muttering thunder without lightning. With tears running down his cheeks, the old man raised his voice to a thin high wail and chanted: "In sorrow I am sending a feeble voice, O Six Powers of the World. Hear me in my sorrow, for I may never call again. O make my people live!"[3]

Neihardt described the acknowledgment of the Thunder Beings. "For some minutes the old man stood silent, with face uplifted, weeping in the drizzling rain. In a little while the sky was clear again."[4]

And that is why I call that sacred place Thunder Being Mountain.

PART THREE

AIR

Bringing Forth Your Own Mother Earth Wisdom

If you're going to learn to swim, you're going to have to immerse yourself in the water.

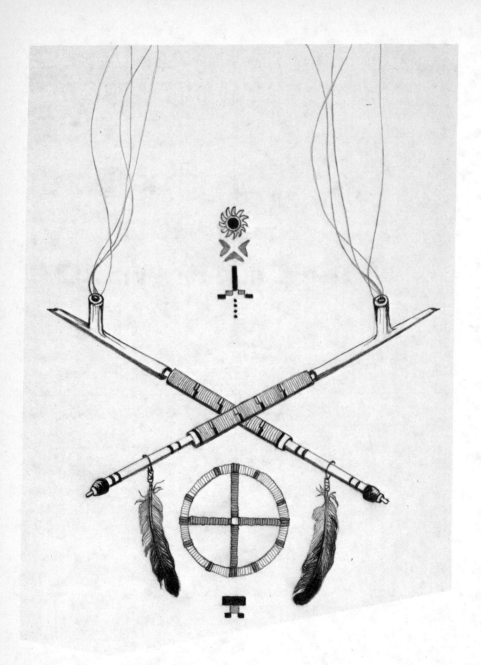

15

The Making of the Pipe

Before the Sioux migrated to the headwaters of the Mississippi, they carried ceremonial pipes made from ceramic clay. After Buffalo Calf Woman appeared to them on the plains bearing a red peace pipe, a special emphasis was placed on the red catlinite pipes as a way of honoring her and her special instructions. As a result, a Sioux peace pipe is usually made of red pipestone or catlinite, a red, semihard clay material quarried by hand by Sioux tribal members, from the pipestone quarries in Minnesota. Since all stones are from Mother Earth, however, all can be equally useful or holy in making a pipe. Chief Eagle Feather, the holy man whom I occasionally assisted, had a medicine pipe made of green jade. Judging from the power and strong activity in Chief Eagle Feather's ceremonies, evidently the spirit world did not mind that he was not using a customary catlinite pipe.

The peace pipe is a highly respected item among Indian people. Some Sioux have objected to "outsiders" using red catlinite for their pipes. Many Sioux Indians do not object, however, and even carve the pipe from the red stone and make the pipe available. Some Indians believe that the more the dominant society becomes acculturated from learning Indian spiritual concepts the sooner we will all progress toward a healthy Mother Earth spirituality.

I like to avoid conflict, and yet I do not believe in sweeping important matters under the rug. I find it difficult to fault the respectful and well-meaning use of certain items for ceremonial purposes by a person who has a healthy respect for a religious item and sincerely uses it to connect to the Great Spirit and who of course is very concerned about the health of our Mother Earth. We Indian people have suffered severely from religious institutions that set themselves up as God, and I believe that we should never fall into that way of thinking.

For those who wish to avoid conflict along this subject, I hope that you will be very respectful in the use of your pipe. Your pipe can also be made from other stone than pipestone. There is a very beautiful, soft, ivory stone from Nevada and a black stone, argillite, that was used by many tribes. For centuries, Eskimo people have carved totem animals from the black argillite. In your travels, if you come across any peace pipes that seem old and abandoned or discover they are not being used for respectful ceremony, ask the owner to return the pipes wrapped in red cloth to traditional Indian people. I believe these endeavors will soften criticism by some tribal members.

It is not difficult to make a peace pipe from pipestone or a similar material of hardened clay. Red pipestone or the cream to white Nevada ivory stone can be cut with a hacksaw or flint. The Nevada stone comes also in light green (for Mother Earth) and also has waves of pipestone-colored rust-red in the cream-white grain and carves easier than pipestone. You first cut a T at least an inch thick from a natural block of whatever stone you have chosen. (See the illustration on page 134.) If the bowl is to have ornately carved figures upon it, then you should start with thicker material. The bowl may simply be tapered slightly from top to base. (See the illustrations on pages 50 and 74.) The end or the point of the pipe, especially a Sioux pipe, is usually tapered considerably. When peace pipes are leaned against the pipe rack in the Sun Dance, the pointed end thrust into Mother Earth helps hold them more securely.

When drilling a hole in a pipe, a small drill, ¼ inch or less, should be used and care should be taken so that the drill bit does not go too far and punch through the bottom of the pipe. A hole is drilled down deep enough into the bowl of the pipe so that it intercepts the hole drilled into the butt of the pipe for the stem. After the holes intersect, a larger drill bit is used. It is also important not to make the holes too large, or the walls of the pipe become too thin or weak. Usually the hole for the bowl is only slightly larger than that for the pipe stem.

After the drilling, the pipe may be shaped and sanded smooth. I find the sands of a lake an excellent place to shape and smooth a peace pipe. A file, or several files of varying roughness, will help in the shaping. Sandpaper of various grits may be used for finishing. After the smoothing step, a final polish with an emery cloth will prepare the pipe for finishing.

The finishing step is to immerse the pipe in hot beeswax. This gives an added luster to the stone. If you do not have beeswax, neutral paste shoe polish will also work.

A pipe stem can be made of any kind of wood. Sumac is a popular stem material because of its colored outer layer and the ease in making a hole. A hot wire is repeatedly inserted into its pith and will easily bore its way through the length of the stem.

In times past there were pipe makers. Many warriors had peace pipes, and all chiefs and leaders of the Sioux had their own ceremonial pipes, for their leadership was regarded as a spiritual role as well as a political one. The pipes came into their possession either as a gift or through barter. Sometimes a chief or mystic warrior would want a pipe with special designs or animal totems, in keeping with a dream or vision. A pipe maker would be sought out, and payment in the form of goods would be given for such a special pipe to be made.

I have owned over a half dozen peace pipes and have made only two of them myself. Some were given to me as gifts. One was large and elaborate, but it was not a practical pipe for the many ceremonies that my pipes usually experience, so I gave it away to a close Yankton Sioux friend for a smaller pipe. It seems that I do not have the time or the high degree of talent to always make my own pipe. I am grateful to the Sioux pipe makers at Pipestone who laboriously dig the red stone by hand. They forbid the use of power tools in the quarries and, therefore, do not take it the easy way. After they have obtained the catlinite, they spend many hours cutting, filing, and shaping the peace pipe. Their portable altars have helped people of all colors understand the beseechment of the four directions and ultimately the relationship of the two-leggeds with Mother Earth.

The following account was written by Deborah Chavez (Red Pipe Woman), a close rainbow friend of mine. It is the story of how the making of a peace pipe took a rainbow person on a special journey. Obviously, her "coming into her pipe" was meant to be.

Coming into the Pipe

If someone had told me six months ago that I would be the proud owner of a peace pipe I had made, I would not have believed it. Yet here I am, writing about a spiritual journey that brought me to phenomenal tranquility and peace. The making of my pipe gave me the key to a door that has been closed for many lifetimes. The light from the door leads me into the unknown but I'm not afraid—the light will protect me.

My story of the making of the pipe began as I made the forty-five-minute trek from Long Lake to St. Paul in a trance. I had experienced my first Sweat Lodge ceremony, and my emotions overwhelmed me because of a vision I had had. A peace pipe was presented to me by the spirit world. In my vision, the pipe was stationary for a couple of seconds, then began to spin around in a clockwise circle. I could see it clearly. The pipe stem was long, with feathers hanging from it. The pipe itself was small (a woman's pipe, I discovered later). I left the ceremony confused, apprehensive, and in a foggy state. The vision seemed important, but I didn't understand its meaning. I was embarrassed to ask the leader of the Sweat Lodge, Eagle Man, the significance of the vision. I didn't want him to think I was bragging about my experience. I tried to minimize the experience by telling myself he'd probably say, "Oh, yeah, people get those visions all the time, it's no big deal," or "I'm so sorry, you'll be dead in thirty days." It was my first Sweat Lodge; what did I know about visions?

After quieting my emotions, I casually approached Eagle Man and said, "By the way, do you know what it means when you see a peace pipe in a Sweat Lodge?"

Eagle Man responded, "You mean the pipe we loaded before the Sweat Lodge?"

"No," I answered. "I had a pipe presented to me in the Sweat Lodge."

Eagle Man looked at me in a strange way. Okay, I told myself, this is it. He spoke softly and slowly, "It's an honor to have a peace pipe sent to you from the spirit world. It is a very strong vision. You are a very spiritual person. You must be strong."

I felt like fainting. I gathered my thoughts, and in a small voice exclaimed, "Really?"

Eagle Man began asking me questions about my job, where I lived, and if I owned a peace pipe. "No," I said, "I've thought about a peace pipe, but haven't wanted to buy one. I didn't want money exchanged for a pipe."

"You must make one, then," he replied.

"Make a pipe?" I squeaked out. "How do I do that?"

Eagle Man proceeded to tell me about the pipestone he had at his house and told me to pick up the stone the next day. I barely heard him. All I could think was, What does this mean? Do I have to leave the people I love and live like a hermit or, worse yet, become a nun? (I was raised Catholic.) What does this mean?

I was in a state of shock for a week. I floated through work, told a few close friends about my vision and waited—for what I didn't know; I just waited. Eight days after my vision I found myself standing in Ed's garage selecting stone for my pipe. Pipestone is a red claylike material, somewhat soft, but harder than sandstone. When it's carved into a pipe it turns into a portable altar used in ceremonies and rituals. It is very interesting to hear the story about the Buffalo Calf Woman and how the pipe came to the Sioux people.

I selected my piece of pipestone from many stones. My stone was small in comparison to others, but I didn't want a gigantic pipe that would be uncomfortable to hold. My stone had a hairline crack, and Eagle man was worried that it would break when I worked it, but I felt comfortable with it.

Eagle Man's twenty-one-year-old son, John, was there that day, and taught me how to use the power tools. My pipe was the first pipe he had ever worked on, and he was as excited as I was. First, we sketched an outline of the pipe onto the stone and cut the outline out with a special blade saw. The outline was shaped like an upside-down T with the front end angled like a thumb. Eagle Man suggested this style rather than the traditional flat end. This style prevents the end from breaking off when the pipe is placed in Mother Earth while ceremonies are taking place. The saw blade became dull almost immediately, so I chased to the hardware store to stock up on blades. I didn't realize I was covered with pink dust from the stone until the clerk asked me what I was working on.

I stumbled for an explanation. I couldn't tell the truth, so I answered evasively, "I'm working on a project."

He laughed and said, "It sure must be dusty."

I smiled and left the store quickly. This became my first of many experiences in balancing the white world with the Indian spiritual world.

The pipestone outline was the crude image of a pipe. One side of the pipe was thin and unevenly angled. John told me I wouldn't be able to sand this side to a smooth finish without damaging the pipe bowl. My options were to cut another piece of stone or accept that the pipe would be imperfect. I was satisfied with the stone and continued. I learned a very important lesson. The rough side of the stone flourished into a beautiful work of Mother Earth. It was not imperfect after all. Many images are contained in the rough indentations: a young woman, an old woman, an eagle, an Indian chief, a buffalo, and an Egyptian woman, and all of these images were specially put there by the Creator millions of years ago just for me to discover. The Great Spirit's work—hardly imperfect! Simply but powerfully put, my portable altar carries very strong and natural symbols that add supernatural quality to it.

My next step was to drill a hole into the top for the bowl and into the end for the stem. I was nervous that the stone would break and also hesitant at touching the stone. It seemed to have a power surrounding it which initially frightened me. (Later I became aware that the stone demanded respect, which I earlier reacted to with fear.) We drilled carefully, because at any time the pipe could break or crack at its weak points. We used several sizes of drill bits on the bowl, which made the bowl's center wide and the top narrow. All went smoothly, and Eagle Man commented that he had never seen a pipe made that quickly.

I needed a stem, so John suggested we find a sumac tree and chop down a branch with a slight curve in it. We followed a path down to a lake close by; I thanked the sumac tree for its gift to my pipe and sawed a limb off the tree. As we walked back to the house, I began to feel peace within myself in a way I had never experienced before. What a beautiful feeling!

I asked Eagle Man for instructions on how to make the stem. He told me to let the branch dry for about a week and then strip away the bark. The rest was up to me. I decided to work on the stem after I finished the pipe. As a preventive measure, Eagle Man suggested connecting the pipe and stem with a dowel. He explained that if the pipe was accidentally dropped or stepped on, the dowel would break first and could be replaced more easily than the entire stem. He made a dowel out of a large twig, stripped away the bark, and drilled a small hole in the center. I was amazed. I would have gone to a lumber store to find a wooden dowel. It took four hours to complete the stone cutting. We couldn't believe how quickly and smoothly the process went. Before we had started the project, Eagle Man commented that it would take me a week to cut the pipestone.

He said, "Having your pipe today was meant to be."

I was anxious to begin the next process. I brought the pipe home and began the long process of shaping the hard, cold pipestone into a loving peace pipe. I started filing with a borrowed file that had four different types of teeth on it. These four types of teeth represented the four directions. It was a sign from the spirit world, letting me know I had chosen the right path. The file was too large to fit comfortably in my hands and slipped out often as I chipped away at the stone. After three hours, I was frustrated with the file, having lost a couple of fingernails over it. I put the pipe away for the night, wrapping it in a cotton towel. I always wrapped the pipe in this towel when I wasn't working on it. I didn't understand the reason—only that I was "supposed" to do it.

I later learned that my pipe has the ability to communicate with me in similar ways that a crystal does. Some of the messages I received included: it must be in a protective covering when not in use, it didn't want to be touched by others while I was working on it, and I should use borrowed tools unless it was absolutely necessary to purchase one.

The pipe was on my mind while I was at work the next day, Tuesday. I thought of various ways I could decorate it. I was concerned about the rough side. It was very thin and jagged. I wasn't sure if I could design anything on that side without breaking the stone, so I decided to leave it natural. I was worried, though, that this wasn't the "right" way to decorate the pipe. The left side was semismooth, and I knew that with laborious sanding I could make it smooth enough to etch designs in it.

Now, you need to know I do not consider myself an artist. My drawing ability consists of making bunny rabbits, trees (using the ever-popular V approach), and stick people. Making this pipe was a giant leap toward trusting my spiritual self. I let go, and spiritual powers took over. The pipe wanted to be made in a specific way, and my hands were the tools.

I came home that night, driven to work on the pipe. I asked my dad if he had small and narrow files. He opened a drawer in the print shop he owned and pulled out four small files (again, representing the four directions). I was surprised and excited because I wouldn't have to buy files.

My dad asked me, "What are you going to do with these?"

I hesitated in answering him. My dad's a rather traditional person and would think I was crazy if I told him the truth. I opened my mouth and blurted out, "I'm making a peace pipe and need to file the pipestone down."

I was shocked at myself. Great, I thought, now I'm really losing my mind. I can't even control my speech.

I glanced at my dad, avoiding direct eye contact with him, expecting a ton of questions to be lashed out at me. Instead of quizzing me, he shrugged his shoulders and mumbled, "Oh, ummhmm." Whew, I really got off easy, I told myself. I grabbed the files and made a quick exit.

I filed for about five hours that night, forcing myself to stop for supper. I was covered from head to toe in pink dust, but I didn't care. I had learned through my psychic development that the color pink bathes a person in happiness, contentment, and peace. Eagle Man had also mentioned that pipestone dust brings luck.

I canceled my evening plans for the entire week. Each night after work I physically and emotionally withdrew into the pipe. I filed—and filed—and filed. I wasn't sure if what I was doing was correct, so I contacted the library in hopes of finding a book with photographs of peace pipes. The librarian searched the computer and found one book on Native American pipes. I couldn't believe it. One book! I asked him to read the information from the book. He read that the pipes were used as a symbol of peace among North American and Canadian tribes, and that the peace pipe had been extinct since the 1800s. I thanked him and hung up. This was really bizarre. I'd just been told that my pipe and other pipes I'd smoked at Sweat Lodge ceremonies were nonexistent. Was I in the twilight zone? After venting my frustration, I accepted that I was on my own, used my intuition, and listened to the pipe.

Wednesday evening my dad had some friends over for dinner. I, of course, was working on my pipe.

They began to ask questions. "What are you making?"

I answered, "A peace pipe," and thought to myself, please don't ask any more questions. No such luck.

"What are you going to do with it?"

"It's for a class on Native American religious ceremonies," I replied. Yes, I stretched the truth, but I had taken this class from Eagle Man.

"It looks like hard work. How long have you been working on it?" they asked.

I mentally summarized the past week and said, "I started Monday and am almost done with the pipe. I still have to make the stem."

"Are you going to smoke it?" the woman asked, crumpling up her nose. She had quit smoking fifteen years before.

"Yes, but only at ceremonies," I reassured her. I'm sure they thought I was weird, but I didn't care.

At the end of the evening, the woman came over to me, looked into my eyes, and said, "I know what you're doing. I want to tell you I think it's beautiful."

I sat back in my chair and gazed into her eyes. They were glazed over and had an empty, faraway look. I thanked her nervously and thought to myself, Something is happening here. I didn't know what it was, but it sure wasn't normal. She continued to chatter about other things, and her eyes changed back to their original sparkle. She then said good night and left with her husband.

I interpreted the experience as a sign from the Great Spirit and Buffalo Calf Woman. My work was acknowledged, and I was told I should continue along this path. My pipe seemed to have powerful connections to the spirit world. I wrapped my pipe in its towel with renewed respect and put it away for the evening.

By Friday, the sanding was finished, and I worked on designs to engrave on the smooth side of the stone. I drew a design with a moon on the pipe bowl and the four directions surrounding it. Lightning bolts on the front end represented the thunder beings, and four arrows at the stem represented the four directions. As I picked up the engraving tool I realized I had forgotten an important lesson—my hands were tools for the pipe and the design was predetermined.

I sat down with my almost finished pipe and listened to the strong energy emitting from it. The pipe didn't want my design on it. I asked myself (and the pipe), Now what?

My intuition told me to smooth the pipe by sanding it with fine sandpaper and then sealing and polishing it. I called Eagle Man and asked him how to seal the pipe.

"You're ready to seal it?" he asked me, sounding surprised.

"Yeah, I want to finish it for the Sweat Lodge tomorrow night," I replied.

"Okay," Eagle Man said, paging through his telephone directory. "Call this guy, Chuck Derby, at Pipestone Quarry. He knows how to seal the stone."

Pipestone Quarry is in Pipestone, Minnesota. The stone has been quarried at Pipestone for many centuries. It's used for amulets and pipes. Today the pipestone can be quarried only by Indians. Non-Indians can obtain the stone by purchasing it from Indians.

After numerous tries, I managed to get hold of Chuck. If there's one thing I've learned in making this pipe, it's to be persistent. He gave me the instructions.

"First, boil the pipe in about three inches of water in a fry pan. Flip the pipe over so all sides are in the water and hot spots won't get on it. Get a good boil going and after a couple of minutes take it out and melt beeswax all over the pipe, inside the bowl, everywhere. Then let it cool in cold water. If you want it to be really shiny, take superfine wet/dry sandpaper and sand the pipe." I read the instructions back to him, thanked him, and began my search for beeswax.

Five craft and grocery stores later, I still didn't have beeswax. I thought beeswax was used to seal canning jars and in candlemaking. I learned that paraffin wax is used in canning and a cheap wax is used to make candles. I was depressed. So close to finishing, and a simple kind of wax was holding me up. I called natural food stores, cosmetic stores, and co-ops. No luck. It was 6:00 P.M. on a Friday night, and I began to give up. Wait until tomorrow, I told myself. I wanted to finish the pipe before the Sweat Lodge on Saturday, but was uncomfortable rushing the process. Then, suddenly, an idea popped into my head. The Yellow Pages—look in the Yellow Pages. Sure enough, under "Beekeepers," a supply store was listed. I called and found out that not only did they have beeswax, but they were only about three miles from my house and were open until 9:00 P.M. I left immediately and picked up one pound of beeswax. You've never seen anyone that excited over beeswax.

By 8:00 A.M. on Saturday, I was working on my pipe. I was extremely driven to complete my task. I *never* get up early on weekends, yet here I was, sanding the final touches and preparing my pipe for the finale. I was apprehensive about placing the pipe in boiling water because of the hairline crack on the end. Looking back, it's funny that I was so concerned about the crack, when I'd be burning tobacco in it the same evening. The boiling process went smoothly, although I burned my fingers a few times on the hot stone. I learned my lesson and used salad tongs.

After lifting the pipestone out of the water and placing it on a cloth, I ran the hard, cold wax over the steaming stone. The wax was like cold butter on a hot ear of corn. The stone absorbed the wax and a beautiful smell came from the stone: chocolate. I had given up sugar a couple of months before and really missed chocolate. How could my pipe smell like chocolate? I licked the wax to make sure it was actually beeswax. Isn't it amazing how the mind plays tricks—or was it the mind?

I boiled and sealed the pipe four times. Yes, four times. I wasn't aware that I was protecting my pipe. My pipe, on the other hand, felt the need to be protected repeatedly. I did what my hands wanted me to do. My intent in coating the pipe so many times was to seal it thoroughly and shine it. Unfortunately, it didn't work out that way. My pipe had wax caked on it and looked dull. There was nothing I could do about it; I had to leave for the Sweat Lodge. Surprisingly, I wasn't upset over the waxing. I knew it would be okay.

My pipe was initiated at the Sweat Lodge that night. I didn't get the pipe stem finished, so Eagle Man let me use a pipe stem he had carved for his pipe. My pipe was smudged with sage before the Sweat Lodge. Smudging is done by lighting the herb, sage, and drawing the smoke around the object or person. This cleanses and protects the object or person from negative spirits. It's similar to protecting yourself with a shield or a white or pink light.

I was excited and proud that night. It was one of those special events I will always remember. I felt I was "graduating" to a higher level of spirituality. Eagle Man surprised me by announcing to the group that I would be given a Sioux Indian name, *Luta Chanupa Winan*, Red Pipe Woman. I was honored, shocked, and stunned by this. I asked myself, "What does this mean?" I began to worry about the responsibility of having an Indian name. I calmed my logical mind and allowed myself to feel the beautiful white glow that surrounded me when I rehearsed the pronunciation of my name. I held my pipe toward the moon and chanted my name to the heavens. Power surged throughout my spirit and body.

A few days after the Sweat Lodge, I unwrapped my pipe and inspected the beeswax. It was still caked to the stone. I began rubbing the stone with the towel I had used to wrap it. Amazingly, the wax began to rub off, and shiny red stone peeked through the hard wax. I rubbed the stone furiously until all the wax disappeared. I held my pipe in my hands and looked at it in awe. It was beautiful!

It took a couple of weeks for me to come off my high from the Sweat Lodge. I wasn't ready to start working on the stem yet. I didn't know why, but the time didn't feel right. I visualized different symbols to carve onto the stem. However, I knew the pipe had its own ideas for the stem. I decided to respect that process. I continued with my daily living, attending Sweat Lodges biweekly until a tragic event hurled me into completion of the pipe.

The event that propelled me into a working frenzy was the death of my seventeen-year-old foster son, Tracy Eagleman. Tracy had entered into my life five years before, and I loved him as a son. On a Thursday night a month after I was named, I received a telephone call from the group home where he was living at the time. His counselor told me that Tracy had taken his life. I was numb with emotional pain. The funeral would be at his reservation, Fort Totten, North Dakota, the following Monday. I glanced over at my pipe, which was sitting in a corner in my bedroom, and I knew I had to finish it. It was time.

Two days before Tracy's death, I had asked him if I could use his beadwork (for which he had won a first prize) on my pipe.

Tracy had said, "Sure, Deb, I don't mind."

I knew the pipe wanted the beadwork on it, and I wanted his spirit on the pipe. I needed his permission to have the beadwork on my pipe; it seemed disrespectful not to ask.

Friday, the day after his death, I plunged into carving the stem. I picked up strong messages that my pipe was needed for a ceremony. I didn't know the details, only that my pipe was needed.

I picked up the dried sumac branch and began stripping off the bark with my dad's fish fillet knife. It came off swiftly, and I shaved through five layers of wood: green, blond, brown, white, and black, until I came to the shape I wanted. I was stripping away more than just wood; I was also stripping away the layers of defenses I had wrapped around myself in order to cope with Tracy's death.

I finished the whittling in about four hours. The stem was semi-smooth and needed to be sanded to get the knots and bumps evened out. I used the sandpaper I had used on the pipestone and sanded for the rest of the evening. As I worked on the stem, friends called to express their love and sadness about Tracy. Several friends wanted to attend the funeral, but it was more than three hundred miles away. They asked me if I was willing to have a funeral in St. Paul for him. The thought terrified me. How could I have two funerals for Tracy? I could barely make it through one! They asked me to think about it while I was in North Dakota. I promised them I would.

Saturday I picked up blond calf leather for a pipe bag. This sounds easier than it actually was. I was in a state of shock, and decision making overwhelmed me. I spent an hour deciding on the color and type of leather. I probably shouldn't have been shopping in my frame of mind, but I knew this was important. I had to finish making the pipe. I finally chose a bolt of leather and asked for a couple of yards.

"Sorry," the clerk said, "you have to buy the entire hide."

At $8.00 a yard, it would have been more than $100.00. I didn't need that much leather, so I rummaged through a remnant bin and settled on a blond piece with a few defects in it.

I had no idea how to make a pipe bag because I had never seen one before. I trusted my intuition and cut out a pattern by laying the pipe and stem next to each other on the folded leather. I figured I'd have to sew the leather together with leather laces. I didn't know how to put the lacing holes into the leather without ripping it. Luckily, a friend asked her dad if I could use his leather punch. He loaned the tool to me, and I punched the holes out. I made the bag large enough to completely cover the stem and wide enough to cover the pipe. Later I learned that the pipe transforms into a sacred object when connected to the stem; therefore, the pipe bag had to hold the pipe and stem separated from each other. At the time I made the bag I had no knowledge of this; I only knew the pieces needed to be separated.

I felt good while I worked on this bag. The smell of leather grounded me into Mother Earth, which I needed to help me through the emotionally draining time. My friend's mom called her favorite shoemaker and located leather laces for me. Within a few hours the bag was complete. I fitted the pipe and stem into the bag, and a sense of peace enveloped me.

I took a piece of remaining leather, fringed it, and began sewing Tracy's beadwork on it. The leather encircled the pipestem.

It was almost ready. For what?

At 6:00 A.M. on Sunday, I was on the highway heading toward North Dakota. During the trip I thought more seriously about my friends' requests to have a funeral for Tracy. I sifted through my emotions. Could I endure another event that acknowledged his death? I was angry at my friends. How could they ask this of me? Can't they take care of themselves? How can they expect me, in my emotional state, to pull something like this together? I want people to take care of *me*.

Then I began to think about the loss they were experiencing and how much they had loved Tracy. I couldn't decide what to do, so I let it go.

The next three days were a nightmare. I was (spiritually) tested day and night. I used my crystal and pipe to protect myself. I was relieved that I had brought them. I would have been extremely vulnerable to negative spirits without these sacred objects. During this time I thought a great deal about Tracy and his life with me. I asked his spirit how he wanted his life to be remembered. He answered me indirectly, by leading me into a decision to have a Pipe Ceremony for him with the people who shared his life in St. Paul. It would be a celebration of his entrance into the spirit world. I received strong messages that he was graduated by his death to a higher level of spirit as a warrior. This must be celebrated by people who loved him, and my pipe was the spiritual tool. It's so easy to look back and see how the plan was laid out for me, yet when I was living through it I couldn't see the forest for the trees. Just like life, I guess.

The next weekend, I had a Pipe Ceremony for Tracy. My pipe was complete, with his beadwork circling the pipe and the four directions represented by red (east), yellow (south), black (west), and white (north) beads surrounding the pipe. The fringes had jingle beads with two feathers in them: a red feather, given to me by a Blackfoot Indian woman from her ceremonial dress, and a black and white feather I had found in front of the house of the priest who had performed Tracy's funeral service.

People were invited to the ceremony who had contact with him in the previous six years. I'm sure Tracy's spirit helped me with the invitation list. Fourteen adults and four children arrived at the Indian Mounds on the east side of St. Paul. I had never led a Pipe Ceremony before, but I knew that whatever I did (with respect to the Great Spirit) would be fine—and it was. We smoked *kinnic kinnick* (a combination of tobacco and red-willow tree bark) that I had purchased at a store on the reservation. Many tears were shed, sadness was released, and love was sent to Tracy. Tracy's spirit was released from each person's heart and joined with him in the spirit world. His love and happiness surrounded us. It was a beautiful way to end his journey on earth and send him on his way to a new path.

The making of my pipe was a journey into the spirit world. The closure of my pipe making was the passing of a human spirit into the spirit world. I am honored to have been chosen as a pipe maker and pipe holder. Two eagle men helped me through the pipe making process: Eagle Man and Tracy. I'm privileged to have helped celebrate my son's passing of life with my pipe. I wonder if this may have been the reason my pipe making went so smoothly? Only Tracy and the Great Spirit are able to answer this question.

16

Building a Sweat Lodge

Building a sweat lodge is not particularly difficult, but careful consideration should be given to various details.

Choosing a Location and Siting the Lodge

A quiet and secluded area is the obvious setting for a sweat lodge. Privacy is essential, yet the area must also be accessible. Once you have found a private but accessible site, you must then choose where you wish to place the lodge itself.

There is no hard and fast rule that the doorway of a sweat lodge must face a particular location. The lodge doorways at the base of Spirit Mountain in the Black Hills face west. Most Sioux and Ojibwa sweat lodges face east or west, but you must consider the terrain, location, and setting of the entire lodge area when selecting your lodge opening. In the interest of fire safety, you may have to select your fireplace area first. This will determine the direction of the opening for you, since lodges almost always face the fire. I recently built a sweat lodge that faced south because there was only one choice for a safe fireplace area, and the only clear space for the lodge was north of the fireplace.

There is another good reason for facing a lodge opening north or south if you so choose. Black Elk said that the north and south road was a road of good. From the north blows the cleansing white wind that gives us courage and endurance. From the south comes growth and the yellow hoop.

Other than the early morning Sun Dance sweat lodges, most lodges I have been associated with are held in the evening. I usually begin the ceremony close to sunset, and therefore prefer the opening to face east or west. But I always try to consider the aesthetic view for the ceremony participants. On one occasion, the breathtaking view of the setting sun was not interfered with and the quiet solitude and privacy of the lodge was enhanced by sound-cushioning cedar trees only by setting the lodge and fireplace on a north-south lineup. At a "full moon sweat," I consider the direction of the rising moon.

But if the direction the doorway should face is not a major concern, fire safety is.

Fire Safety

Fire safety is of extreme importance in selecting the lodge site and choosing the location of the fire pit. At times, fire pits may have to be dug deeper than what might seem necessary and their location will have to take advantage of windbreaks or shelter from the wind. Even if it is a calm day, assume that the wind could become a factor. Seldom is a sweat lodge built for only one evening's activity; therefore, always consider that high winds can come up during the time the fire is heating the rocks for a later ceremony and resulting sparks and drier conditions could result in a fire.

A friend of mine who lives in the western United States not far from a national forest has a sweat lodge in his back yard. The area can become quite dry, especially in the summertime, and has suffered destructive forest fires. My friend goes to great lengths to check with the local fire department for a wind and dryness report before he considers doing a Sweat Lodge ceremony. The fire department has been cooperative and respects his beliefs and desire to do the ceremony; they cooperate with one another because of their concern for the safety of the forest.

My friend is a Sioux and is from the same reservation I was born on. He has taken some guarded precautions in the interest of fire safety. In wetter locales I would not see the need for such extremes, but his example is worth looking at.

If it is windy, my friend simply cancels the ceremony and holds it at a later time. His fire pit is dug deep into the ground and has high sides made from the spent rocks that have been used in the ceremony. He has also erected a high, wooden slab fence around the entire sweat lodge area. The fence has a twofold purpose. It affords wind protection and also adds to the privacy of the lodge.

Fortunately, in the eastern woodlands there is an abundance of lush, green foliage most of the time; in fact, dry wood is often difficult to find if it has been lying on the ground for a length of time. If your Sweat Lodge ceremony is held in the wintertime or the woods are saturated with spring or early summer rains, then fire damage does not have to be as serious a consideration compared to drier, more arid areas, but fire safety must always be considered when doing a sweat ceremony. The best rule to follow is to cancel the ceremony when in doubt.

Heating the Rocks

Early on, assign several participants to gather firewood and rocks. Put one or two persons in charge of preparing the fireplace, building the fire, and heating the rocks. If you start the fire early, the rocks are usually hot by the time the lodge is finished.

Be sure that the fireplace is far enough away from the lodge so that ceremony participants can have some privacy. Many times there will be two successive sweat ceremonies, and people usually wait their turn sitting around the comforting fire. Their conversations could be distracting to the ceremony if the fireplace is too close to the lodge.

When old trees have died, instead of using the trunks for firewood, cut the trunk crosswise with a saw into one-and-a-half- to two-foot lengths and use them for sitting stools, especially the trunks that are ten to eighteen inches in diameter. Wider portions of a large tree can be used as tables.

Rocks should be limestone or granite, without significant cracks. Use rocks a little larger than a softball, or the size of a cantaloupe. Never use sandstone or other porous, water-absorbing–type stones. Wet sandstone can explode when heating in the fireplace. Lava rocks are probably the best rocks to use because they seem to retain their heat and also convey unusual images when they are heated to a red glow and are observed within the dark confines of the lodge. The form and makeup of a lava rock is an added safety feature in that the rock does not have a tendency to possess hairline cracks or fissures wherein water can be trapped.

Several hatchets, a shovel, and a pitchfork are useful tools for the fire and stone heating, although I have held sweat ceremonies without them. I do not object to modern tools and recommend their use whenever they are available. A shovel is useful for digging out the fireplace area before beginning the fire. Heavy-duty fireplace tongs are very useful for handling the rocks.

Building the Frame

If everyone pitches in, you can build a sweat lodge frame in three to four hours. All it takes is a knife, a hatchet, and a ball of string. The frame is usually made of willow, but any sapling will do. I once made a nice lodge from available sumac on a secluded spot on my brother-in-law's farm.

The average-sized lodge will comfortably seat eight to twelve people, but, with the ever-increasing popularity of the ceremony, I suggest considering a lodge for twelve to fifteen. To estimate the size, first draw a circle two feet in diameter in the center of the lodge site. This will be the rock pit that you will dig later. Sit cross-legged on the ground facing the circle, and leave at least a foot or two between your knees and the center circle's outer edge. Place a stick with a string tied to it in the center of the circle. Run the string a few inches behind your sitting position. The string serves as a radius for the lodge, and you can then draw the circumference on the ground.

A nine-foot diameter lodge will seat twelve people comfortably. A ten-foot diameter lodge will seat fifteen to sixteen people. Remember, though, that a large lodge can be difficult to heat, unless it is well insulated. With the black tarp found in so many hardware stores and the blankets people bring, however, a large sweat lodge can be built that will hold the heat. Sweat lodges seldom hold more than twenty people. Bear in mind that you can hold several sweat ceremonies in the same evening.

Cut twelve saplings with a base approximately the size of a quarter or fifty-cent piece. I prefer to use twelve because it acknowledges the twelve Indian moons or months with which we are annually blessed. In the Sun Dance, we tie twelve chokecherry branches to the Sun Dance Tree for the same reason. In the Indian Way, we constantly recognize and express our appreciation for *Wakan Tanka*'s creating our means and way of life. In a sense, even the making of a humble little lodge frame is a form of prayer or acknowledgment.

Sixteen to twenty saplings may be needed to form the radius of the lodge if a fifteen- to twenty-person capacity lodge is to be considered. A private sweat lodge can have a smaller capacity, but if a lodge is being built for a conference where there are a considerable number of people who wish to experience the ceremony, then the lodge should be made to hold more than a dozen participants. There is a limit, however, as to size. Much more than twenty will occasion a long third endurance because everyone prays individually at that time. As noted, large lodges are also difficult to heat, especially in the wintertime. If you plan to do winter sweats, size has to be a consideration.

After the saplings have been brought to the lodge area, remove the branches and sharpen the bottoms. If you have selected willow, use the soft branches and leaves as a flooring for the lodge, at least for several ceremonies. The willow has a pleasing aroma that adds to the evening's enjoyment. Although willow is the usual preference of most tribes when and where it is available, do not restrict yourself to this tree only, and never spend too much time trying to find a suitable stand of it. Bear in mind that the Indian people were great adapters and made use of what was available. I have seen many Native American sweat lodges made of saplings that were not willow.

When making a large lodge, you will have to pre-bend your saplings because they should be thicker and stronger. Mother Nature usually provides a "bending vise" whenever I need one. Simply place the thick end of the thicker saplings between two trees that are growing a few feet apart and impart a bend about four feet from the sharpened base of the sapling. Place the sharpened ends into the ground at an equal distance around the drawn circumference, leaving an opening for the doorway. You may use a heavier pointed stake to make the holes for the saplings, or use a hunting knife if the ground is very hard.

Be sure that the saplings are embedded far enough into the ground so they hold firm when they are bent and tied together to form the domed frame. The bend of the sapling should allow for a large man to sit comfortably. Don't build your lodge too tall or it will be difficult to heat. Bind the saplings with string, fishing line, or willow bark peeled in long strings. (A precautionary note: Do not discard any extra fishing line or lengthy string ends on the ground. Throw these into the fire. I have seen more than my share of wild birds ensnared near lakes and streams as a result of careless fishermen throwing spent leaders and line into the water or on the shore.)

To strengthen and reinforce the lodge, tie sapling crossbraces horizontally to the upright saplings. As you do this, think about the strength that man and woman derive from one another. Think about the strength that like-minded groups of people derive from one another.

While work is progressing on tying the saplings together, send part of the group out to gather grass, sage, cedar, or leaves to place on the floor for people to sit on. Once, asked to do a sweat lodge and naming ceremony near a marsh, I found that reeds make an excellent base for the lodge flooring. If wildflowers are available, a sprinkling within the lodge adds a pleasant aroma. When placing the seating material, leave room for the rocks to be rolled into the lodge, usually a foot-wide path from the doorway to the rock pit.

After the frame is finished, dig a pit approximately eighteen to twenty-four inches deep and two feet or more in diameter for the rocks. Remove all roots and burnable debris from the pit. The red hot rocks will cause a serious smoke problem if the pit is not cleaned. Also remove all protruding roots, stones, and other uncomfortable objects from the sitting area.

Covering the Sweat Lodge

Tarps are excellent for covering the sweat lodge frame. They are waterproof, and if it rains, participants will find a dry haven inside the lodge. (It is my experience, however, that if rain does fall, it usually comes after we have completed the ceremony. This is also the experience of my close friend, Thunder Owl.) The best method is to cover the frame with a tarp and then cover the tarp with clean blankets. The blankets provide heat and sound insulation and also block out all light (some tarps are semi-transparent). I prefer a pitch-black lodge, and one as soundproof as possible. The more blankets draped over the frame, the better the insulation, and the fewer rocks you will need. If it is colder weather, drafts will not penetrate inward. Use a thick blanket, or several blankets, for the doorway. For an adequate supply of blankets, ask each participant to bring one or two. To prevent the blankets from sliding off the lodge, use twine to tie the corner of each blanket to the corner of a counter-balancing blanket draped on the opposite side of the lodge.

Transporting the Rocks

The ceremony can begin when some of the rocks are glowing red. A long-handled pitchfork is a convenient tool for adjusting rocks around a hot fire and transporting the rocks to the lodge. Unlike a shovel, a pitchfork prevents coals from being brought in with the rocks. Coals emit smoke that make the lodge interior uncomfortable. In the old days, Indians used deer or elk horns for moving the rocks. It is surprising how certain shaped deer horns can transport hot rocks. Deer horns are also very handy inside the lodge for guiding the stones from the pitchfork to the pit. Stout sticks are most often used inside the lodge for shifting the stones within the pit. A shovel is not necessary, but it is a good substitute, in case a pitchfork is not available.

You will also want to have several five-gallon water containers both for the ceremony and for dousing the fire when everyone is ready to leave the area. Usually fewer than five gallons are required for the ceremony itself. You will also need a dipper and a two- to three-gallon pail for splashing water onto the heated rocks.

If you are holding more than one ceremony in an evening, the group waiting around the fireplace should keep their conversations low. If yours is a permanent fireplace area, one that will heat many sweat lodges, place logs around the fire for comfortable seating. When the ceremony is over, most people do not want to leave. They usually sit around the fire enjoying each other's company.

When the lodge is completed, everyone can look on with pride and satisfaction. You required no donations, no building drives or other superfluous distractions. The cost was a simple ball of string. All the rest was provided by Mother Earth, the greatest temple of all. Most importantly, a deep spiritual ceremony can begin, and its impact will last for a lifetime.

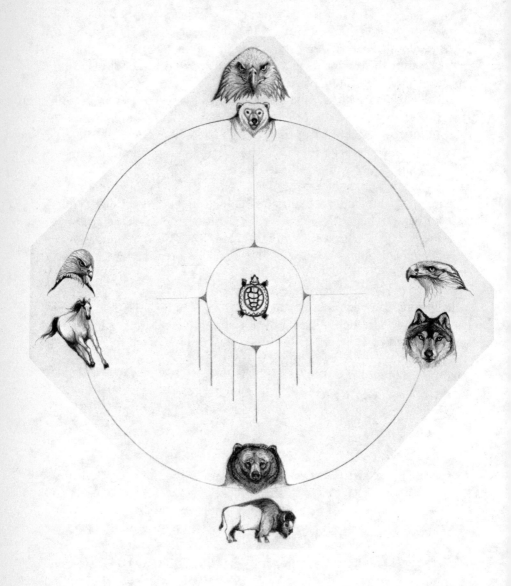

17

Shield Making and Understanding the Sacred Hoop

A tripod bearing the warrior's shield was set up outside each tipi in the Sioux camps back when the tribe was mobile and free on the plains. In their woodland days, the Sioux painted shield symbols upon their canoes. On the plains, certain symbols found on their shields were also painted upon their tipis and on their own bodies when they danced in the Sun Dance.

In the old days, a Sioux war shield was made of buffalo hide. The head of the buffalo was the thickest and was often selected for shield making. For a larger, decorative shield, other areas of the hide were used. Because the warriors on horseback did not want their freedom and agility restricted, Sioux war shields were not large. Many warriors did not carry shields into combat.

A war shield was thickened and toughened by placing a green hide (raw hide) over a cottonwood fire and steaming it. Cottonwood was preferred for specialized fires such as shield making and tanning because the wood did not have the tendency to throw sparks as many woods do. Over cottonwood coals in a recessed fire pit a fresh hide was spread and staked out on one or several sides; the opposite side was held down by some large rocks. Occasionally the hide would be lifted from the rocks, and water would be poured into the coals to make steam. The steam would make the hide pliable for shaping and would shrink and thicken the hide as would the heat from the hot coals. After the hide was thickened, it would be covered with buckskin, and the bearer's symbol or symbols would be painted on the buckskin.

A shield reflected the symbology of a warrior's medicine. "Medicine" to the plains tribes carried a broader scope in its meaning than simple medical healing for physical affliction or injury. Medicine reached into all facets of a person's life. Protection in combat, success in the hunt, success in lovemaking and mate selection, protection from evil doing, and success in visions and dreams were major petitions and were reflected in the symbols found on the Sioux shields.

Dreams and visions that recurred were considered messages from the spirit world. Animals that appeared to a hunter under normal circumstances or repeatedly in dreams became medicine symbols and were included on the shield of that individual. If a night animal repeatedly appeared to a warrior in the daytime, it was recognized as a message from nature. Special stones or other sacred items, feathers, or bones were also attached to the shield.

Present-day shields usually center on a person's natural name; from that center, the shield reaches out in much the same symbolic fashion as did the shields of the warriors of the past. We want to be safe, successful, socially accepted, and spiritually whole. These desires create a commonality with the shields of our ancestors. We have a journey in this lifetime, and our shields can also be an expression of our purposes or directions. Like the animal world, all two-leggeds are blessed with unique gifts. Each of us should recognize his or her special gifts and use this Creator-endowed specialness. Possibly, this uniqueness can find its reflection upon a symbolic shield. It will always be a pleasant reminder, an encouraging acknowledgment.

A shield projects confidence on the part of the bearer. It is circular. This is a significant symbol in itself. A circular shield bearing no symbol at all would still convey many messages and attribute many strengths. The circle represents the great circular way of the Great Spirit's creation. All things are unending like the circle. We will all leave this planet some day, but the circle is the indicator, the ultimate symbol that our spirit life is unending. A plain, circular shield sends this message for all to see.

A shield bearer may have a lone four-legged or a flying one depicted on his or her shield, just a plain shield and the feathered or four-legged. This solitary depiction places emphasis on the power and gifts of that particular creature. Usually the shield bearer is familiar with the unique attributes of the animal and may regard the animal as a special spirit helper for his or her life journey. At the end of this chapter, certain flying and four-legged ones are described relative to their natural gifts and endowments.

It is an extraordinary gift to make a shield for another. After Thunder Hawk was tribally named and we became blood brothers, he presented me with my shield. It is made of four pieces of leather sewn together in four equal quarters: muted buckskin yellow, black, eggshell white, and red. *Wakinyan* (lightning, which can also represent thunder) is painted on the black west quarter, paired rainbows flow across the north quarter, and an eagle flies its way into the red east. The yellow is plain and bears a power of the hoop symbol attached to it. The buffalo that we once held a ceremony for has its hair on the east and west periphery. Four eagle feathers hang from the center of the shield for the four Sun Dances in which I was pierced.

Thunder Hawk's shield is similar to mine and made of the same colored leather. A pair of hawks flap their wings on the red field. The paired rainbows and *Wakinyan* are similar to the symbols on my shield. One lone eagle feather centers his shield.

When Thunder Hawk conducted his first Sweat Lodge ceremony, a pair of hawks led him to a power line in the middle of the day preceding the sweat. He went over to the power line platform to look at the hawks. They were almost tame in their reaction, letting him get so close that he could almost touch them. Then, suddenly, he knew why they were behaving in such an unusual way. They were leading him to the body of one of their brothers.

A crumpled red hawk was lying in the grass below the platform, electrocuted somehow by the power lines or by the night's lightning storm. In any event, the six powers wanted Thunder Hawk to have the feathers of this hawk. The skull of the hawk, painted black and white, decorates the top of the shield. The feathers adorn the left side, the red side of knowledge and wisdom because Tim is a messenger and must bridge both worlds. This he is deeply committed to do. A buffalo that had gone on into the spirit world has given its hair to keep its power and spirit flowing into Tim from the west.

To make a shield, simply find some light saplings or branches. Willow is very pliable almost any time of the year, even in winter, although you must bring it in and thaw it out. Bend the branches or saplings around a circular container or large bowl. Overlap the ends and tie them together to make a circle.

You can use a variety of kinds of leather for the shield: suede, buckskin, tanned leather. You may even choose to make the shield surface of cloth or some other material. What is important is that the surface should be strong enough to attach things to, or if you plan to paint it, that it will take paint well. A woman friend is a weaver and has woven the surface of her shield with yarn that she has spun herself. Choose something that feels right to you.

When the hoop has dried somewhat, spread your hide over the circle and trim the back side, leaving enough extra to use to tie on the leather. Punch holes in the leather overlapping the back with a leather punch or scissors. Tie the back side with twine or leather thongs. You can make extra thongs from the edge of the hide before you apply it to the frame. Or if you have trouble finding leather thongs, try the leather shoelaces that are sold for workboots.

Smooth out the hide by tugging here and there and tying with extra thongs to keep the surface even. Braid several thongs together and make a handle on the back. You may also want to add a loop at the top of the shield for hanging it on the wall.

The next step is to determine what symbols or objects to put on the shield. Don't rush this step. Take the time to decide which things are meaningful to you in your spiritual and personal path. If you only have a few, use those and then add others later as they come to you. This shield reflects you and your earth walk and will be different for each person.

Images may be painted on the surface: beads may be strung and then attached to the surface or may be hung from thongs along the edges of the shield. If you have feathers and/or beads, animal claws or teeth, or personal decorations that are meaningful to you, these may be attached in some way. Be sure to include colors for the four directions, perhaps as red, white, yellow, and black beads.

If you like the look of the white tassels that are seen on many shields sold as decorations, you can use these. Go to a weaving store or a place that sells crafts supplies and ask for "roving." This is wool that is carded and ready to be spun. It comes in lengths that can be cut and tied to your shield.

There is no "right way" to create a shield. Since it is a symbol of your spiritual self, it is important that you design it with care. It is not something that can be copied from another person. There is no rush. Take your time in finding just the right things for your shield. Or begin by creating the shield surface and gradually add symbols and decorative items as your spirituality develops.

Attributes and Gifts of Winged Ones and Four-Leggeds

Chief Crazy Horse of the Oglala Sioux was regarded as one of the best warrior chiefs of the whole Sioux nation. Crazy Horse was described by fellow warriors who had witnessed his conduct in combat as being absolutely fearless when he confronted enemy forces. He was also clever and exploited enemy weaknesses. Although a chief, he was exceptional in that he did not wear a warbonnet made of eagle feathers in battle; rather, he wore a hawk ornament at the side of his head when he went into combat. The hawk is viewed by the Sioux as exceptionally fearless and feared by all other winged. Obviously, Chief Crazy Horse was very sensitive to this winged one and managed to secure some of its powers. The hawk's elusiveness, cunning, and effective striking ability were characteristics that also were reflected by the famous Oglala chief.

Following are descriptions and recognition of the special attributes and gifts endowed to certain winged ones and four-leggeds by *Wakan Tanka*. They are offered for those who seek a deeper sensitivity for a particular animal. They are also offered to help the two-leggeds align the gifted powers and characteristics of the natural guides (the animals, birds, finned ones, and insects) with the particular gifts that emanate from the four directions.

The children of the earth, *Wakanyeja makah*, are our winged, finned, insect, and four-legged friends who have a special knowledge of Mother Nature and the corresponding four directions. Each creature child of the earth can become a helper for two-leggeds to aid our seeking of universal knowledge. The four directions, the four quarters with the power of earth and sky and all related life is regarded as the sacred hoop.

East Direction, East Wind

Red Hawk (Cetan Lutah)

Red Hawk *(Cetan Lutah)* was Crazy Horse's medicine: fearless, aggressive, and swift moving.

The red hawk is a messenger. It is close to the eagle, and its gifts are very similar to those of its larger flying relative. The hawk is keen-eyed and observant. Like the hawk, we must all become keen-eyed and observe

The Sacred Hoop

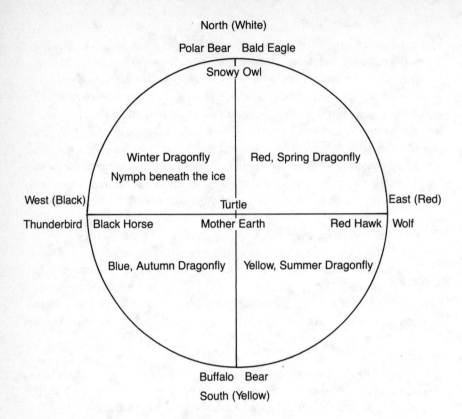

North (White)

Polar Bear   Bald Eagle

Snowy Owl

Winter Dragonfly   Red, Spring Dragonfly

Nymph beneath the ice

West (Black)   Turtle   East (Red)

Thunderbird   Black Horse   Mother Earth   Red Hawk   Wolf

Blue, Autumn Dragonfly   Yellow, Summer Dragonfly

Buffalo   Bear

South (Yellow)

The children of the earth, *wakanyeja makah*, are our winged, finned, insect, and four-legged friends who have a special knowledge of Mother Nature and the corresponding four directions. Each creature child of the earth can become a helper for two-leggeds to aid our seeking of universal knowledge. The four directions, the four quarters with the power of earth and sky and all related life is regarded as the sacred hoop.

the signs that the environment is sending us. We must keep ourselves aware of the notable happenings that we perceive from each new day.

Red Hawk is linked with the rising dawn of the east. It is a communicating messenger for knowledge. The hawk spends most of its lifetime observing all that is viewable as it soars high in the sky. It has the freedom to move in all directions, the freedom to go everywhere to view the revealing beauty of Mother Earth. Its swift, quick movements, sharp vision, and penetrating talons insure that it seldom has to worry about its next meal. It seems that this creature was especially gifted to feed itself and therefore can spend the majority of its time watching, studying, circling, and contemplating. In this day and age, many have the same opportunities as the hawk. They are free to look, listen, and view new surroundings and take in new knowledge. From what I have seen in Hawk's projection of relationship to certain of my rainbow friends, this usually reclusive winged one is not reluctant to come down and reveal itself to those who make a special effort to seek its companionship.

Selecting or seeking Hawk for a nature guide means that one of your efforts or goals will be to bridge the world from Mother Nature and its ally, Native American knowledge, into the present-day modern industrial world. Maybe you can reach into avenues to disperse your newfound knowledge where others cannot. This can prove to be a challenging task, yet many are finding this journey to be highly rewarding.

East Direction, East Wind

Wolf (Shuunka Manitu)

Wolf, like many humans, is a misunderstood animal. True, Wolf is a predator. It chases down its prey and kills with its powerful jaws and lengthy incisors, but it is only fulfilling the Great Spirit's overall plan for natural selection and reduction.

Wolf is a great deal like many of the two-leggeds. It is territorial, hunts or seeks provisions through group effort, and is a loyal and dedicated family participant along with having an equally dedicated tribal bond to its wolf pack.

Wolf mates for life yet manages to cover a lot of ground. No doubt the security that Wolf gains from its close family and tribal connection gives it the courage and curiosity to seek out the knowledge that it gains by its long travels into every nook and cranny of vast forests, tundra, and range lands.

If Wolf appears in your dreams, no doubt you should consider aligning yourself with this four-legged teacher who returns to the pack with knowledge of its travels and information of enemies, game, or forthcoming weather. If danger approaches, the wolf pack will quickly move to a different location, carrying young pups in their mouths if they have to. If better hunting conditions exist, it is the wolf scout that will relay this information to the pack. Be like Wolf, seek adventure, explore the world, then report back with your new-found information.

Long ago there was a woman from my tribe who was called the Wolf Woman. She received her name after she had spent several seasons with a den of prairie wolves. One time, Wolf Woman hurt her leg and could not travel with the tribe. In those days, when the plains people followed the buffalo herds, they had to live on the move for survival. When a tribal member became too sick or injured to travel, the incapacitated one would have to be left behind. It was the law of tribal survival, and all tribal members respected this custom.

So when Wolf Woman hurt her leg, the people contributed some of their remaining supplies of dried meat and left her camped close to a clear stream. They promised they would circle back if the buffalo herds returned. Although times were hard, they tried to leave her a winter's supply of meat. They left her a horse in case she mended, and hoped that she could rejoin them.

The Sioux woman's leg took a long time to mend; in the meantime, her horse ran off, winter was approaching, and she was running out of food. She noticed the repeated presence of a female wolf near her camp and took it upon herself to explore the wolf's den, crawling on her hands and knees to get there. The den was a little cave tunneled into the side of a bank not far away. The Sioux woman waited until the she-wolf was out hunting and crawled into the den. Inside the den a pack of wolf cubs snarled at her while they feasted on a fresh rabbit. Hungry for fresh meat, she crawled further into the den and helped herself to what was left. The wolf cubs snarled and growled retreating to the back of the den.

The female wolf returned with a deer carcass and, discovering the presence of the human, left the meat at the entrance to the den. The woman helped herself to the meat but made sure that the cubs received their share also. The she-wolf continued to bring food to the den and eventually accepted the newcomer to her pack.

The woman lived all winter in the confines of the wolf den. Her leg mended, and she was able to travel and even helped to hunt with rabbit snares.

For several winters the woman lived with the wolves. The cubs grew into adulthood and accepted her as a relative. The wolves had a language of their own, and in time she learned to communicate with them.

One day, one of the wolves, a scout for the pack, told her that her people were coming and within a few days would be close by. She began to smell a strange smell that increased in its intensity as the days passed by. The scout wolf told her that her people were camped only a day's distance at their rate of travel and told her to get ready, for he would lead her toward them the following dawn. Already the strange smell seemed almost overpowering to her, and she did not like it.

The next morning the scout wolf led her to the top of a hill where she could look down on her people camped in their tipis. When they saw her they ran to greet her, but she had to tell them to stay back, for the human smell which she had not been accustomed to was too much for her. She told them she would follow at a distance until she got used to them.

Eventually, she joined them and was known as *Tashuunka* Woman, Wolf Woman, and The One Who Lives with the Wolves. Thereafter, she had the ability to tell the band of approaching blizzards and storms, for she could interpret the songs of the wolves singing to the moon. She told her people how the wolves talked to each other and in many ways were like the two-leggeds.

Maybe Wolf will come into your dreams. Wolf will be telling you to go forth and be a teacher for Mother Earth. Wolf will tell you to go out and teach the rest of the two-leggeds to reach out to a higher plane, a higher consciousness, and to expand upon the great truths that nature has to reveal.

South Direction, South Wind

Buffalo (Tatanka)

The buffalo was sustenance and life to the Sioux. It was also shelter and warmth. Our spiritual messenger, the Buffalo Calf Woman, even took the form of the buffalo, a white buffalo calf, after she appeared to us in human form and taught us the use of the sacred pipe within our ceremonies.

Buffalo is provisions, shelter, and thanksgiving. What Buffalo symbolizes usually takes form in the summer; therefore, the buffalo is strongly associated with the south. After the summer buffalo hunts, it was a time of rich provisions. The hot, dry plains air at that time of year effectively dried the buffalo meat for winter storage. Our tipis were made of buffalo hide, and after the summer hunt the Sun Dance for thanksgiving to *Wakan Tanka* was held.

It is almost overpowering to stand next to a live buffalo, especially when it looks directly at you, eye to eye. I am fortunate to see this majestic being very closely when I vision quest at Spirit Mountain. I have often expressed how awesome a buffalo truly is. I think if the Great Spirit ever wanted to take earthly form, it would resemble more the overpowering, dominating form of the buffalo than it would the small-headed two-leggeds.

Seldom have I heard of two-leggeds who have had the buffalo appear in their dreams or visions. Maybe this four-legged is a symbol reserved for thankfulness and appreciation. When we do see Buffalo, we should always remind ourselves of prayer and gratitude for all that the Great Spirit has allowed for us as we journey here upon our Mother Earth.

The Sioux regard the buffalo also as abundance. For those who are sincerely seeking help in educating, awareness programs, and earth-saving technology, I wish you strong buffalo medicine and that your labors shall reap abundance in order to carry forth your worthwhile goals.

South Direction, South Wind

Bear (Mato)

Bear is an excellent representative for the warm south direction. Bear's claws dig into Mother Earth for her herbs and roots. Bear is a symbol and a strong totem for those who seek earth's medicines. Medicine plants abound throughout the world. Their leaves, stems, fruits, and roots are to be gathered when they are at their strength and can more potently impart their particular gifts to heal sickness and disease. We are losing many special medicine plants because large portions of the tropical rain forests are destroyed.

Bear is a reminder of summer, the season that represents the warm south. Spring is the awakening of the annual cycle of seasons, and east represents awakening. Fall is representative of preparing the Bear's long winter sleep. The leaves fall like shadows, and the west is associated with autumn. The white north and winter's snow is an obvious association. Summer is related to the south direction where the heightened, intensified sun rays bring forth their growth and harvest by warming Mother Earth into her rich bounty of provisions, medicines, and shelter from the wood of the standing ones (trees).

Bear makes full use of summer and then goes into hibernation when the snows fall. The long sleep brings the winter dreams.

In my tribe, there were medicine men who were "Bear Dreamers." Bear would come to them in their dreams and reveal certain herbs or roots useful for medicine. If your dreams are of Bear, you should be studying plant life and thinking about the special effects certain plants in your area can be used for in regard to the way in which they were used by early pioneers and the Native Americans. Possibly, if your Bear dreams are persistent, *Mato* may be wanting to show you a particular remedy for some of the ills that we are faced with today. You could become a modern Bear dreamer of this new rainbow way or the Natural Way.

Like most animals, the bear does not want to have any trouble with humankind. Bear will usually avoid you if given early warning. But when cornered, the bear will stand and fight. Likewise, it will even attack if it is threatened or fears for the survival of its young.

Bear, like Wolf, has many two-legged tendencies. It even has vanity and likes to look at itself in the water.

I am not in favor of some wild animals having to appear in zoos and circuses. I think that with the modern media presentations and their professional ability to portray wild animals, the public is better served by viewing real, natural freedom, "happy freedom," rather than seeing such creatures penned unhappily in captivity. Nevertheless, especially in the circus, the bear reveals how it can adapt for human entertainment. It is a very clever, personable animal and can even clown and have humor. But in the end, I wish all bears could be free from their captivity and be allowed to spend their lives back in the wilds of Mother Nature.

Perhaps if *Mato* appears in your dreams and visions and is not pointing out a particular herb or root, he (or she) is asking you to help all creatures, all children of Mother Earth to regain their natural freedom.

West Direction, West Wind

Thunder Being (Wakinyan)

The thunderbird is symbolic of the power within the thunder and the lightning of the great life-giving rains *(wichoni minne)* that roll out of the west.

"I have the power to make live and the power to destroy," Black Elk was told by the west power. Surely the lightning can destroy, but more life comes forth from the towering westwind thunderstorms.

The golden eagle is a symbolic bird for the thunder being, but it is usually illustrated in petroglyphic form and often illustrated with lightning. Lightning streaking across a black background is another depiction of *Wakinyan* power upon a shield.

Growth from the earth is a power of the thunder being. The thunder is the Great Spirit's earth voice. Before the rain, so much life in all forms is about to spring forth that earth and sky communicate. The two-leggeds and all creatures are being told that the lifeblood, the water is about to descend. The next time you see a thunderstorm approaching, greet it appreciatively and as a relative. Sense the immense connection approaching and revel in the awesome workings of *Wakan Tanka's* nature. Have the courage to stand out in this drenching, vital force and let it anoint you to become a mystic rainbow warrior in your cause for our Mother Earth.

West Direction, West Wind

Horse (Tashuunka Wakan)

When the Sioux first saw the horse and a man riding it they called it *Shunnka* (dog) *Wakan* (holy). They called it holy dog because it could carry man about, and this allowed the buffalo to be hunted much more efficiently. It lived with man like a dog, yet it had so much power; therefore, holy dog was a very befitting name. Later the horse was called *Shunnka Tanka* (a very large dog).

The black horse in Black Elk's vision symbolized the first power of the universe, the west power. The black horse as a creature symbol on the sacred hoop of life represents Black Elk's powerful vision. A white horse, a roan (red) horse, and a buckskin or yellow horse would equally be representative of Black Elk's vision, and the four of them together would represent the first four powers of the rainbow-covered lodge.

Down through time, the horse has enabled communication to progress. Messengers on horseback relayed and advanced communication thanks to horses' acceptance of domestication. Communication now is an all-important tool to be used for the projection of environmental understanding.

The preservation of Black Elk's vision by John Neihardt could be interpreted as a powerful fruit of the spirit power of the west. The vision was life-giving spirit rain. The particular revelations of the six powers were entered into the disk of humanity through the Sioux. This guidance was preserved, stored, and locked away from the tampering of nonharmonic, narrow-minded forces who would have ejected or erased it from access by all humankind, for their power was awesome during that time. It seems that communication among the two-leggeds had first to be improved.

The connection to relationship of all was put forth to humankind through a simple, yet deeply spiritual man who could not write or speak the language of his captors, and now his words have blossomed forth in many languages thanks to a courageous, unpretentious man, John Neihardt, whose vision was akin to the old prophet's. Black Elk told Neihardt that his Indian name, *Pta Wigmunke* (Flaming Rainbow), came from a vision wherein Black Elk saw little flames drop from a rainbow and where they landed, flowers bloomed. Truly, for everyone who reads of Black Elk's vision, a new flower of peace and harmony does bloom forth.

The thundering spirit of the west told Black Elk long ago that he would be helped and his vision would be called upon. Obviously, the invincible interest of the six powers brought forth the old man's story, and now his revelation is being called upon by many environmental and spiritual people. I see the black horse rearing up, in a powerful kicking stance like thunder and lightning, ready to back up worthwhile environmental endeavors.

The horse upon a shield or on a painting can be a recognition of the great vision. It is also an encouragement that the powerful spirit forces have not forgotten the Natural Way and will be there to help if called upon.

North Direction, North Wind

Polar Bear (Mato ska)

The polar bear ranges the frigid Arctic, living where no other four-legged can survive. Patience, resolution, and a solitary life are some of its major characteristics, but endurance is the key word that stands for this representative of the north.

Other than a female with cubs, *Mato ska* keeps to itself out on the pack ice where it spends most of its life hunting its favorite food, the ringed seal. The bear's white camouflage, keen sense of smell, sharp claws, and patience enable it to catch the seal when it surfaces to breathe at holes or openings in the leads or edges of the ice. Its strength, stamina, and speed make it a feared animal when it leaves the pack ice and comes south for a brief time to mate. Males can attain a standing height of nine feet and weigh up to fourteen hundred pounds.

The great white bear is a success symbol for environmentalists. This magnificent four-legged was once hunted from airplanes and became endangered, but that hunting method is now prohibited by federal law—the Marine Mammal Protection Act of 1972—thanks to a concerted outcry of concerned environmental groups. Present hunting regulations are severely restrictive, and as a result, the bear population is increasing.

Polar Bear tells us to keep endurance in mind as we journey and explore along the Natural Way. Polar Bear wants us to remember the earth knowledge that we receive. "Let the worthwhile information endure within you so that you can better protect the animals and Mother Earth."

North Direction, North Wind

Snowy Owl (Hinhan ska)

While Polar Bear is far away prowling the Arctic ice, Snowy Owl *(Hinhan ska)* is the bear's north-wind messenger; it watches out for us, especially during the long northern nights.

Owl is the swift, silent hunter of the night. The old-time traditional Sioux admired this bird so much for its ability to catch its prey in the dark that warriors who had excelled in combat were allowed to wear a cap of owl feathers as a badge to signify their bravery. An old-time society of the Sioux was called The Owl Lodge. This society believed that nature forces would favor those who wore owl feathers and, of course, their vision would become increased. The Indians recognized that animals and birds had powers that humans did not possess. The owl is a good example of a creature that possesses special powers that the two-leggeds have not been endowed with.

Many Sioux people to this day consider the owl a bird of warning. When it comes to you in the night and calls out repeatedly, it is believed that the bird is warning you to be careful of your movements the next day, lest an accident befall you or an enemy seek to do something harmful or speak untruths that can harm you. The bird is telling you to keep your senses alert so that you can better protect yourself from danger.

Many cultures regard the owl as a bird of wisdom. If Owl should come into your dreams and visions, no doubt it is telling you to look for total truth, to look at the great depth and revelation of all that surrounds you. Explore now your nature side, the side of you that has too long been ignored. Explore your inner self, for your own self is also a part of the great natural world. Like the owl's special vision, by looking into yourself and blending this seeking with your explorations of nature, you will be surprised how well the study of each helps reveal the profound wisdom of the other.

Some tribes have the superstition that Owl is a bird to be frightened of and to be avoided. But many holy ones believe that the Great Spirit does not make any creatures bad; they are all good. Man is the only creature that can learn that which is bad or harmful, and even we two-leggeds start out as good when we are innocent children. The rest of the creatures all obey totally the Great Spirit's direction. There are no bad animals, no bad winged, no bad stones, no bad standing ones (trees), etc. Unfortunately, some bad people have conjured up untruths about certain of our four-legged and winged friends, no doubt to control and deceive for their own self-gain and attempt to increase their own power in satisfaction of their misguided egos. Look how distorted were the records of early white men when they told so many untruths about the Native American in order to justify the taking away of their lands. Unfortunately, too many bad people (the blue man in Black Elk's vision) have gained much power in this world, mainly because of greed and unhealthy exploitation of our Mother Earth. Many of these two-leggeds have caused the animals of the world to suffer considerably as a result.

For the good of all humanity and the preservation of our creature relatives, we must become like the owl and hunt around the clock to track down these offenders of the environment and take away their power.

Owl teaches us to be like the north wind. Face the elements and learn endurance; from endurance gain courage. Like the driven snow, seek purity in your goals and endeavors. Keep a clean body and surroundings. These habits are helpers in keeping a clean spirit and a pure heart. The north wind is harsh at times, but it leads us to a healthy respect for truth. Truthfulness and realization of what the Great Spirit has placed before us teach us that there are no Creator-made taboos. If you look for them in God's nature you will not find them, and you will come to realize that taboos, so-called bad spirits, and black magic are all untruths composed by the blue man of Black Elk's vision. Armed with natural truth, Owl will help you to get on with your tasks and natural path that lie ahead.

North Direction, North Wind

Bald Eagle (Wanblee)

The bald eagle *(Wanblee)* is a symbol of leadership, and to the Indian it is the creature symbol of greatest power because it flies so high, close to the Great Spirit, and is regarded as the eyes of the all-seeing powers of *Wakan Tanka*, the one above who created all things.

The Indian wore the feathers of the eagle, but this great bird is so highly regarded that each eagle feather had to be earned by the wearer. Deeds of bravery, generosity, self-sacrifice, or provident wisdom could result in the wearing of an eagle feather.

An eagle has such good vision and great caution that seldom could a hunter get close enough to it to bring it down with a bow and arrow. It was regarded so highly that it was believed bad luck would befall any hunter who would shoot such a magnificent bird. A special ritual for its capture was regarded as the only dignified and allowable means to take it and obtain its feathers.

The ones who sought to capture an eagle would be purified in a sweat lodge and then with the help of several assistants would sit for days in a covered hole in the ground or a pit camouflaged with branches with a dead jackrabbit or a prairie dog attached to the captor by a length of thong. If the captor and his helpers, who remained at a distance, were deceptive and careful enough, an eagle would take the bait; the captor would have to be quick to catch the eagle as the bird attempted to take off with the bait. The bait could also draw a bear or a pack of wolves, and therefore this ritual, like the Sun Dance, was done only by brave men.

If the captor or his helpers made a mistake and did not conceal themselves well enough, the eagle's extraordinary vision would pick out the men's errors and the catching party would come back empty-handed. If the captor was successful and managed to catch the eagle, the bird would be dispatched swiftly, for its talons and beak were formidable weapons. The body of the eagle would be placed on an altar, and a Pipe Ceremony would be held before taking any of the eagle's feathers. After the feathers were removed, the body would be taken back to where it was captured and given back ceremoniously to the Great Mystery. This was done to show that the great bird was respected.

Eagle is regarded as the connection to *Wakan Tanka*. Its feathers are regarded as having brushed the face of God and are used as powerful healing tools. Eagle feathers are also believed to help an individual to gather courage and to maintain courage for a fearless drive to perform a good task or a worthwhile deed under difficult conditions.

Eagle usually will appear in real life more so than in dreams. When you first see *Wanblee* in flight, the white head and white tail feathers will stand out so clearly that most people will carry its image in their memories for a lifetime. This winged is truly endowed with special power. Eagle is telling us, "See, how I stamp myself in your memory. What you do or do not do, good and bad; when you had courage; when you lacked courage—these are stamped into the memory of time and mostly within your own endless circles. Lies, deceit, greed, and harm will not be erased. Neither will the good deeds of generosity and caring be erased."

If Eagle soars toward you or circles above, stop and regard this happening as a great natural blessing. I was very fortunate, once, to have an eagle hover above me for a long time as I was just starting to come down from a mountaintop to end a Vision Quest. I had been prepared in a Sweat Lodge ceremony before ascending the mountain, and now that I had vision quested it seemed that the wild bird so close above me knew it. I could have hit it with a stone, yet it was unafraid. In fact, it was totally oblivious to me, knowing I would not harm it as it moved only its head searching for game in the mountain valley below.

I was spellbound as I stood beneath the eagle. I watched every feather for movement as it held its position so effortlessly. After a while, the eagle lowered a wing and dropped down, then glided upward into the morning sun. There, it held its position in the blinding ball of the rising sun and seemed to disappear. "Maybe it has disappeared," I thought. "Maybe this eagle, that lets me get so close, is really my imagination." I was tired and hungry from the long, cold night, and at that stage, I thought possibly this was some form of imagery. The eagle came out of the sun, however, and came right back above me. Never, I realized, could I get so close to a wild eagle in free flight. Then something communicated, "You have been in ceremony." I had just been in the Vision Quest, the Sweat Lodge, and performed a Pipe Ceremony. "This is the power of ceremony," something was saying. Was this majestic bird, which was hovering so unusually close, speaking to me in a form of thought transference? I knew that Wolf Woman heard the wolves speak to her. My mother told me that.

"This is the power of ceremony. See how we respond," the eagle or something seemed to say. Finally, the eagle flew off and I walked down the mountain.

Mother Earth

Turtle (Keya)

Turtle is the symbol for Mother Earth. Maybe in these troubled environmental times, everyone's shield should bear some recognition of turtle.

In the old days when the Sioux saw turtles leaving a pond or stream, in time the pond or stream would become dry. Of course, these little creatures were regarded as knowing beforehand. Their exodus was a weather warning that dry times were coming; therefore, they were called water carriers. The Indians said wherever they went they carried water. When they left, the water would go with them.

The turtle has a shield that surrounds and encloses it. It is even able to totally withdraw its head and appendages within the protection of its hard shell. At one time when humankind was few in numbers, humans were like the turtle.

The two-leggeds lived in caves and withdrew themselves into the literal protection of Mother Earth when fierce predators threatened. Now this world is becoming so overpopulated that if the two-leggeds keep increasing at the present alarming rate, the resulting pollution from energy needs and overmaterialistic consumption will surely hasten the thinning of the protective ozone layer high in the earth's atmosphere.

If the world heats up, those two-leggeds that manage to survive will no doubt have to return to the caves that once protected our cave people ancestors long, long ago. This thought is so sobering, I believe I will attach a small pipestone turtle that I recently purchased at the Pipestone quarries to my medicine shield as a reminder of what can happen to our Mother Earth if we cease to be environmental and spiritually centered. Maybe you, too, will paint a turtle symbol somewhere upon your shield or attach a turtle effigy.

The turtle has two habitats, water and earth. Our two-legged bodies are reflective of the turtle's habitats. We are made up of water and earth, and like the turtle are dependent upon the sun for our energy source. The hard-shelled one has a long winter's sleep beneath the icy pond of winter when the sun's energy is the least. Turtle makes use of the long summer sun by soaking up the sun's energy whenever it has the opportunity. Turtle tells us to make use of the creative energies of Father Sun. Maybe modern technology can someday harness sun energy or other related "clean fuel" in order to hold off or remove the threat of the thinning ozone layer.

The Four Quarters, The Four Seasons

Dragonfly (Tusweca)

Dragonfly *(Tusweca)* is the Indians' answer to Plato's allegory of the cave, in which Plato taught us that the life we understand and comprehend today is but a mere shadow on the wall compared to the complete reality that lies beyond.

Dragonfly spends its beginning life under the stones and pebbles of a mountain stream, a pool, or a pond, crawling from hiding place to hiding place in its search for food; it is a favorite meal of various fish. Trout fishermen create many wet-fly imitations of the dragonfly nymph and have success on trout streams casting their man-made nymphs into the swirling waters and letting their tiny lures drift beneath the surface.

The nymph undergoes metamorphosis and instead of being a fiercely ugly little crawling creature that resembles a miniature dragon, it develops wings and rises to the water's surface. If a trout or a panfish doesn't feast upon it, it flies into the air and looks down at where it came from. It is suddenly in a new medium, a medium that would be vastly inconceivable by water creatures such as it had been under the surface. Its configuration and physiology undergo such a total change that it could be somewhat analogous to comparing it to a two-legged's spirit when it rises up and enters the spirit world.

If the dragonfly is a knowledge seeker, it now has an opportunity immeasurably greater than it could ever have conceived of when it was so restricted under the water's surface. There it was unaware of the vast, new, inconceivable reality that exists. Dragonfly can now discover, search, and grow, by a simple beat of its wings.

The Indian says that the Great Spirit reveals many of its secrets and bits of knowledge by the example of what it creates. We two-leggeds can learn from the knowledgeable Plato and our little friend that skims across the waters and hovers so close by for us to study and comprehend.

Dragonfly also reminds us of the four quarters and the four seasons. Red Dragonfly comes to us in the spring, when the waters warm just enough for it to sprout its wings. Yellow Dragonfly zooms across the ponds in the heat of summer. Blue Dragonfly tells us that fall is upon us and the long winter is approaching. Blue Dragonfly also reminds us that blue is considered a representative color for the west because of the life-giving rains, the *wichoni minne,* that come primarily from the west. Winter Dragonfly stays under the white snow that covers the icy ponds and pools, crawling about in its hiding places and being limited in its vision at the bottoms of the waters.

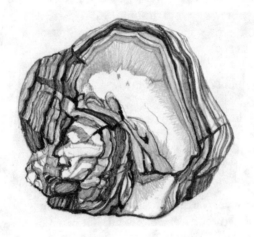

18

Receiving Your Earth Name and
Finding Your *Wotai* Stone

It is comforting to have a natural name, one that connects you explicitly to Mother Earth. It is also a good feeling to have a stone, a stone that conveys a special meaning to you and has come to you in a special way. It may also bear special symbols that speak out and assure you that a minute portion of Mother Earth (the stone) was created just for you, millions upon millions of years ago.

Special stones and natural names ("Indian names") are often closely related to each other. I will tell the story of Red Hawk Woman to clarify. Lorelei joined a group of rainbows to go to Spirit Mountain to vision quest. She had attended many Sweat Lodge ceremonies and had a talent for making beautiful, well-balanced beaded necklaces and earrings. In the ceremonies, her prayers during the third endurance were especially spiritual and meaningful. Once she brought a group of her women friends, and the lodge ceremony exhibited strong powers. The heat seemed to rise only so high in the lodge as if the group together were having some control on the elements of fire, heat, and steam.

En route to Spirit Mountain, Lorelei rode mainly with Red Pipe Woman (Debbie Chavez). Debbie had received her name during an earlier Sweat Lodge Ceremony. Before Debbie's naming, the stars above the lodge showed the outline of a traditional peace pipe. She also had an intense journey during her making of her own pipe, as was described earlier, so Red Pipe Woman seemed to be a very fitting name. In the ceremony, the name seemed to have a special "ring," and she accepted it with enthusiasm.

Lorelei's natural name first showed itself in the form of a smooth stone that she came across at the Cheyenne River where the group stopped. She had had dreams several times in which a red bird appeared. She didn't know what kind of bird it was, however. When she asked me about the bird from her dreams, I had the feeling that her Vision Quest would help solve the identity. It has been my experience that people who have particular questions that are perplexing to them have those questions answered within a few days or weeks of their quest. Lorelei was excited about her find. The red bird was clearly imaged in her stone, and the color was definite, but the exact species was still unclear. When she returned to the car to resume her journey, a red-tailed hawk flew close, circled several times, and flew away.

At Spirit Mountain, a Sweat Lodge was held, and several within the lodge received their natural names. Animals and birds that appeared in thoughts or dreams were described by the vision seekers. Some had strong identification with inanimate symbols, such as crystals, rainbows, thunder, dance, and feathers. Earth Song, Rainbow Crystal Woman, and Water Spirit Woman are some examples of natural names associated with these symbols. Eagle Woman, Two Hawks, and White Wolf are natural names associated with animals that have been adopted by the rainbow tribe.

During that ceremony, Lorelei was still unsure of the identity of the red bird that had appeared in her dreams and was portrayed on her stone. She was satisfied that she had found her stone, but was not yet certain that the red hawk was the correct bird. Since she was uncertain, I suggested that she wait for her name. In time, nature, the Earth Force, or whatever power resides in the earth would make it known to her. She accepted this decision.

During her Vision Quest, she did not receive any more signs regarding her natural name. She was not impatient, however, and fulfilled her Vision Quest in harmony with the six powers of Black Elk's vision and the Great Mystery. I rode back with her when we left the Black Hills. On the way, we stopped at Pipestone and visited with one of the Indian pipemakers. We asked if we could see some finished pipes that would possibly be for sale.

Lorelei zeroed in on one pipe in particular. Out of several pipes placed on a table, she picked up one and was immediately bonded to it. "This is the pipe I must have," she exclaimed and handed it to me for inspection. I took the pipe and carefully studied its grain and features, which I am accustomed to doing when I study a stone. Pipestone is more than a hardened piece of red clay. Pipestone has colors in it ranging from white to yellow to orange to red-orange dots or granules. Some pipes also exhibit images. Some pipes look as if they are sprinkled with a galaxy of stars.

Before Lorelei had handed me her pipe, I had been fascinated by a pipe that had a bright yellow ring that encircled its base amid a galaxy of stars. "The yellow power of the hoop," I thought. Lorelei's pipe had some yellow within its grain also, and it too had galaxies of stars; but what was most astounding was the clear image of a woman, her hair sweeping back like streamlined feathers. This woman represented a bird woman, and her hair was like feathered wings, giving her the appearance of one flying through the heavens. The image strongly suggested a hawk woman, since her features were sharp and forceful. We purchased both pipes.

We did a Pipe Ceremony in a secluded spot at the Pipestone quarries. Nature provided a serene setting. Several different species of birds flew down to inspect us closely as we beseeched the four directions. After the ceremony to the four winds, I conducted a naming ceremony for Lorelei. After all her experiences and now that she had found the hawk woman pipe, her natural name was to be Red Hawk Woman, *Lutah Cetan Winan*. Several other birds dropped down to inspect us. I had the feeling that a red-tailed hawk would drop in on us, and almost expected one to do so.

It was still daylight when we left the quarries. Not far out of town, we saw a large bird up ahead on the highway. At first, I thought it was a raven or a crow, but when it rose from the highway, I could see that it was an eagle or a hawk. It flew toward us, coming down the road on the driver's side. As it drew closer, it crossed over toward the right side of the car and banked sharply to reverse direction and fly with us on Lorelei's side. The bird was clearly a red-tailed hawk, and acted as if it was looking inside our car.

As we drove away, there was no question in Red Hawk Woman's mind that she had just received a special acknowledgment from the forces of nature. She now sees hawks considerably more than she used to, and their presence, like her *wotai* stone, gives her a special comforting feeling.

If an animal or several animals come to you in your visions or dreams, you should consider an earth name that links you to them. In Lorelei's experience, the bird and the stone and the pipe were in harmony. This does not mean that your *wotai* stone necessarily has to have your animal sign on it. It simply is a stone that draws your attention and has a special feeling to you.

I have had two *wotai* stones. One had my natural name sign on it, the other did not. The first *wotai* clearly had the mark of an eagle, and this was its most distinguishing symbol. This was the *wotai* stone that came into Fools Crow's *Yuwipi* Ceremony held for me before I left for Vietnam. It gave me extreme confidence and courage in combat, and I wore it faithfully on my combat missions.

As a child, I was named unceremoniously by Ben Black Elk. He simply remarked while he watched me play one day, "Ho, *Wanblee Hoksila* [Eagle Boy]," he stated, and that was my Indian name. I was just a child, more interested in a child's adventures, so I had to be reminded as I grew older that I had an Indian name, even if I did receive it from someone as renowned as Ben Black Elk.

After I returned to dance in the Sun Dance and Ben Black Elk had me carry his father's pipe in the dance, I was ceremoniously given my name *Wanblee Wichasha* (Eagle Man) by Ben Black Elk, Bill Eagle Feather, and Fools Crow, the presiding Sun Dance chief.

After my second Sun Dance, I discovered my second *wotai* stone. It flashed rather dramatically from a clear mountain stream in the Black Hills while I was waiting for my sister to arrive at a swimming spot from the Sun Dance encampment. I had been pierced, and was hot, dusty, and tired from the four-day ordeal, so I had left while my sister and brother-in-law were still preparing to hook up their camper.

My nephew, who was in his early teens at the time, was playing along the creek bank and had flushed a snake from its hiding place. The snake came upstream, and scared me momentarily because it came out of the water and glided across my foot. I jumped and scared it back into the water, and it went across the stream. All of a sudden, a flash at the bottom of the shallow stream captured my attention. A snake swimming in the rapid current is a compelling sight, but the flash was much more interesting.

The snake disappeared in the grass at the edge of the opposite bank. A second time, whatever it was flashed again from the stream bottom. The bright August sun was at its midafternoon height, and the water was quite clear. It is easy to explain the reflection of something from the sun through the rushing current, but this was an unusually bright flash. I waded out into the water when the flash occurred a third time.

I honestly cannot remember my exact thoughts as I walked out into the stream. I think that I expected to find a bright tin can that shouldn't be polluting such a crystal clear stream. I remember complaining to myself that people shouldn't throw their cans away, but I also can honestly say that I was somewhat mesmerized and my thoughts were unclear at that moment. When I came almost directly over the flashing area, I debated whether or not I should reach down and remove the "tin can" from the water. While I was debating, the "tin can" flashed a fourth time, long, hard, and bright, as if it were commanding me to reach down and pick it up.

I obeyed, reached down, and at first did not realize what a beautiful tipi canyon agate I had found, for I also had come up with a handful of mud and moss. When I washed the stone off in the current, I was delighted that I had found such a beautiful agate with a crystalline center and a rainbow rim. I showed the agate to my nephew, who was more concerned with chasing out another snake. My sister appreciated my find, but neither of us took the time to look for any images within the stone. We were more interested in cooling off in the stream.

Several months later, Bill Eagle Feather paid me a visit, and while I was relating my finding of the stone, he asked to see it. After studying the stone, he pointed out the powerful images within it. They were so clearly discernible that it was somewhat embarrassing that neither my sister nor I had seen them.

The most obvious figure in the agate is a stern, strong-faced warrior named Charging Shield. It is as if the spirit actually lives within the stone. Superimposed is another figure which, surprisingly, bears some resemblance to myself wearing what could be a Sun Dance crown of sage. Opposite to these two figures is a powerful woman with long, flowing hair. And when the stone is turned, the silhouette of Fools Crow can be seen clearly.

People who study the stone usually find these features easily and always seem to point out a new feature or two. One four-legged symbol, the mountain lion, stands out for me and seems to hide itself from many friends. The stone tells me, "Be like the mountain lion."

Bill told me that the stone was *sicun*. He said the word *wotawe*, meaning "a personal charm" and then said *wotai*. He said the stone's spirit was obvious. You could see or feel it. It had come in a powerful way at a powerful time, after my first piercing. *Sicun* means a soul or a spirit lasts forever like the circle. It is capable of being reinvested in another object at one's death. Charging Shield is a very dominant spirit within this stone. Bill went on to say that my first *wotai*, the stone that had been with me in combat, would leave me and not to worry about it. After that the rainbow rimmed agate would be my *wotai*.

After I vision quest at Spirit Mountain, I often go to the same mountain stream to swim and refresh myself, because there are warm springs there. I have placed my *wotai* in the same place in the water, and even when the sun has been in approximately the same position, I have never experienced a flash from it again.

I will admit that this is a rather dramatic way for a stone to come into my life, but I am most appreciative of it. If it leaves me, then I hope that it will be replaced by another, but I do take precautions to safeguard it. I draw great comfort from this uniquely designed creation of nature and am at times in awe of its many features and symbols. It clearly says that the Great Spirit designed this stone for a reason and that I was meant to have it. I also believe that it is a reward for having the courage to take a stand when I had to for the Sun Dance.

I have a friend who found his *wotai* in a garage sale, of all places. This stone has a profound representation of the four colors of the four directions. My friend is as fond of his *wotai* as I am of mine. Another friend purchased hers in a gift shop, and after she showed it to me, I pointed out the very distinct image of the Buffalo Calf Woman holding a peace pipe. *Wakan Tanka* put this beautiful image within her stone.

Wotai stones can and will come in various ways, although they are usually discovered along a path or stream. Many are also found in lapidary stores or at shows or conventions where crystals and stones are sold. It doesn't make any difference whether you have purchased the stone rather than found it. What is important is that you have come together.

Discovering your natural name can be as spontaneous as finding your *wotai* stone. For some a profound spiritual event is the basis for a natural name. My friend Thunder Hawk received his name in this way, and it was the beginning of a journey that gave him what he had asked. Another friend, Thunder Owl, had a similar experience with an owl, and this particular bird now reinforces his dreams and visions. Occasionally, an owl drops low and flies over his sweat lodge fire when he is about to conduct a ceremony.

Once, Thunder Owl and I were about to conduct a sweat lodge and naming ceremony for a woman who had given us the use of her land for a lodge site. Before the ceremony and before the rest of the participants had gathered, a beaver was eating along the bank as we approached. Instead of being alarmed, the beaver took a good look at us, saw we were Indians about to conduct a ceremony, and calmly swam out into the current. It did a water ballet right in front of us as we stood above it looking down from a low footbridge. The beaver demonstrated that it was unafraid. Four times the animal circled slowly in front of us. Then, when it heard more people coming, it splashed its tail and swam away. The woman was named Water Spirit Woman. She is spiritual and has been close to the water since childhood, canoeing and swimming.

In the old days, a child was given a child's name, and after he or she became an adult, was given an adult name. Some natural names are listed in the appendix; if one of these rings true or conveys a special feeling, adopt it. Or seek out your own special name in dreams, signs, or visions.

There is no special ceremony for a naming. You can name yourself without a group, although some kind of group ceremony seems to make it "official." What is important is that the bearer feel comfortable with the chosen name. Sweat Lodge ceremonies are unique settings to convey natural names. The spiritual veil is thinned, and it gives an intensity to the receiving of a name tied to the creation of the Great Spirit.

Some Indian people believe that a natural name allows them to take the form of the animal or bird in the spirit world. This is just a supposition and is not regarded as fact; but if I were to allow myself a lament, considering the theological suppositions that have been unfairly imposed on us, I think we are entitled to a few suppositions of our own. We of traditional bent like to preface our statements by saying that everything is a mystery and nothing is as certain as one would like to imagine.

There are some cases, especially in a *Yuwipi* Ceremony, in which some ancestors come into the ceremony in the form of an animal. Grey Weasel, Bill Eagle Feather's spirit guide, is an example of this. We assume that the natural name or a visiting spirit guide could be a reflection of an animal, bird, or other image that is part of the transformation into the spirit world that lies beyond.

For Indians, four-legged and winged ones, stones, and trees are regarded as holy, in that they harmoniously live upon this earth, following exactly the plan of the Great Spirit. They are well rewarded for their balance and harmony. They are housed, clothed, and fed with little or no agitation or anxiety of the type that plagues the free-willed beings walking around on two legs on this planet. We should not look down on any creature that lives free in the wild—far from it, for they are enjoying a life of natural freedom that is quite enviable.

In ceremony, the animal or bird forms serve as a mysterious connection that we cannot totally comprehend, but we know that they are present. Those who have a portion of their name as *Wakinyan*, Thunder, for example, could be considered to embrace the form of thunderbirds, of which the eagle or hawk could be representative. Having a natural name, therefore, gives a concrete identification with the natural world, which many Indians feel could be useful in the spirit life.

Some religions believe that woman should never be allowed to do ceremony and should be subservient to man, because their concept of God has decreed that this should be so. Others have their women wear black coverings when they are in public, and the women can be beaten at will. Others require that their priests drink alcohol in their ceremonies and be celibate all their lives. One reports that only a certain mathematical number can reach the spirit world; they recently adjusted this number upward since their membership has grown. The wildest of all has been the supposition that a great armed clash is imminent and that it will result in the world population believing all in one way, their particular way.

So I guess that we Indians should be allowed a few gentler persuasions like our belief in harmless little rocks that speak to us. And we should also be allowed our association with our four-legged and winged friends, both here and in the spirit world. So it is, and in the end, we will all arrive, in one way or another, in the same spirit world.

In summary, the *wotai* stone that comes upon a seeking person's path may be an answer should there become a large increase in numbers of those who will be beseeching the natural powers based on Black Elk's vision.

Both Red Pipe Woman and Red Hawk Woman had either a powerful vision in ceremony or direct corroboration from the natural world in positively acknowledging their pipes or their name coming into their lives, and this was several years ago. A ceremonial vision or an assurance by nature is not to be downplayed nor is it to be considered negatively.

On my last trip to the Pipestone quarries I sensed that there is a limited availability of pipestone. It is comforting to know that the remaining amount will be quarried only by hand. Maybe those pipes that have been made were to help bring about the present progress toward peace, harmony, and environmental thinking that we are experiencing. Maybe earlier pipes have journeyed out into the world and have done their job, and now the quarries must be given a rest and revert back mostly toward traditional Native Americans that come some distance in need of stone.

This is not to rule out those who have received strong supportive visions and have gone to an experienced traditional for advice and direction. This is again only human supposition, but in light of all the positive change that has been happening, maybe it could be so. I have talked to the keeper of the Sacred Pipe and he indicates so.

In this area, one's personal stone or crystal can fill the void as a beseechment article. I even find myself using my *wotai* stone in place of my pipe as a means for beseechment when I call upon the six powers or the four directions. When people desire a grace before a meal, it is convenient to bring forth one's stone or crystal to beseech those powers that are ultimately responsible for the food upon the table or the presence of all at the meeting. I think we who are of different colors and backgrounds can all have a closer commonality for spiritual beseechment if we use our stones or crystals as our portable articles. There are stones everywhere and we certainly are not going to run out of those. A personal *wotai* stone that comes to you can become a very close spiritual identification to all the powers that affect us daily.

PART FOUR

FIRE

Healing Mother Earth in Your Own Community

When you understand relationship, you can
bring back the stewardship that once worked so
well for Mother Earth.

19

Conducting Ceremony

Ceremony usually involves the participation of a group of people, except when the individual beseeches the six powers by himself or herself. In group participation, such as in the Sweat Lodge, Sun Dance, or Spirit-calling Ceremony, the leader serves as the medium to connect across the bridge to the spirit world or at least to give the ceremony direction and structure based on traditional practice.

To learn traditional practices involves assisting one's elders who have spent a lifetime conducting ceremony and of course practicing and walking the red road. For aspirants, nothing is more valuable than learning ceremony from a willing and knowledgeable teacher.

I was fortunate to have had the opportunity to assist Eagle Feather in some of his ceremonies, namely Sweat Lodge and *Yuwipi* ceremonies. I was also able to observe the leadership of Fools Crow in the Sun Dances in which I participated, and assisted him in the *Yuwipi* and Sweat Lodge. Both Eagle Feather and Fools Crow prepared me for the Vision Quest, and it was to them that I told my vision quest experience.

Both men insisted that to properly conduct ceremony, absolutely no alcohol or other chemicals were to be consumed, and this included the cactus bud called peyote. "We get our visions from our own juices," Bill would tell me. Both holy men were total abstainers, and it is my strong recommendation that if you are considering taking a leadership role in ceremony, you abstain from all alcohol, drugs, or mind-altering substances. You should maintain total sobriety for as long as you are involved in conducting ceremonies.

Native Americans had no alcohol before the white man came to these shores. For centuries upon centuries, there was no poisoning of man's brain in this land. Our leaders were honest and truthful; like the land, their minds were unpolluted. I have said many times that the Indians took their examples and signs from God-created nature. Animals and winged ones do not consume foreign substances that the Great Spirit did not intend for them. If it is not natural or does not grow here, it is not to be used.

Questions are often asked regarding what is put in the peace pipe besides tobacco. First, the smoke from the tobacco in the pipe is not usually inhaled. It is a symbol of one's visible breath, so that what we say upon a pipe is to be a truthful and meaningful statement. It is as if an audience of knowledgeable spirit beings are looking on with the capacity to convey the purpose of the ceremony to the greatest mystery, *Wakan Tanka*. With that kind of audience, one would want to be extremely respectful and honest. The tobacco smoke is to remind the participant that one's visible breath, one's words, must be true.

The Sioux were formerly from the Carolinas, where they were peaceful corn planters. They also had access to tobacco from this area and brought it with them as they migrated westward to avoid the white man. They brought tobacco into the headwaters of the Mississippi and on out into the Great Plains. Upon the plains, they used buffalo hides and pipestone as trade items to barter with southern tribes for tobacco. They also learned to substitute the bark of the red willow and sumac leaves for tobacco when their supply became scarce.

Holy men and holy women who are schooling aspirants look for the absence of ego in their protégés. Egocentricity is considered an unwelcome trait for those who seek leadership in ceremony. One who has a large ego, even with the counterbalancing traits of sharing and generosity, would still be considered a poor risk for the powerful position that the holy man or holy woman occupies. We have all seen how some religious leaders on television have severely misused their spiritual stewardship. Native American spirituality has not projected itself on such a grandiose scale, but the disheartening and harmful results can be very similar.

Freedom from excess materialism is another prerequisite that Native American spiritual leaders look for in their aspirants. Little explanation is needed on why this is considered an important trait. The winged ones and our animal brothers and sisters were given freedom from selfishness, greed, and excess accumulation of wealth. If the Great Spirit made the holy ones of fur, fin, and feather in this manner, is *Wakan Tanka* not saying that we also should take only what is needed and not take in excess? Excess materialism distracts from the spiritual path. Knowledgeable spiritual people must center on their paths and not on material gain. It is my belief that spiritually balanced people with good intentions should be welcomed to conduct ceremony, and they should not be fearful. The holding of one's crystal or *wotai* stone to the dawn and recognizing that new knowledge can result from each new day is a form of ceremony. Turning to the south and recognizing that energy, health, growth, and shelter result from the sun's warmth and light is a version of ceremony. If one beseeches all the four directions, then the beseechment can be regarded as having come full circle. This beseechment is not restricted to Native Americans or holy men or holy women.

The four directions and their powers are for the whole world, not just the Native Americans. And open-minded, knowledgeable Indians will welcome respectful beseechment, especially when it helps impart a Mother Earth relationship that is beneficial for the entire planet.

To conduct an elaborate Sweat Lodge that beseeches through four endurances or to conduct a related Spirit-calling Ceremony is a different matter. I do not recommend that the conduct of a Sweat Lodge Ceremony be attempted by a novice. It helps considerably to have been in several such ceremonies before you attempt to do one on your own. If there are no teachers available, however, then some will have to strike out on their own.

I can understand that there will be many truly sincere rainbow people who will want to build a sweat lodge and experience the ceremony. There may not be teachers available for all of them. The building of a sweat lodge is not a difficult task. The finding of land and privacy may be a little more difficult, but Mother Earth still has sites for many sweat lodges. There are special considerations of safety that must be addressed and will always have to be kept in mind. A number of these have been discussed in detail in chapter 16.

Establishment of a sense of purpose and relaxed surroundings are essential for conducting ceremony. Fasting before conducting the ceremony is also a worthy preparation. Politeness, respect, brevity, straightforwardness, truth, and impeccable honesty are strict prerequisites to being a ceremonial leader. Double-talking, skepticism, ulterior motives (such as pleasing or impressing your audience), and self-aggrandizement are to be avoided in a leader. Being smart-mouthed, rude, or inconsiderate are also obstacles to the successful conduct of a ceremony. Avoid the grandiose. Be sincere.

Spirits or whatever mysterious forces show their presence in ceremony seem to exhibit the human characteristic of appreciating a degree of formality and respect when being beseeched or asked for special requests. They do not care for abruptness in beseechments. When two-leggeds meet or visit, there is a protocol or formal way to do so. This is true in all cultures. Being hasty, inconsiderate, or bossy are all obstacles in worldly social exchanges and are equally so in the spirit world.

Before conducting your own ceremonies, you should endeavor to assist more experienced leaders and to enhance your own understanding of ceremonial functions and styles. Doing what is asked by those who are more spiritually informed is another means of enhancement, especially when these tasks are primarily to increase your own knowledge.

My road led to many ceremonies in which I was called to assist the holy ones. I also did what they asked of me. When they requested that I should vision quest before my next Sun Dance, I did it, and by doing so, I learned that one ceremony can profoundly impact your receptivity for another ceremony. For example, a Vision Quest can broaden your understanding and insight into the Sweat Lodge and can make you a better leader of the Sweat Lodge Ceremony.

In time, I was asked to perform a ceremony by the holy man Bill Eagle Feather, who told me to build a sweat lodge and do the ceremony since he would not always be available. Many sweat ceremonies later, it seems that the spiritual veil has become considerably thinner, and there seems to be a higher degree of presence manifestation in sweat lodge. Personal preparation alone does not make this possible; the high spiritual state of the attending people, mostly appreciating and respectful rainbow people, have a lot to do with it.

Language use is also very important in Native American ceremonies. Most traditional Indians are very good speakers. For this reason, I encourage you to learn to pray aloud without being self-conscious. You may also want to learn enough of the Sioux language to address the six powers and *Wakan Tanka* in the traditional ways. This will add to your sense of connectedness with the red way or Natural Way. In an appendix at the end of this book, I have included the references to the six powers of the universe so that you may incorporate them if you wish.

The Pipe Ceremony is the basis for all other ceremonies conducted by the Sioux. Rainbow people should use their stones or crystals for beseechment in a similar manner if they do not have a peace pipe. Pipe holders don't always have their pipes available when they wish to express themselves in ceremony. They may have their *wotai* stones or their crystals, however, and these may certainly be substituted for the pipe.

A ceremony can be very brief and spontaneous. I occasionally return to the Black Hills and revisit the place where I met my present *wotai*, the crystal agate with the rainbow rim. I immerse the stone in the stream where it came from. I hold the stone up to the four directions and thank the powers for its entrance onto my path. This is a brief, personal thanksgiving ceremony. Actually, just a simple acknowledgment to the rising dawn or taking time out to watch and appreciate the awesome power of an advancing thunderstorm is, in itself, a personal ceremony.

Some spontaneous ceremonies can be very effective. One such ceremony that I was involved in has given me lasting confidence that the Natural Way that is reemerging from the Native American traditions is a good way.

Thunder Hawk called and told me that a buffalo was to be killed on a farm outside of town and that I was welcome to go there and do a ceremony for the buffalo. You have to follow your own instincts about some things, and my intuition was that I should do what Thunder Hawk suggested.

He was waiting for me at the farm. It was a cold day, and there were several inches of snow on the ground. A small buffalo herd could be seen on the south side of the corral feed yard. I noted the sign posted on the yard fence.

Buffalo Are Dangerous.

Do not cross the yard unless you can do it in 9.9 seconds.

The buffalo can do it in 10.

Buffalo are surprisingly quick, and the cows are especially protective of their calves, not unlike domestic cattle. And every year, it seems, some tourists in the Black Hills discover how quick the large animals can be.

I was told that several of the buffalo were destined for the packing plant and watched one yearling buffalo that had already been shot through the head being loaded by a tractor onto a pickup truck for the trip to the processing plant.

A very large bull was next to be shot, and I was asked to perform a ceremony for it, since it was the leader of the herd. I understood that for genetic purposes (a new bloodline), a new bull was being introduced to replace it. I looked at the big bull standing at the opposite end of the feeding yard. Behind the yard, the land opened to a stand of woods surrounded by a heavy-duty fence. The bull approached, taking a few steps before standing, solemnly staring, while I assembled my peace pipe.

Being an Oglala, I always get a strange feeling when I look eye to eye with a buffalo. It is like a brief immersion in a beautiful past, beautiful not only for the two-leggeds but for the majestic buffalo as well. I spoke to the bull, telling it that soon it would be entering the spirit world and that I was there to conduct a ceremony honoring it. I would thank it and all its ancestors for keeping my people alive when my tribe was once free on the Great Plains.

The bull seemed to understand. He pawed the ground a few times, and his eyes remained fixed on me as if to acknowledge what I had to say. I offered my pipe briefly to the four directions and began to load it with tobacco. After the pipe bowl was filled, I capped it with a piece of sage and took out my drum. I chanted a song to *Tatanka*, the buffalo.

After I finished, the farmer took his gun and approached the bull. The bull backed away and walked slowly toward the trees. It stopped once to charge the farmer, sending him scurrying for the corral fence. After awhile, the farmer maneuvered into a shooting position and fired a shot into the head of the buffalo with a high-powered rifle. The bull dropped. But as the farmer walked over to slit its throat so that the blood could be drained away by the pumping of the heart, the bull pawed him away and struggled to its feet. It fell several times, rose one last time, shook its head, and walked steadily back to rejoin its herd.

The farmer, Thunder Hawk, and I looked on in disbelief as the bull formed up its herd and took the onlooking cows and calves into the wooded cover. I walked back to my car and decided to leave at that moment. I wanted my last vision of this buffalo to be when it was alive and still leading its herd. I drove away and spoke to the spirit of the buffalo as I went down the road. I told it that I understood its great act of power. Yes, they can shoot our Indian spirit right in the head, yet it will not die. This force is so powerful that it will not die, and you, buffalo bull, just gave all of us a powerful sign and renewed confidence in our way.

So it is with ceremony. Some ceremonies are formal and well planned. Others just happen. And from every ceremony, you can receive another earth walk journey teaching.

Earth Day Ceremony

As we have learned, the Sioux beseeched the Creator in various ceremonies, but the tribal beseeching took place at the annual Sun Dance. It was the ceremony of thanksgiving for all that the Creator had abundantly provided them.

On August 16, 1987, a worldwide consciousness took place in the form of ceremony for the expression of peace and harmony to spread throughout the planet. Globally, two-leggeds gathered and beseeched their concept of the Higher Power for a communicative peace to flourish across the continents, across the oceans. It didn't take long for positive, peaceful steps to happen. This date was called the harmonic convergence. It worked! The Berlin wall cracked and world governments seemed to change overnight. Troop reductions and defense budget curtailments began to be discussed among major world powers. Despots and dictators that denied basic freedoms were overthrown.

Although there have been some setbacks, global peace has begun to spawn, but now we are facing a more severe phenomenon. Global warming is being seriously discussed by leading scientists around the globe. We as offspring of the planet all face the same serious consequences. We can actually lose our planet if global warming and overpopulation keep advancing. The situation is so serious that we two-leggeds should beseech the mystical powers for the life of this planet. Our beseechment can lead us to a coming together that is sorely needed. Earth Day ceremonies on a national scale, on a world scale, should be held more often than every twenty years. The forthcoming calamity of environmental disaster should call for a global Earth Day recognition at least every four years. (Since many of the natural, native peoples placed strong emphasis on doing ceremony or ceremonial aspects in fours, every four years would seem to be a good recommendation for a global Earth Day.) If the environmental dilemma keeps advancing, then we will have to become like the Sioux. We will have to beseech annually for spiritual help and insight for the saving of our planet.

Let us take heart in the success of the harmonic convergence that has brought positive results. The following is an account of my experience on that commemorative time with the rainbow people. Let us take a close look at this ceremony and other similar ceremonies that happened across the land that day and let us begin to shape our ceremonies for the future in which we will all seek to commemorate the forthcoming earth days, earth weeks, and earth thinking.

Several hundred two-leggeds gathered in Minnesota near Lake Minnetonka (Great Water) upon a tract of pasture surrounded by woods. It was the day preceding the harmonic convergence. Throughout the continent, thousands were gathering in groups to welcome in a new era of wisdom and understanding.

A sweat lodge had been constructed several months before, and a Sweat Lodge Ceremony was to be held that morning for early arrivals. My close friend, Thunder Owl, was with me. We were the only Native Americans present. He is Dakota Sioux and I am Lakota Sioux. Our ancestors named this state Minnesota (*minne ahtah*, land of much waters). Many surrounding towns and landmarks bear our language: Shakopee, Wayzata, Chaska, Winona, Minnetonka, etc.

Black Elk's vision was a theme on which the Minnetonka gathering centered. A tree would flower some day, and around it many races would gather. Black Elk went on to say that a new people would respect, deeply, all of creation and in such a manner that great peace and harmony would flow throughout humanity, not unlike the sacred manner that the animals (furred ones and flying ones) exhibit. Black Elk may have lamented in his waning years that the tree did not flower, and he was understandably saddened before he departed into the spirit world; but I am sure his spirit leaped with joy when he looked down upon the Minnetonka gathering.

We erected a tall tipi a week preceding the harmonic convergence. At the beginning, Thunder Owl and I didn't understand what this was all about; but our friends were involved, and they had asked for our help. Thunder Owl and I called it the ceremony of harmony among the two-leggeds.

After the tipi had been erected, the group organizing the harmonic convergence ceremony decided that a cottonwood tree somewhat similar to the Sioux Sun Dance tree "around which the people would gather" should be raised and planted close to the tall tipi.

A cottonwood tree was selected. A felling party approached it and gathered at the tree base. A woman—a pipe holder—first spoke to it as she held her peace pipe. She asked that the tree forgive the gathering for having to take its life and then explained the good purpose for which the tree was intended. The woman then took an axe and took the first cut upon it. All present were well aware of Sioux tradition, which places a high emphasis on the participation and leadership of the female in the ceremonies.

At Minnetonka, the tree was brought to the ceremony area to be decorated with red, yellow, black, and white cloth, the colors of the four directions and the four races of humankind. Above these colors were draped a blue cloth for Father Sky and a green one for Mother Earth.

Close to the top of the tree we placed a rawhide cutout of a dove, which stood for peace and harmony. This dove replaced the buffalo that is traditionally placed on Sioux Sun Dance trees. A rawhide cutout of a woman was placed closest to the top of the tree. This feminine figure replaced the usual rawhide cutout of a man.[1]

A peace pipe bowl was placed in the hole dug for the cottonwood tree, and the tree was raised. I had placed an eagle's claw on the tree. The eagle flies the highest of all creatures and, with this in mind, I asked that all of our prayers fly upward into the Great Spirit's "ear" the following dawn.

The tall tipi and the cottonwood were a beautiful sight. The tree's brightly colored flags fluttered in the Saturday evening breezes. Birds called out evening songs, spiritual people laughed and talked, horses stared at the tree momentarily while they grazed, and even the crawling ones chirped excitedly. It was a good moment to remember.

Between the tipi and the cottonwood, concentric circles were made from fine, colored gravel. This area bore six crystals embedded in the earth, as well as crystals attached to wand holders.

That night Thunder Owl and another volunteer held Sweat Lodge ceremonies, while I made sage wreaths bearing eagle feathers and wildflowers for the people who would represent the four directions and Mother Earth in the following day's ceremonies.

The ceremony at dawn was preceded by silent meditation, harmonic om's, and violin music. But the gray skies made us hold off for more than an hour. As Good Spirit Woman and I stood on a knoll, she eyed a long black cloud. A semblance of daylight appeared underneath and behind the cloud, a sign that the weather would clear. It was time to begin. I started down the hill beating an old buckskin drum in a Sioux dance beat.

The Great Spirit blessed our efforts strongly that morning. That huge black cloud roared toward us. It looked like a giant crab shell with horns, and it came over low with a great volume like rolling thunder. Tiny needles of rain tingled my body, yet I did not get wet. Swirling wind rolled from the edges of the cloud. The trees in the woods bent and rocked, but our ceremonial tree and tents were unharmed. High in the sky to the east, a pair of birds held their position with little effort. I pointed to them with my drumstick and let out a pleased yell. They were doves, but exactly what species I was not certain. The doves and the roaring cloud were both very, very powerful signs (*lelah wakan*, we would say in Sioux) that the Great Spirit was giving this day a strong blessing. The people held up their arms and cheered in acknowledgment.[2]

Then the ceremony began. The first beat was cracked on a barrel-sized drum suspended on four poles beside the tipi. The crowd was asked to gather between the tipi and the cottonwood. After they had assembled, we looked to the southwest. Good Spirit Woman took her position on the crest of the hill, to signal the coming of the horses that would portray Black Elk's vision: the horses of the four races, the four directions, and the flowering tree of life.

A gold horse with sun circles on its eyes, ridden by a woman clad in gold cloth, pranced over the hill and picked up the booming beat of the barrel-sized drum. The horse was very spirited and acted as if it loved what they were doing—dancing to the new dawn. Horse and rider danced down toward the gathered crowd, circled once clockwise, and then took their position. They represented the rising sun and the dawn of the new age. A small girl approached the horse and stood beside her. She was also clad in gold and had yellow hair, representing a sunbeam. When the four directions and races had assembled, the sunbeam would spread incense of smoking sage and sweet grass throughout the crowd.

A bay horse with a powerfully faced woman rider appeared on the crest. Black Elk's prologue was read as the horse and rider peered down upon us. The horse and rider could easily have been directly from the spirit world, for they were detached, mysterious, and somehow ominous.

"Black Elk's story," I began with a loud voice, "is the story of all that is holy. It is good to tell of us two-leggeds sharing with the four-leggeds and the wings of the air and all green things, for these are the children of one Mother, and their Father is One Spirit.

"Black Elk was borne up into the heavens. He was told by two men speaking together, as he stood in the middle of a great plain, 'Behold him, the being with the four legs.' Black Elk looked and saw a bay horse standing there. 'Behold me!' the bay horse spoke. 'My life history you shall see.' Then the horse wheeled about to where the sun goes down and said, 'Behold them! Their history you shall know!'"

In our ceremony, the bay horse and its rider galloped straight toward me as I stood out to the western edge of the crowd. The horse stopped on a line before me while I read of Black Elk's vision; then it wheeled about to disappear to the west, returning shortly with a black horse. This horse wore a necklace of bison hooves and had lightning painted on it.

"I looked," I read again from Black Elk, "and there was a black horse yonder with a necklace of bison hooves, and it was beautiful; but I was frightened, because its mane was lightning and there was thunder in its nostrils." (Black Elk spoke of several horses, but I translated his vision into a single horse for our ceremony.)

The bay horse wheeled about and returned with a white horse. "Its mane was flowing like a blizzard," I read, "and from its nose came a roaring and, above, white geese soared and circled." (The evening before, Thunder Owl and I had noted a flock of geese circling the cottonwood tree from the north.) After the bay delivered the white horse, it wheeled about to bring the sorrel horse, representing the red that stands for the east.

"The sorrel horse," I continued to read, "comes from where the sun shines continually. It had a necklace of elk's teeth and stood abreast with eyes that gleamed like the daybreak star and a mane of morning light."

The bay wheeled one last time to bring the yellow buckskin horse representing the south. "I saw the buckskin horse with horns painted on its head and a mane that lived and grew like trees and grasses. The bay horse said, 'Your Grandmothers and Grandfathers are having a council. They shall take you, so have courage.'

"Then the horses went into formation, four abreast—the black, the white, the sorrel, and the buckskin—and stood behind the bay who turned to the west and neighed.

"'See how your horses all come dancing!' I looked and there were horses, horses everywhere—a whole sky full of horses dancing around me.

The reading from Black Elk was over. By this time, four women had assembled to the west, and they were now approached by the bay leading the four horses.

The first woman was dressed in a fringed red dress and wore a garland made of sage and flowers upon her head. Two eagle-wing spikes were inserted prominently in the crown. The red woman carried a peace pipe. She reached for the sorrel horse's reins and led it and its rider to the eastern edge of the gathered crowd close to where the cottonwood stood.

Next, the yellow-clad woman, carrying a yellow hoop and an ear of corn, took the buckskin horse and led it to the south edge of the wood.

The black-clad woman wore a fringed black dress and carried a black vase of water. She led the black horse to its respective position.

The woman in white, who led the white horse to the north, wore a white dress and a dove necklace made from mother-of-pearl and white beads. She carried both the sacred herb, sage, and white feathers representing doves' wings.

After the women of the four directions took their places, a slow drumbeat began, and the red woman approached the center of the crystal area. She held forth her peace pipe. It was a beautiful pipe—very feminine in its construction. It was a traditional Sioux ceremonial pipe, in that its pointed end was quite pronounced, for placing into Mother Earth.

"I am the east," said the woman. "My color is red. I bring new knowledge of this new day. Behold this pipe! Behold this pipe!" she exclaimed four times. She then held out the pipe to me with its pointed end. I thanked her as a sister and placed it in the ground. The stem was pointed east to the rising sun of this important day. The red woman took her position a few yards from the pipe.

Next the woman from the south came forward. "I am the south. Yellow is my color," she spoke. "I stand for growth, the warm south wind." She held up her yellow hoop to the crowd. "Behold this hoop! It is the hoop of the world. All hoops are holy, and some day all shall join together." She placed the hoop upon the ground, surrounding the peace pipe, and set the ear of corn within the hoop.

The woman in black came from the west, bearing a black vase of water. "I am from the west, from the spirit world. The spirits of our ancestors send their blessings. They shall be with you. Look! I shall pour spirit water within this hoop." She then poured part of the vase's water within the hoop. "This water shall bring strong growth to all that stands for this day today." She then poured the remainder of the water onto the cottonwood tree.

The woman from the north then came to the center of the gathering. She placed her dove feathers and sage within the hoop. "I am from the north, I am white, I bring the cleansing snow, and with this cleansing power I bring endurance and strength. This sage represents truth and honesty. It is these virtues that shall bring forth peace and harmony in this new age."

Then, out of the tipi, Mother Earth came forward, dressed in a mul-
ticolored dress and a garland of sage. "I am the Mother of you all. I have
fed you, clothed you, housed you. Every particle of your body comes
from me." She held her arms upward and swept an arc from the east to
the west. "The old order is eclipsing." She turned to face the sun, pointing, and said, "This is the dawn of the new age that shall bring peace
and harmony."

At that moment, Father Sky, in a war bonnet with a trailer to the
ground, came forth from the tipi. He spoke briefly while Mother Earth
passed out sage to the gathered crowd. "I am Father Sky. My energy, the
sun, brings forth life from Mother Earth. Our daily communion is
responsible for you all. Give health back to Mother Earth in this new
age, protect her environmentally, and she will give health back to you."
Then Father Sky turned and took the peace pipe. He took tobacco and
loaded the pipe, offering it in the four directions, down to the earth, up
to the sky, and then to the Great Spirit.

The big drum sounded, and Mother Earth motioned for all to gather
in a large circle around the tree of life. The crowd circle-danced clockwise
to the beat of the drum. Flowers were placed at the base of the cottonwood tree while the horses danced, also clockwise, just beyond the edge
of the crowd.

The leaden skies parted for the sun to beam brightly down upon the
flowering tree of life and the Minnetonka ceremony of harmony. Black
Elk's vision of the flowering tree was fulfilled. Knowledge, wisdom, peace,
and healing will spread outward. Eventually, the hoops of the world will
be united.

Earth Day Ceremony

A ceremony acknowledging Earth Day could be held in a similar manner
as the preceding harmonic convergence ceremony. Just as Sioux ceremonies were adapted for the convergence ceremony, ceremonial adap-
tation can be made for an Earth Day ceremony. Whereas peace and harmony were essential goals in the convergence ceremony, the survival of
our planet is now the ultimate endeavor.

Instead of cutting down a ceremonial tree, a new tree can be planted
or transplanted, and its full maturity should be assured. Around this
tree the people can gather, and it can be addressed in respect for the life-
saving function it performs for the planet. The people can promise to

try to protect its brothers and sisters and give them the chance to reach full maturity.

The four directions can be addressed in a manner that the two-leggeds will recognize and admit the folly of past wasteful and harmful practices and values. They will address the east power in regard to needed knowledge and wisdom that can combat the perils of overpopulation, pollution, and destructive agriculture. Communication knowledge will be addressed in reducing military tensions in order to use the resources now spent on wasteful military expenditures for environmental projects. The south power will be called upon to recognize the change in eating and shelter habits that will be needed to reduce agricultural and timber consumption. The west power will be called upon for a strong spiritual enlightenment to replace the excess of materialism and harmful egocentricity. The north power will be asked for its endurance and strength to carry forth these goals.

Mother Earth can come forth and hand out tree seedlings. Those who receive the trees will declare their intentions that the new trees will reach maturity and that many other trees will also be cared for. Father Sky can come forth and pass out a small stream stone to each participant to signify that all are related and that each stone is a part of Mother Earth. It is to be our daily reminder that we must all strive daily to protect and respect her.

Mitakuye Oyasin:
We Are All Related

The plight of the non-Indian world is that it has lost respect for Mother Earth, from whom and where we all come.

We all start out in this world as tiny seeds—no different from our animal brothers and sisters, the deer, the bear, the buffalo, or the trees, the flowers, the winged people. Every particle of our bodies comes from the good things Mother Earth has put forth. Mother Earth is our real mother, because every bit of us truly comes from her, and daily she takes care of us.

The tiny seed takes on the minerals and the waters of Mother Earth. It is fueled by *Wiyo*, the sun, and given a spirit by *Wakan Tanka*.

This morning at breakfast we took from Mother Earth to live, as we have done every day of our lives. But did we thank her for giving us the means to live? The old Indian did. When he drove his horse in close to a buffalo running at full speed across the prairie, he drew his bowstring back and said as he did so, "Forgive me, brother, but my people must live." After he butchered the buffalo, he took the skull and faced it toward the setting sun as a thanksgiving and an acknowledgment that all things come from Mother Earth. He brought the meat back to camp and gave it first to the old, the widowed, and the weak. For thousands of years great herds thrived across the continent because the Indian never took more than he needed. Today, the buffalo is gone.

You say *ecology*. We think the words *Mother Earth* have a deeper meaning. If we wish to survive, we must respect her. It is very late, but there is still time to revive and discover the old American Indian value of respect for Mother Earth. She is very beautiful, and already she is show-ing us signs that she may punish us for not respecting her. Also, we must remember she has been placed in this universe by the one who is the All Powerful, the Great Spirit Above, or *Wakan Tanka*—God. But a few years ago, there lived on the North American continent people, the American Indians, who knew a respect and value system that enabled them to live on their native grounds without having to migrate, in con-trast to the white brothers and sisters who migrated by the thousands from their homelands because they had developed a value system dif-ferent from that of the American Indian. There is no place now to which we can migrate, which means we can no longer ignore the red man's value system.

Carbon-dating techniques say that the American Indian has lived on the North American continent for thousands upon thousands of years. If we did migrate, it was because of a natural phenomenon—a glacier. We did not migrate because of a social system, value system, and spiritual system that neglected its responsibility to the land and all living things. We Indian people say we were always here.

We, the American Indian, had a way of living that enabled us to live within the great, complete beauty that only the natural environment can provide. The Indian tribes had a common value system and a common-ality of religion, without religious animosity, that preserved that great beauty that the two-leggeds definitely need. Our four commandments from the Great Spirit are: (1) respect for Mother Earth, (2) respect for the Great Spirit, (3) respect for our fellow man and woman, and (4) respect for individual freedom (provided that individual freedom does not threaten the tribe or the people or Mother Earth).

We who respect the great vision of Black Elk see the four sacred colors as red, yellow, black, and white. They stand for the four directions—red for the east, yellow for the south, black for the west, and white for the north.

From the east comes the rising sun and new knowledge from a new day.

From the south will come the warming south winds that will cause our Mother to bring forth the good foods and grasses so that we may live.

To the west where the sun goes down, the day will end, and we will sleep; and we will hold our spirit ceremonies at night, from where we will communicate with the spirit world beyond. The sacred color of the west is black; it stands for the deep intellect that we will receive from the spirit ceremonies. From the west come the life-giving rains.

From the north will come the white winter snow that will cleanse Mother Earth and put her to sleep, so that she may rest and store up energy to provide the beauty and bounty of springtime. We will prepare for aging by learning to create, through our arts and crafts, during the long winter season. Truth, honesty, strength, endurance, and courage also are represented by the white of the north. Truth and honesty in our relationships bring forth harmony.

All good things come from these sacred directions. These sacred directions, or four sacred colors, also stand for the four races of humanity: red, yellow, black, and white. We cannot be a prejudiced people, because all men and women are brothers and sisters and because we all have the same mother—Mother Earth. One who is prejudiced, who hates another because of that person's color, hates what the Great Spirit has put here. Such a one hates that which is holy and will be punished, even during this lifetime, as humanity will be punished for violating Mother Earth. Worse, one's conscience will follow into the spirit world, where it will be discovered that all beings are equal. This is what we Indian people believe.

We, the Indian people, also believe that the Great Spirit placed many people throughout this planet: red, yellow, black, and white. What about the brown people? The brown people evolved from the sacred colors coming together. Look at our Mother Earth. She, too, is brown because the four directions have come together. After the Great Spirit, *Wakan Tanka*, placed them in their respective areas, the *Wakan Tanka* appeared to each people in a different manner and taught them ways so that they might live in harmony and true beauty. Some men, some tribes, some nations have still retained the teachings of the Great Spirit. Others have not. Unfortunately, many good and peaceful religions have been assailed by narrow-minded zealots. Our religious beliefs and our traditional Indian people have suffered the stereotype that we are pagans, savages, or heathens; but we do not believe that only one religion controls the way to the spirit world that lies beyond. We believe that *Wakan Tanka* loves all of its children equally, although the Great Spirit must be disturbed at times with those children who have destroyed proven value systems that practiced sharing and generosity and kept Mother Earth viable down through time. We kept Mother Earth viable because we did not sell her or our spirituality!

Brothers and sisters, we must go back to some of the old ways if we are going to truly save our Mother Earth and bring back the natural beauty that every person seriously needs, especially in this day of vanishing species, vanishing rain forests, overpopulation, poisoned waters, acid rain, a thinning ozone layer, drought, rising temperatures, and weapons of complete annihilation.

Weapons of complete annihilation? Yes, that is how far the obsession with war has taken us. These weapons are not only hydraheaded; they are hydroheaded as well, meaning that they are the ultimate in hydrogen bomb destruction. We will have to divert our obsession with defense and wasteful, all-life-ending weapons of war to reviving our environment. If such weapons are ever fired, we will wind up destroying ourselves. The Armageddon of war is something that we have all been very close to and exposed to daily. However, ever since that day in August when people gathered in fields and cities all across the planet to beseech for peace and harmony, it appears that we are seeing some positive steps toward solving this horror. *Maybe some day two-leggeds will read this book and missiles will no longer be pointed at them.*

The quest for peace can be more efficiently pursued through communication and knowledge than by stealth and unending superior weaponry. If the nations of the world scale back their budgets for weaponry, we will have wealth to spend to solve our serious environmental problems. Our home planet is under attack. It is not an imagined problem. This calamity is upon us now. We are in a real war with the polluting, violating blue man of Black Elk's vision.

Chief Sitting Bull advised us to take the best of the white man's ways and to take the best of the old Indian ways. He also said, "When you find something that is bad, or turns out bad, drop it and leave it alone."[1]

The fomenting of fear and hatred is something that has turned out very badly. This can continue no longer; it is a governmental luxury maintained in order to support pork-barrel appropriations to the Department of Defense, with its admirals and generals who have substituted their patriotism for a defense contractor paycheck after retirement. War has become a business for profit. In the last two wars, we frontline warriors—mostly poor whites and minorities—were never allowed to win our wars, which were endlessly prolonged by the politicians and profiteers, who had their warrior-aged sons hidden safely away or who used their powers, bordering on treason, to keep their offspring out of danger. The wrong was that the patriotic American or the poor had to be the replacement. The way to end wars in this day and age is to do like the Indian: put the chiefs and their sons on the front lines.

Sitting Bull answered a relative, "Go ahead and follow the white man's road and do whatever the [Indian] agent tells you. But I cannot so easily give up my old ways and Indian habits; they are too deeply ingrained in me."[2]

My friends, I will never cease to be an Indian. I will never cease respecting the old Indian values, especially our four cardinal commandments and our values of generosity and sharing. It is true that many who came to our shores brought a great amount of good to this world. Modern medicine, transportation, communication, and food production are but a few of the great achievements that we should all appreciate. But it is also true that too many of those who migrated to North America became so greedy and excessively materialistic that great harm has been caused. We have seen good ways and bad ways. The good way of the non-Indian way I am going to keep. The very fact that we can hold peace-seeking communication and that world leaders meet and communicate for peace shows the wisdom of the brothers and sisters of this time. By all means, good technology should not be curtailed, but care must be taken lest our water, air, and earth become irreparably harmed. The good ways I will always respect and support. But, my brothers and sisters, I say we must give up this obsession with excess consumption and materialism, especially when it causes the harming of the skies surrounding our Mother and the pollution of the waters upon her. *She is beginning to warn us!*

Keep those material goods that you need to exist, but be a more sharing and generous person. You will find that you can do with less. Replace this empty lifestyle of hollow impressing of the shallow ones with active participation for your Mother Earth. At least then, when you depart into the spirit world, you can look back with pride and fulfillment. Other spirit beings will gather around you, other spirits of your own higher consciousness will gather around you and share your satisfaction with you. The eternal satisfaction of knowing you did not overuse your Mother Earth and that you were here to protect her will be a powerful satisfaction when you reach the spirit world.

Indian people do not like to say that the Great Mystery is exactly this or exactly that, but we do know there is a spirit world that lies beyond. We are allowed to know that through our ceremonies. We know that we will go into a much higher plane beyond. We know nothing of hell-fire and eternal damnation from some kind of unloving power that placed us here as little children. None of that has ever been shown to us in our powerful ceremonies, conducted by kind, considerate, proven, and very nonmaterialistic leaders. We do know that everything the Great Mystery makes is in the form of a circle. Our Mother Earth is a very large, powerful circle.

Therefore, we conclude that our life does not end. A part of it is within that great eternal circle. If there is a hell, then our concept of hell would be an eternal knowing that one violated or took and robbed from Mother Earth and caused this suffering that is being bestowed upon the generations unborn. This then, if it were to be imprinted upon one's eternal conscience, this would surely be a terrible, spiritual, mental hell. Worse, to have harmed and hurt one's innocent fellow beings, and be unable to alter (or conceal) the harmful actions would also be a great hell. Truth in the spirit world will not be concealed, nor will it be for sale. Lastly, we must realize that the generations unborn will also come into the spirit world. Let us be the ones that they wish to thank and congratulate, rather than eternally scorn.

While we are shedding our overabundant possessions, and linking up with those of like minds, and advancing spiritual and environmental appreciations, we should develop a respect for the aged and for family-centered traditions, even those who are single warriors, fighting for the revitalization of our Mother on a lone, solitary, but vital front. We should have more respect for an extended family, which extends beyond a son or daughter, goes beyond to grandparents and aunts and uncles, goes beyond to brothers, sisters, aunts, and uncles that we have adopted or made as relatives—and further beyond, to the animal or plant world as our brothers and sisters, to Mother Earth and Father Sky and then above to *Wakan Tanka*, the *Unci/Tankashilah*, the Grandparent of us all. When we pray directly to the Great Spirit, we say *Unci* (Grandmother) or *Tankashilah* (Grandfather) because we are so family-minded that we think of the Great Power above as a grandparent, and we are the grandchildren. Of course, this is so because every particle of our being is from Mother Earth, and our energy and life force are fueled by Father Sky. This is a vital part of the great, deep feeling and spiritual psychology that we have as Indian people. It is why we preserved and respected our ecological environment for such a long period. *Mitakuye oyasin!* We are all related!

In conclusion, our survival is dependent on the realization that Mother Earth is a truly holy being, that all things in this world are holy and must not be violated, and that we must share and be generous with one another. You may call this thought by whatever fancy words you wish—psychology, theology, sociology, or philosophy—but you must think of Mother Earth as a living being. Think of your fellow men and women as holy people who were put here by the Great Spirit. Think of being related to all things! With this philosophy in mind as we go on with our environmental ecology efforts, our search for spirituality, and our quest for peace, we will be far more successful when we truly understand the Indians' respect for Mother Earth.

Lakota Mother Earth Relationship Word List

Reviewed by J. Dearly, Oglala Lakota (Sioux), Lakota Linquist and Language Instructor.

This is a list of words that may be heard in ceremony or that are associated with Sioux spirituality. Spelling of most Sioux words is not consistent; the list below is usually spelled phonetically.

Ate (Ahtay)   Father
Awanyanka   protect
Awanyanka Ina Maka (Ina Maka awanyanka)   protect Mother Earth
Can (chan)   a tree, wood; prefix for things made of or related to wood
Can cega   drum
Cangleska   a hoop
Cangleska wakan   the sacred hoop
Canli wapahte (chanli wapahkteh)   tobacco bundle offering
Cansasa (chan sha sha)   red willow-bark tobacco
Cante (chanh teh)   the heart
Canwi yuza   small sharp stick for hanging meat
Canwi yuza waopo   sharp piercing peg for a sun dancer
Castun   naming
Catku   place of honor
Chanupa   peace pipe
Chanupa lutah   red pipe
Chanupa Wakan   Sacred pipe
Hanblecheya (hanblechia)   crying for a vision
Hanblecheyapi   vision quest
Hau   exclamation, yes, agree, hello
Hehaka   elk
Hehaka Sapa   Black Elk

Hetch etu   it is so; amen

Hetch etu aloh   it is very much so; it is so indeed

Heyoka   a sacred clown; to act contrary, to do things backward, to be humorous

Hinhan   owl

Hinhan Ska   Snowy Owl

Hiya   no

Hocoka   camp circle or sacred space

Hoksi (hokshi)   a child

Hoksica kiyapi   Releasing the Soul Ceremony

Hoksi cala   baby

Hoksi chan kiya   root or seed

Hoksila (hokshila)   boy

Hunka   ancestor, relative

Hunkapi   Making of Relatives Ceremony

Hupa gluza   raising one's pipe in prayer

Hunkpapa   entrance to the camp circle; band, tribe of the Sioux Nation

Hununpa   two-leggeds

Hutopah   four-leggeds

Icaga   to grow

Icanya   to cause to grow

Ihanblapi   they dream of

Iktomi (unktomi)   spider, the tricky spider-fellow in Sioux stories

Ina   my mother

Ina Maka   Mother Earth

Inipi   Sweat Lodge Ceremony

Inktomi lowanpi   spider sing

Inyan   rock, stone

Inyansa   red stone

Ishnata Awicalowan   Preparing a Girl for Womanhood

Ista (ishta) , the eye

Itancan   camp chief, leader

Itokaga   south

Itokaga ouye   power of the south (prayer for the south)

Kinnic kinnick   tobacco

Koda   friend in Dakota dialect

Kola   friend in Lakota (Oglala) dialect

K'u okrya   to help out by giving

Kunshi, unci   grandmother

Lakol wicohan   Indian way

Lakota   allies, friends, Indian name for the Western Sioux
Leksi   uncle
Lelah wah ste wakan   very good and spiritual
Lelah wakan   very powerful signs, very holy
Lutah   red, color for the east (*sha*, also red)
Maka   Earth
Makpiyah Ate   Father Sky
Mato   bear
Mato ska   white bear, polar bear
Mini   water
Minne   water
Minne ahtah   much water, much rain, heavy rainfall
Minne mitak oyasin   water for all my relatives
Mitak oyasin   all my relatives
Mitakuye oyasin   all my relatives; we are all related; all are related
Otuha   give away ceremony
Paha Sapa   Black Hills
Pay sha   hair roach
Peju ota   sage, sacred herb of the north
Pejuta   medicine
Pejuta Wichasha   Medicine Man
Pejuta Winan   Medicine Woman
Pejuta makah wakan   the medicine world
Pilamaya   thank you
Pilamaya aloh   thank you very much
Ptecincala Ska Wakan Winan   White Buffalo Calf Woman
Sapa   Black (color for the west)
Sha   red (color for the east)
Shakopeh Ouye Wowanyanke Hehaca Sapa   six powers of the Universe of
  Black Elk's vision
Shakopeh Ouye   six powers of the universe
Shuunka Takan   very large dog (horse)
Shuunka Wakan   holy dog (horse)
Sica (shicha)   bad, wrong, not good
Sicun   that aspect of the soul that lasts forever and is capable of being
  reinvested in another object at one's death
Sicun wotawe   special stone that has been invested with a spirit
Sicun wotawe wotai   a definite stone whose spirit is obvious and comes
  to the bearer in a special way
Ska   white (color for the north)

Tankashilah   Grandfather

Tapa Wanka Yap   Throwing the Ball Ceremony

Tate   Wind

Tashuunka Wakan   wolf

Tatanka   buffalo

Tiyospaye   extended family (band)

Tokata   future

Tokata wicocage   future generations

Topa Tate   four directions, four winds

Unci   Grandmother

Waga chun   cottonwood tree

Wakan   holy, sacred

Wakan Tanka   Great Spirit, Great Mystery

Wakangli   lightning

Wakanyeja Makah   children of the earth

Wakinyan Cetan   thunder hawk

Wakinyan   thunderbird, also means lightning or thunder

Wakinyan tanka   thunder beings

Wakinyan hotonpi   thunder

Wamakaskan oyate   the animals

Wanagi   soul, ghost, spirit

Wana olowanpi   sing now

Wanblee (Wanbli)   eagle

Wanunyanpi   offerings

Washichu   white man

Waste (washtay)   good

Waziya   north

Waziya ahtah   big storm, strong north wind

Waziya ouye   power of the north (prayer for the north)

Wichasha pejuta   medicine man, primarily a healer

Wichasha wakan   holy man, ceremonial leader who also performs healings

Wichoni mini   life-giving rains

Wichoni minne   life-giving rains

Wigmunke oyate (Wigmuunke)   rainbow people

Winan Wakan   holy woman

Wiwanyag Wachipi   Sun Dance Ceremony

Wiyo Ate   Father Sun

Wiyoheyapa   east, rising dawn

Wiyoheyapa ouye   east power; rising dawn of the east (prayer for the east)

Wiyo ichoni   high sun, Sun at its height is giving life

Wiyopeyata   west, the sun is setting
Wiyopeyata ouye   west power; power of the setting sun
Wotai   personal stone that has appeared to you, you carry it at times
Wotawe   personal charm, can be a personal stone
Wowas ake Iyuha   all powers
Yupayo   close it, close the door
Yuwipi   Spirit Calling Ceremony, they tie him up
Zi zi (Zhee zhee)   yellow (color for the south)
Zintkala oyate   the winged people

Prayer to the Six Powers of the Universe

Bright Earth Warrior (Judith Favia), one of my rainbow friends, has been very moved by the prayers in the sweat ceremonies that she has attended and asked if she could write a prayer for this book. Below I have included her prayer. She has been very consistent in praying with her pipe and has become comfortable with the four directions and the six powers and their unique attributes and characters. Although your prayers need not be so long in every case, hers will give you a sense of how your own beseechments may be made.

> Ho. *Wiyopeyata ouye*, power of the setting sun. We call on you. Have pity on us that the people may live.
>
> *Wakinyan*, thunder beings of the black west, we call on you. You are the source of both the power to live and of destruction, who ride the back of *minne wichoni*, the life-giving rains.
>
> For long years, the way of the people has been weak and there has been fear. Many have said that the red road would disappear and that the six powers and *Wakan Tanka* would turn their faces from us.
>
> It is true that many of the old ways have been lost. But just as the life-giving rains restore the earth after the drought, so your power will restore the Way and give it new life.
>
> We ask this not only for the red people but for all the people that they might live. In ignorance and carelessness they have walked upon *Ina Maka*, our Mother. They did not understand that they are part of all beings, the four-legged, the winged, grandfather rock, the tree people, and our star brothers. Now the earth and all our relations are crying out. They cry for the help of all people. And many are hearing. Once again, the people call on the six powers and try to walk in a sacred way upon the land.

Power of the west, we call on you to bring life to their efforts. To once again bring rain to the desert.

Wakinyan, have pity on us that the people may live.

Mitakuye oyasin.

Ho. *Hetch etu aloh.*

Ho. *Waziya ouye,* white giant of the north.

For time out of time, you have made us strong and helped us to walk the holy path. Your white blanket covers our Mother as she sleeps and dreams. And from her dreams come the spring and renewal of life. Even so are the people purified and made strong by your cold breath.

As our Mother sleeps, we too dream and pray. It is a time of holiness and preparation. And from this time, the people become strong and they endure.

Waziya, bringer of sleep, our ceremonies also have slept. And like the earth, they have dreamed deep dreams. Now we ask that these ceremonies blossom forth renewed, as do the flowers in spring.

Giver of the sacred herb, remind us that every act is sacred, since all are performed on the body of our Mother and beneath the eye of *Wiyo Ate,* Father Sun. Purify our intentions, that each ceremony may be performed for a holy purpose, that the people may live.

Mitakuye oyasin.

Ho. *Hetch etu aloh.*

Ho. *Wiyoheyapa ouye,* power of the rising sun of the east.

From you come wisdom and understanding. To you we send a voice.

You are the power of the red dawn and the home of the morning star. We call on you to bring forth new knowledge and understanding among the people that the earth and all our relations may live. Once you brought us *Ptecincala Ska Wakan Winan,* the White Buffalo Calf Woman. She brought to us the sacred pipe and the seven rites, that the people might live. Today, we again need the power of the pipe to show us the sacred path. It is a time of new ways, and we ask that those ways be right and holy. With each new day we pray to you for wisdom. And we know that with this gift comes the obligation to use it for the good of all our relations.

Mitakuye oyasin.

Ho. *Hetch etu aloh.*

Ho. *Itokaga ouye,* yellow power of the south.

You are the power of the hoop, the hoop of all the peoples.

With these ceremonies, may the people come together as one, united with all our relations.

South power, we pray to you for healing and for abundance, that in the warm sun of the south, we may bring forth the flowering tree of Black Elk's vision. Let the sacred way of the people include all, red, yellow, black, and white, that we may join together that our Mother the Earth may live. Heal the hurt and enmity of the past. Light for us the good red road that leads us to harmony and balance among all the beings of the earth. Teach us that no one lives unless all the people live. And let us recognize that every other being is simply ourselves in another skin.

Power of the south, we call on you. Have pity on us that the people may live.

Mitakuye oyasin.

Ho. *Hetch etu aloh.*

Ho. *Ina Maka*, Mother Earth.

It is you who feed us, shelter us, teach us, heal us. And like unthinking children we squander your riches, taking without thought for the future.

Mother, we are ashamed of our ignorance and our greed.

It is our wish to live in a holy way, in harmony with you and with all our relations. We commit ourselves to a new reverence for life, for you, and for ourselves and our place in the universe. Mother, most of all, have pity on us that the people may live, for without you we are nothing.

Mitakuye oyasin.

Ho. *Hetch etu aloh.*

Ho. *Wiyo Ate*, Father Sun.

We thank you for the fire in our lives.

Sunmate of Mother Earth, you provide us with heat, light, and the passion for growth. It is your power, made gentle, that we see in the campfire. It is your power, stored for us millions of years ago, that today provides our heat and light. You warm us in summer and cheer us in winter.

We understand that we have been wasteful with your gifts and we ask for the passion to find new ways. We send a voice to you Father Sun. Have pity on us that the people may live.

Mitakuye oyasin.

Ho. *Hetch etu aloh.*

Name Glossary

Below are some of the natural names that have been received in ceremony by both Indian and rainbow people.

Bear Woman
Brave Warrior
Bright Earth Warrior
Buffalo Eagle
Buffalo Spirit
Chanting Squirrel
Children's Warrior Woman
Crystal Eagle Woman
Crystal Feather Man
Crystal Woman
Dancing Eagle
Dancing Grizzly Bear
Dancing Lion
Dancing Moon
Eagle Elk
Eagle Hawk Man
Eagle Spirit
Eagle Wolf
Eagle Woman
Eagle of the Spirit Water
Earth Dance
Flaming Rainbow Woman
Flying Fox
Friend to All
Good Shining Woman
Laughing Heart

Laughing Wolf
Little Crow
Looking Hawk
Looking Wolf
Midnight Fire
Midnight Owl
Mountain Lion
Mountain Lion Woman
Owl's Mother Earth Warrior
Power Butterfly Woman
Rainbow Bridge
Rainbow Crystal Woman
Rainbow Eagle Woman
Rainbow Shield Woman
Rainbow Warrior
Rainbow Water
Raven Horse
Red Dawn
Red Dawn Fox
Red Dawn Wolf
Red Hawk
Red Hawk Dog
Sacred Waters
Shining Porpoise
Singing Eagle
Singing Red Hawk Woman
Soaring Eagle Woman
Star Fire
Star Water
Sundance Eagle
Talking Bear
Thunder Owl
Thunder Wind
Thunderbird Woman
Water Spirit Woman
Whispering Willow
White Buffalo Eagle
White Wolf
Wolf Moon
Wolf Spirit

Sweat Lodge Checklist

For Building the Frame

Hatchets
Hunting knives
String, twine, or fishing line
Tarps
Several clean blankets

For the Fireplace

Hatchet
Shovel
Pitchfork (or deer horns)
Matches or lighter
Limestone or granite rocks (approximately twenty per ceremony, cantaloupe size)
Several five-gallon water containers

For Inside the Lodge

Two- or three-gallon pail
Dipper
Drums, rattles
Eagle-bone or wooden whistle
Sage

Personal Items

Change of clothing and towel
Tobacco bundles
Special amulets, stones or crystals, medicine bags
Peace pipe (if you have one)
Mineral water, soda, or juice; absolutely no alcohol*
Food contribution for supper
Cooking and eating utensils
Potholders
Garbage bags

---

*For thousands of years the Native North Americans beseeched and acknowledged in ceremony without any form of drugs or alcohol. Their spiritual path led them to a highly harmonious lifestyle, socially and environmentally. They also reaped a high self-esteem and positive self-worth. Respect Indian ceremony and its proven history. For thousands of years our Mother Earth was very respected. Respect the deep dignity of these spiritual ways.

Notes

Introduction

1. Albert Einstein quoted in *Center for Respect of Life and Environment* (Washington, D.C.: Environmental Public Relations Pamphlet, 1988), pp. 6–7.
2. Fyodor Dostoevski, from *Brothers Karamazov* in *ibid*, p. 7.

Chapter 3

1. Jack Weatherford, *Indian Givers* (New York: Crown, 1988), p. 123.
2. Bruce E. Johansen, *Forgotten Founders* (Ipswich, MA: Gambit, 1982), pp. 12 and 61.
3. Weatherford, *Indian Givers*, p. 135, 136.
4. Weatherford, "Indians and the Fourth," *Baltimore Evening Sun*, July 3, 1989.

Chapter 4

1. Jack Weatherford, *Indian Givers* (New York: Crown, 1988), p. 126.
2. Ibid., p. 128.
3. Ibid., p. 129.
4. Henry Steele Commager, *The Empire of Reason: How Europe Imagined and America Realized the Enlightenment* (Garden City, NY: Doubleday, 1978), p. 54.
5. Weatherford, *Indian Givers*, p. 129.
6. Thomas Paine, *The Rights of Man* (Middlesex, England: Penguin, 1969; originally published 1791), p. 223.
7. Weatherford, *Indian Givers*, p. 146.
8. Willard E. Rosenfelt, *The Last Buffalo; Cultural Views of the Plains Indians: The Sioux or Dakota Nation* (Minneapolis, MN: Denison, 1973), p. 66.

9. Ibid., p. 67.
10. John F. Bryde, *Modern Indian Psychology* (Vermillion, SD: University of South Dakota, 1971), p. 1.

Chapter 5

1. Every word of this spiritual epic was spoken in Sioux by Nicholas Black Elk to the writer John Neihardt through the Oglala holy man's son, Ben. Ben always referred to the book as "my father's book."

   John Neihardt was an unusual writer for his time. He did not exhibit the usual paternalistic, superior attitude toward Indians that most writers then did. He wrote down the "straight" interpretation and did not alter or bend the Indians' words merely to please the authorities. Black Elk, who had turned down other writers who sought his story, sensed the man's sincerity. Many Native Americans, including me, are very grateful for his truth, integrity, and courage.

Chapter 8

1. Today at Spirit Mountain, several lodge frames are available at the base of the mountain. The state park department must be commended for its consideration. The park rangers even provide firewood and request that tourists respect the privacy of Indian ceremonies.
2. William K. Powers, *Oglala Religion* (Lincoln, NE: University of Nebraska Press, 1977), p. 180.
3. In my opinion a mild introduction is better than a hot introduction. A ceremony is primarily for prayer: it is not an endurance contest. Many first-time participants are apprehensive as it is. A light application of the dippers of water initially makes it easier on the apprehensive ones, giving them a better chance to concentrate on their prayers, and the percentage of participants staying through all four endurances is much higher. The timid and the fearful gain a great deal of confidence if they endure the complete ceremony. Therefore, they should be initiated gently, if possible. Also, a Sweat Lodge leader should ask any of those who think they might be apprehensive or claustrophobic to sit up close to the doorway. If they become too frightened they can simply leave. In most cases, those sitting close to the door never ask to leave, and their imagined fears are calmed considerably.

Chapter 9

1. The Department of Interior Parks Department has set out signs at many of the plants, explaining their usefulness to the Indian people and the early settlers, and this makes the area all the more interesting.

Chapter 10

1. For a step-by-step version of the Sun Dance, an academic description should be sought. Anthropologists, sociologists, and other academics as well as ministers and priests have produced numerous analyses of all aspects of the Sun Dance. Some are so academic that they even provide the scientific names for our cottonwood tree, sage, and the red willow bark that we call *cansasa*. In their need to be scientific, they are prone to point out skeptically the inconsistencies in our ceremonies—that the sweat lodge rock pits are different diameters, for instance, or that holy men conduct the ritual differently. Many ultimately trap themselves in paternalism by trying to compare our rituals to those honoring the white man's God. Ceremony is not measurement, however. Ceremony is spiritual openness, beseechment in humility, acknowledgment of blessings, and thanksgiving. Changing times, changing locales, changing circumstances bring variations in presentation and reflect the adjustments that a tribe has made in their lifestyle. The central essence of ceremony—communication with a higher realm—does not change.

Chapter 11

1. William Stoltzman, S. J., *How to Take Part in Lakota Ceremonies* (Pine Ridge, SD: Heritage Center, Red Cloud Indian School, 1986); William K. Powers, *Yuwipi: Vision and Experience in Oglala Ritual* (Lincoln, NE: University of Nebraska Press, 1982).

Chapter 12

1. Cynthia Bend and Tayja Wiger, *Birth of a Modern Shaman* (St. Paul, MN: Llewellyn, 1988).

Chapter 14

1. See *Black Elk Speaks, Being the Life Story of a Holy Man of the Oglala Sioux as told to John G. Neihardt (Flaming Rainbow)* (New York: William Morrow, 1932; rpt. Lincoln, NE: University of Nebraska Press, 1961); and Joseph Epes Brown, *The Sacred Pipe: Black Elk's Account of the Seven Rites of the Oglala Sioux* (Norman, OK: University of Oklahoma Press, 1953).
2. *Black Elk Speaks*, pp. 272–74.
3. Ibid., p. 274.
4. Ibid.

Chapter 20

1. It is my understanding that feminine power and harmony are to become very strong in this new age onward; and as I look around when in spiritual gatherings, I see that it is womankind who is most represented. The old world order with its restrictive, male-dominated regime is being eclipsed. It is good to see that women are finally taking up their spiritual roles, as womankind is more peaceful, and this aspect is sorely needed. In this time of dangerous atomic weapons, peaceful people must have the stronger voice. This new age, with its indications of a new spirituality, give Native Americans great encouragement and relief.
2. In the six Sun Dances of which I have been a part, I have seen similar mystical acknowledgment. Once, during the first Sun Dance in which I was pierced, a lone cloud came over the Sun Dance crowd, out of a cloudless sky, and rained lightly on us. Another time, a lone eagle hovered over us. But this acknowledgment at Minnetonka was far more powerful to me.

Chapter 21

1. John F. Bryde, *Modern Indian Psychology* (Vermillion, SD: University of South Dakota, Indian Studies Department, 1971), p. 1.
2. David Humphreys Miller, *Ghost Dance* (Lincoln, NE: University of Nebraska Press, 1959), p. 65.

Suggested Readings

Bend, Cynthia, and Tayja Wiger. *Birth of a Modern Shaman*. St. Paul, MN: Llewellyn, 1988.

Boyd, Doug. *Rolling Thunder: A Personal Exploration into the Secret Healing Powers of an American Indian Medicine Man*. New York: Dell Books, 1974.

Brown, Joseph Epes. *The Sacred Pipe: Black Elk's Account of the Seven Rites of the Oglala Sioux*. Recorded and edited by Joseph Epes Brown. Norman, OK: University of Oklahoma Press, 1953.

Bryde, John F. *Modern Indian Psychology*. Vermillion, SD: Department of Indian Studies, University of South Dakota, 1971.

Carey, Ken. *Return of the Bird Tribes*. Kansas City, MO: Uni Sun, 1988.

Eastman, Charles A. (Ohiyesa). *From the Deep Woods to Civilization*. Lincoln, NE: University of Nebraska Press, 1916.

Fire, John (Lame Deer), and Richard Erdoes. *Lame Deer: Seeker of Visions*. New York: Simon and Schuster, 1972.

Goodman, Jeffrey. *American Genesis: The American Indian and the Origins of Modern Man*. New York: Summit Books, 1981.

Johansen, Bruce E. *Forgotten Founders: How the American Indian Helped Shape Democracy*. Ipswich, MA: Gambit, 1982

Miller, David Humphries. *Custer's Fall: The Indian Side of the Story*. Lincoln, NE: University of Nebraska Press, 1957.

Neihardt, John G. *Black Elk Speaks, Being the Life Story of a Holy Man of the Oglala Sioux as told to John G. Neihardt (Flaming Rainbow)*. New York: William Morrow, 1932, rpt. Lincoln, NE: University of Nebraska Press, 1961.

Powers, William K. *Oglala Religion*. Lincoln, NE: University of Nebraska Press, 1977.

———. *Sacred Language: The Nature of Supernatural Discourse in Lakota*. Norman, OK: University of Oklahoma Press, 1986.

———. *Yuwipi: Vision and Experience in Oglala Ritual*. Lincoln, NE: University of Nebraska Press, 1982.

Rosenfelt, Willard E. *The Last Buffalo; Cultural Views of the Plains Indians: The Sioux or Dakota Nation*. Minneapolis, MN: Denison, 1973.

Ross, Allen Charles. *Mitakuye Oyasin*. Ft. Yates, ND: BEAR, 1989.

Sams, Jamie. *Medicine Cards*. Santa Fe, NM: Bear and Co., 1988.

———. *Midnight Song*. Santa Fe, NM: Bear and Co., 1988.

Sandoz, Mari. *Crazy Horse: The Strange Man of the Oglalas*. Lincoln, NE: University of Nebraska Press, 1961.

Stoltzman, S. J., William. *How to Take Part in Lakota Ceremonies*. Pine Ridge, SD: Heritage Center, Red Cloud Indian School, 1986.

Vestal, Stanley. *Warpath*. Lincoln, NE: University of Nebraska Press, 1984.

———. *Warpath and Council Fire: The Plains Indians' Struggle for Survival in War and in Diplomacy, 1851–1891*. New York: Random House, 1948.

———. *Warpath: The True Story of the Fighting Sioux Told in a Biography of Chief White Bull*. Boston and New York: Houghton Mifflin, 1934.

Weatherford, Jack. *Indian Givers: How the Indians of the Americas Transformed the World*. New York: Crown, 1988.

Willoya, William, and Vinson Brown. *Warriors of the Rainbow: Strange and Prophetic Indian Dreams*. Healdsburg, CA: Naturegraph, 1962.

Wolf, Fred Alan. *Parallel Universes: The Search for Other Worlds*. New York: Simon and Schuster, 1988.

———. *Taking the Quantum Leap: The New Physics for Nonscientists*. New York: Harper & Row, 1981.

About the Author

Eagle Man was born on the Oglala Sioux reservation and is an enrolled tribal member, OST 15287. Following the earning of an undergraduate degree in biology, he joined the Marine Corps to become a fighter pilot. After volunteering for combat duty in Vietnam, he was summoned by the Oglala holy man, Fools Crow, for a warrior's preparation ceremony. Eagle Man returned from 110 combat missions and danced in six annual Sioux Sun Dances. The Sun Dance led him to the seven Mother Earth ceremonies under the tutelage of Chief Eagle Feather, the Sichangu holy man who brought back the piercing ceremony. Eagle Man (Ed McGaa) holds a law degree from the University of South Dakota and is the author of *Red Cloud*, a biography of an Oglala Sioux chief.